A TECHNOLOGY OF READING AND WRITING

Volume 3

The Adaptive Classroom

EDUCATIONAL PSYCHOLOGY

Allen J. Edwards, Series Editor
Department of Psychology
Southwest Missouri State University
Springfield, Missouri

Phillip S. Strain, Thomas P. Cooke, and Tony Apolloni. Teaching Exceptional Children: Assessing and Modifying Social Behavior

Donald E. P. Smith and others. A Technology of Reading and Writing (in four volumes).
    Vol. 1. Learning to Read and Write: A Task Analysis (by Donald E. P. Smith)
    Vol. 2. Criterion-Referenced Tests for Reading and Writing (by Judith M. Smith, Donald E. P. Smith, and James R. Brink)
    Vol. 3. The Adaptive Classroom (by Donald E. P. Smith)

Joel R. Levin and Vernon L. Allen (eds.). Cognitive Learning in Children: Theories and Strategies

Vernon L. Allen (ed.). Children as Teachers: Theory and Research on Tutoring

Gilbert R. Austin. Early Childhood Education: An International Perspective

António Simões (ed.). The Bilingual Child: Research and Analysis of Existing Educational Themes

Erness Bright Brody and Nathan Brody. Intelligence: Nature, Determinants, and Consequences

Samuel Ball (ed.). Motivation in Education

J. Nina Lieberman. Playfulness: Its Relationship to Imagination and Creativity

In preparation:

Donald E. P. Smith and others. A Technology of Reading and Writing (in four volumes).
    Vol. 4. Preparing Instructional Tasks (by Judith M. Smith)

Harry L. Hom, Jr. (ed.). Psychological Processes in Early Education

Harvey Lesser. Television and the Preschool Child: A Psychological Theory of Instruction and Curriculum Development

Donald J. Treffinger, J. Kent Davis, and Richard E. Ripple (eds.). Handbook on Teaching Educational Psychology

Kay Pomerance Torshen. The Mastery Approach to Competency-Based Education

A TECHNOLOGY OF READING AND WRITING

Volume 3

The Adaptive Classroom

Donald E. P. Smith

School of Education
The University of Michigan
Ann Arbor, Michigan

ACADEMIC PRESS   New York   San Francisco   London   1977

A Subsidiary of Harcourt Brace Jovanovich, Publishers

ACADEMIC PRESS, INC.
111 Fifth Avenue, New York, New York 10003

United Kingdom Edition published by
ACADEMIC PRESS, INC. (LONDON) LTD.
24/28 Oval Road, London NW1

Library of Congress Cataloging in Publication Data

Smith, Donald E   P
      The adaptive classroom.

      (His A technology of reading and writing ; v. 3)
(Educational psychology)
      Bibliography: p:
      1.   Language arts (Elementary)   2.   Educational innova-
tions.   3.   Open plan schools.   I.   Title.
LB1050.S572   vol. 3   [LB1576]   372.6'044s   [372.6'044]
                                                                                            76-30445
ISBN 0–12–651703–7

CONTENTS

III   MAKING TEACHING METHODS ADAPTIVE

8

A Tutorial Method   269

9

The Basal Reader Method   275

10

An Individualized Language Experience Method   287

11

Programmed Learning and Computer Programs   291

PREFACE

It is commonly said that "methods texts" are, at worst, trivial and, at best, too theoretical. I want to explain why that might be true of some methods texts and why it should not be true of this one.

* * * * *

Many of us in teacher education have had trouble getting together on an answer to the question, What should be taught to the children? There has not been too much disagreement among math and science teachers except on specifics; for example, when to teach number operations—before or after introducing number theory.

In the case of language arts (reading, writing, listening, and speaking), the situation has been much worse. Nobody with the voice of authority has taken a stand on the specifics—on what, precisely, children must know. Instead, most curriculum guides contain objectives like *to appreciate, to gain awareness of, to develop attitudes toward, to be discerning about*; goals like *clarify, verify, examine*, and *gain insight into*; and purposes like *relate, illustrate*, and *delineate*.

If nothing specific is to be learned, books on teaching are reduced to presenting teaching tips, good advice, and things to try. Little wonder, then, that methods courses and methods texts appear ephemeral. Without clear-cut goals and measures, teachers have a problem like that of college students: "If I don't know what I'll be examined on, I don't know when to stop studying." As a teacher, if I don't know what students must learn, I don't know when to stop teaching!

But that isn't all. My colleagues and I have had trouble agreeing on what to teach, but there's one thing that too many of us have agreed on: the idea that it's not good to train a teacher to teach in one way; it makes him rigid; he may never teach in any other way. This "principle" is simply not true. When a learner masters a method that allows him to reach his goal (ride a bicycle, play a cornet, make money in the stock market), his success makes him free. He begins to experiment with variations. The learner who is on the verge of failure is harder to change, most rigid, most intractable.

Nevertheless, the "principle" is widely held. We have avoided imposing our will and our way on our trainees. In fact, we have been very careful to **educate** our teacher trainees—and very careful not to **train** them. And we have been successful: We have produced a bumper crop of well-educated, untrained teachers.

*   *   *   *   *

If there is to be a technology of teaching, we must resolve the problem of the content of language instruction. To do that, Volume 1 of this series, a task analysis, and Volume 2, a discussion of criterion-referenced tests, took a position on the problem of content by defining all competencies judged to be necessary for reading and writing. Those competencies will be scrutinized carefully by other investigators and will probably be modified. They constitute a beginning.

And, if there is to be a technology of teaching, the problem of "best method of teaching" must be resolved. My resolution of it is to show you how to develop any classroom as a self-modifying or adaptive system, a feedback system in which measures of standard learnings are allowed to modify or influence your teaching methods. You can begin with any method (or none at all) and modify techniques by examining their consequences. Materials for use in an adaptive system can be developed, adopted, or adapted by the teacher who has read Volume 4.

*   *   *   *   *

To return to the point: Your peers probably won't call this book too theoretical, but my peers will probably say it is too applied.

The Target: An Adaptive Classroom

SOME ASSUMPTIONS
ABOUT TRAINING

I. Assumptions

I wish I could say that this book is designed to teach teachers how to teach reading and writing. I can't say that. No book can do that. To learn how to teach, you must teach. You must be in a teaching–learning situation; you must carry out behaviors and observe their results. However, you can increase your likelihod of success if you have certain knowledge and skills:

- Knowledge: What must children learn? What measures can be used to evaluate what is learned? What resources are available for promoting learning?
- Skills: How can I arrange a climate of achievement? How can I determine whether or not my materials teach? How can I assess my own effectiveness?

And that is what this book is designed to do: provide certain knowledge and skills.

It differs from most other books on language pedagogy by starting with a different set of assumptions. First, most books on reading and writing aim to **educate** teachers—

- by isolating issues;
- by presenting research findings;
- by avoiding fixed positions on most issues.

3

Such books characteristically eschew prescriptions, cookbook procedures, and "skill-drills." They avoid telling the teacher how to teach ("keep an open mind," "be eclectic").

This book assumes that you have to know some things about language skills and be able to do some things about making materials work before you start. It intends to contribute to training by specifying what must be learned, how it is learned, and what environmental conditions you must arrange in order for learning to happen.

Second, most books on this topic imply that the overriding issue in instruction is the method of teaching:

· They devote much space to comparative evaluations of common methods.
· They conclude by recommending different methods for differing children.

This book begins with the assumption that none of the current popular methods of teaching reading and writing succeeds with more than 70% of the children, but that any of them **can be made to work** for virtually all children. Making a method work requires that you identify its deficiencies and add the missing ingredients.

If the attempt is successful, you will be able to choose a method for teaching based upon available resources. For example:

· If you have one child and only paper and pencil, you can use a tutorial method.
· If you have 30 children and some trade books, you can use an individualized method.
· If you have only a basal reader, you can individualize that.

Each of several methods, from tutorial to computer-assisted, will be described and its correctable deficiencies pointed out.

Third, many books on reading instruction imply that some proportion of children will fail to become literate because of conditions beyond the teacher's control (familial, sociological, or personal shortcomings). This book, on the other hand, is written with the assumption that any child with a minimum of physical equipment can learn to read in **your classroom** and that your responsibility is to arrange classroom conditions so that will happen.

My responsibility is to see to it that you have information, techniques, and a particular outlook about skills and instruction that will help you to help children discover their potential.

II. Plan of the Book

The book has three parts. Part I defines the adaptive classroom and gives six conditions for learning that characterize it. Certain conditions may surprise you and may well test some of your implicit assumptions about child and teacher behaviors. Because your prior learnings may conflict with positions taken here, several conditions are discussed at length. You will not be asked to agree with the positions taken; rather, you will be asked to test yourself only on your understanding of them. Other conditions will be readily understood but will require skills for their implementation. Therefore, you will be asked to complete self-instructional modules on methods of providing information feedback, on procedures for assessing classroom effectiveness, on information about non-standard English, and on techniques for teaching reading and writing.

Whereas Part I concerns an idealized training environment, Part II will define the contents of literacy—the **skill domains** of listening, speaking, reading, and writing—and new techniques for handling hard-to-teach skills. In order to define the skills needed by children, certain cloudy theoretical issues must be dealt with. Concrete expression of the skills is given by means of the criterion tests identified in Volume 2.

Specification of (*1*) the conditions for learning and (*2*) the skills to be learned provides criteria by which to assess strengths and weaknesses of current methods of teaching—tutorial, basal reader, individualized language experience, and programmed (both book and computer). In Part III, each method will be described briefly and techniques for handling deficiencies will be given.

Let us look now at the adaptive classroom. (The reader who is completely new to the teaching of reading, who has no concept of first grade instruction except dim recollections, would do well to turn to Chapter 8, "A Tutorial Method," for a brief introduction before reading Chapter 2.)

THE ADAPTIVE CLASSROOM

Imagine yourself holding an archery bow. Your task is to hit the bull's-eye of a target. You take careful aim and try one shot. You miss the bull's-eye. You then examine the target, estimate the distance and direction of your error, make an adjustment for the distance and direction (and, perhaps, for windage), and try again. You are an **adaptive system**; you used information feedback (in this case, a measure of error in direction and distance) to modify your own behavior, to bring your archery behavior under better control. The events that occurred are called **self-monitoring behaviors, self-determination,** or the **self-control of behavior.**

A classroom may be designed to maximize self-control of learning behaviors by allowing children to function as adaptive systems. After all, the infant learning to drink from a cup is an adaptive system. The beginner on a bicycle is an adaptive system. The child learning to walk, to speak, to draw, to play with others, to build, and to create is an adaptive system. In each case, the child **teaches himself** by modifying his actions in light of their consequences, that is, by responding to information feedback.

The conditions required for learning in the archery example may be stated as follows:

(*1*) The archer can hold and draw a bow. He has mastered certain prerequisite skills.

7

(2) There is a definite, clear target or goal (the bull's-eye) recognized and accepted as a goal by the archer.

(3) The archer can see and focus on the target. The air is clear. The light is adequate. Presumably, there are no distractions.

(4) There is a bow of reliable pull or tension and arrows of similar weight and straightness. These constitute adequate tools or materials.

(5) The amount of error, in distance and direction, can be **seen** by the archer. He does not depend on another person to evaluate his effort.

(6) The archer is free to try again, now or later, to improve his control. On the other hand, he can rest if he wishes or carry on some other activity.

To summarize, an adaptive system will produce self-control of behavior if (and only if) all these conditions are present: a functioning organism, a goal, a conducive practice environment, effective tools (materials), self-evaluation, and opportunity for practice to mastery in the learner's own time.

Classrooms do not often provide **all** these conditions:

(1) A functioning organism: What entering skills (or subroutines) are required of the learner?

(2) Goal: What **is** good reading? How many words must I be able to write? How legible is legible printing? How can I know if I comprehend text well enough?

(3) Environment: Is failure to attend caused by a noisy or emotional environment? How can a teacher know whether the environment is adequate? Who is responsible for maintaining the environment?

(4) Materials: Are the materials appropriate for this child at this time for the skill he is focusing on? Do the materials actually teach or do they merely test? Are they (in fact) make-work to keep the child busy or amused?

(5) Self-evaluation: Are functions so arranged that the learner can compare his efforts with a model and determine adjustments himself—and immediately? Or is evaluation handled by someone else? Is the standard of correctness in the head of the teacher?

(6) Mastery: Is mastery possible? Is less-than-adequate work accepted and merely graded low or is the learner allowed to continue practicing until he achieves mastery? Is he free to shift activities at will and return to the task at a later time?

These are likely to be embarrassing questions to most teachers in today's classrooms. And good teachers will answer with perfect justification: "We're doing the best we can with conditions as they are." Granted. But let me practice what I preach. Let me define the classroom as an adaptive system if only to specify a **clear goal** for aiming purposes.

I. The Brethower Model

The concept of adaptive teaching systems was introduced by Lewis and Park (1966). The "adaptive classroom" was first defined by Professor Dale Brethower of Cleveland State University (1971). To understand his description, let us substitute some terms:

(*1*) For *environment: processing system*;
(*2*) For *self-evaluation: feedback signal*;
(*3*) For *practice to mastery: continuous modification of both child and training system until a standard is reached.*

The following diagram[1] illustrates part of Brethower's "educational system" (adaptive system):

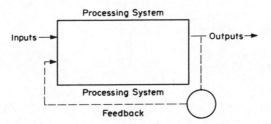

Inputs consist of illiterate children, materials, instruction, and tests; processing consists of receipt of instruction, studying, and taking tests; outputs consist of trained children, the evidence for which is, at the least, a set of test scores. Scores are fed back as inputs: If one or more scores fail to reach the mastery standard, the feedback signal indicates that the processing system must be modified until all children reach mastery.

There is more to the model:

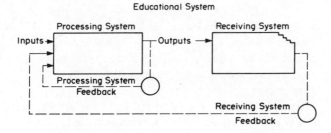

[1] This diagram and the next are from material Professor Brethower has prepared for student use. Reprinted with permission of the author.

The products (outputs) of the processing system are evaluated by a receiving system. For first grade children, the receiving system might be parents, principal, second grade teachers, and so on.

Although the processing system may work perfectly, the receiving system may find fault with its products. For example, parents may say, "Sure he can read. But he can't take a message on the phone and write it down." The second grade teacher may say, "They can spell, but they don't have anything original to say. You squelched their creativity." The principal may say, "Don't you develop any social or citizenship skills?" Signals from the receiving system provide a second kind of feedback to help the system adapt in order to reach its goal.

So much for the theory. How does such a classroom look, in action, and does it really work?

II. Operating the Classroom

A. *Interview with Kimberly*

Interviewer: Kim, I understand that you do a lot of projects in your room.

Kim: Yep, I finished one on flowers that grow in Florida. I did that with one of the boys. We wrote a report and made a big poster. Now we're studying the mouse.

Interviewer: Where did you find out about flowers?

Kim: Oh, anywhere . . . the encyclopedia, flower catalogs. Aunt Kit lives in Florida. She wrote us a long letter.

Interviewer: Is that all you do—projects?

Kim: Oh, no! We do reading and writing and spelling and social studies and science . . . and math. I almost forgot math. I wish I **could** forget math!

Interviewer: You don't like math?

Kim: Well-l-l, I like math. I don't like copying down problems. It takes forever.

Interviewer: You're in the fourth grade. There are other grades in your room?

Kim: Yes, we have second, third, and fourth.

Interviewer: How many?

Kim: Fifty-four. Wow! We don't have seats for everybody. But that's OK. We don't all sit down at the same time. I mean, some kids are in the library, and some are in the Annex Room.

Interviewer: What's an Annex Room?

Kim: That's where you can go to work if people bother you. **Everybody** likes to go there! But only six at a time can be in there.

Interviewer: You don't have desks?

Kim: No, only the ones who are behind in their work have desks. They have to stay there. Mainly those are second and third graders. They haven't caught on yet.

Interviewer: Caught on?

Kim: Well, if you can work by yourself . . .

Interviewer: Independently?

Kim: Yes, if you can work independently, and get your basic work done, you can . . . drift. Of course, no one drifts. They're all too busy.

Interviewer: Tell me about your day.

Kim: Well, we all read until it's time for the flag. Then we have assembly.

Interviewer: What's that?

Kim: Usually we plan the day, special things that have to be done, like that. Then we work by ourselves until 9:30. Then reading groups.

Interviewer: How many are in your group?

Kim: We have seven.

Interviewer: There must be a lot of groups.

Kim: Oh, there are! I don't know how many . . . more than 10. [Actually, 6.] It depends on what book you're in. And some kids get tutored too . . . by mothers.

Interviewer: Does anyone ever change from one group to another?

Kim: Not so far. But some did last year. It's still early in the year.

Interviewer: What do you do in your groups?

Kim: We read out loud—take turns, you know.

Interviewer: You mean round robin.

Kim: Yeah. Then we go to recess. When we come back, we work by ourselves until lunch.

Interviewer: How do you know what to work on?

Kim: Well, we all have our own weekly calendar. It has headings: Reading, Story Folder, Handwriting, Spelling, Math, Science, Social Studies, Centers (like a display of equipment with a study sheet . . . there's one on magnets) and my favorite, Projects. There's lots of projects to choose from. We have to do certain pages in math and reading, and spelling and handwriting. And we have to do one page of writing for the folder each week (you know, a story or a poem or something). Later, we'll probably have pages to do in science and social studies. [Actually, those texts are used as reference volumes.] This is the basic work I mentioned. When that's done we can work on math games, or the centers or projects. If you don't get "OK" on your calendar [basic work completed], you can't go out for third recess.

Interviewer: Who evaluates all those pages you turn in?

Kim: Mainly the teachers. [Two teachers.] Kids give spelling tests to
                     each other—but the teacher grades them.
Interviewer: Doesn't that keep the teachers awfully busy?
Kim: Yes—they don't have time for much else.
Interviewer: Do the teachers do any teaching?
Kim: Some—but mainly we learn on our own—unless we have trouble.
                     Then they help. The kids ask an awful lot of questions.
Interviewer: It must be noisy with all those people.
Kim: Sometimes. If it's just one person, the teacher tells him to be
                     quiet—and that usually works. If the whole group is noisy, she rings
                     a bell and we freeze.
Interviewer: Is it a good place to work?
Kim: Yes, I like it.
Interviewer: What bugs you most?
Kim: Math . . . and kids coming around asking, "What're you doing?"
                     That **really** bugs me. [Kim is used as a model by other children.
                     She has "neat" ideas.]

(Kim's corrections: "No, Daddy, we're studying 'the mouth,' not 'the mouse.'
And we finished **that**. Now it's the **nose**." "And now only four people in the
Annex. Six were too noisy!")

B. An Analysis of Kim's Classroom

Kim's description of her room is quite accurate, as attested by her teachers
Diana Richardson and Suzanne De Vries. This is a **modified open classroom**,
"modified" because basic work is structured (specified) and there are reading
groups. But much of the work is self-selected and self-paced. It is clearly a
superior classroom. With certain changes, it would qualify as an adaptive system.

  (*1*) Subroutines: No information was given on the children's entering skills.
  (*2*) Goals: In this case, the goals are (*a*) pages of work to be completed, each
       page specifying a skill; (*b*) number of words spelled correctly; (*c*) reading
       assignments; (*d*) handwriting pages completed; and (*e*) one page of original
       writing per week. The calendar provides a progress chart (at least for one
       week).
  (*3*) Materials: Most materials are self-instructional; they are somewhat less
       than ideal, according to Kim, who "likes math" but doesn't like **doing**
       math, at least, "writing down problems." The use of reading groups for
       oral reading will be discussed critically in Chapter 9. However, the avail-
       ability of trade books, reference books, and original student work for
       silent reading practice ameliorates this problem.

(4) Environment: The management procedures appear to be effective. Kim produces well here, although "kids bothering her" and her appreciation of the Annex Room suggest a need for either (a) greater privacy or (b) a "Do Not Disturb Others" rule. And privacy is impossible in any classroom.

(5) Self-evaluation: This is a major problem. Procedures for self- and peer-evaluation would benefit both children and teachers.

(6) Practice to Mastery: Teachers keep close track of the productivity of every child and modify materials and techniques in response to those results. Whether children are required to achieve mastery is not indicated in the interview, but the teacher reports that mastery is required.

With the changes indicated, this classroom could approach the ideal that we have heretofore witnessed only in experimental classrooms.

III. The Other Side of the Coin

The description of Kim's open classroom provides an appealing picture. But it is not that easy. The following transcript of testimony is an eyewitness account (rather than the actual court record) of what may be the first legal action of its kind in the country, an attempt by parents to force a school board to remove a teacher for incompetence. Throughout the testimony, the reader should be aware that the teacher had had 7 years of successful teaching in a traditional classroom. Now, however, she had taken on an open classroom, at the request of the principal.

Scene: A courtroom in the county courthouse. The Honorable George A., judge of the circuit court, is presiding (January 10).

Judge: This is a show-cause hearing to determine whether the city Board of Education should not be enjoined from depriving the children of the plaintiffs of their right to an adequate education.

Plaintiffs' Attorney[2]:   Your honor, we intend to show that the so-called open classroom taught by Teacher B at Central Elementary School and consisting of 26 children in Grades 1 and 2 provides an inadequate educational experience as a result of—

                          (1) incompetence of the teacher;

                          (2) poor classroom management; and

[2] The Plaintiffs in this case are the parents.

	(*3*) failure to provide a substantial testing program.
Defense Attorney [3]:	Your Honor, we intend to demonstrate that whatever alleged inadequacies may have existed in this classroom prior to institution of this action are in process of being ameliorated and that this request for relief is precipitous, unnecessary, and should be dismissed.
Co-defendant's Attorney [4]:	A serious charge is being leveled at Teacher B, if only by indirection, and we intend to show that such a charge is without foundation.
Judge:	I remind you that this is a preliminary hearing, not a trial, and we wish to air the issues. Plaintiff, do you have witnesses?
Plaintiff:	I call Principal C. [Duly sworn and identified. Credentials are excellent.] Is the operation of an open classroom a new departure for your school?
Principal C:	Yes, sir.
Plaintiff:	What were the circumstances which led to the decision?
Principal C:	A group of parents requested it.
Plaintiff:	Were you aware of problems in this classroom before the complaint was filed [in early December]?
Principal C:	Yes.
Plaintiff:	When did you first become aware of the problem?
Principal C:	I believe it was during the third week in September.
Plaintiff:	And what did you do about it?
Principal C:	I conferred with the teacher and visited the classroom several times a week thereafter.
Plaintiff:	I call your attention to Plaintiff's Exhibit A, "Performance Evaluation for Teacher B." Did you prepare this report?
Principal C:	Yes, although this is a draft. The final report is not complete.
Plaintiff:	Why?
Principal C:	The teacher has not signed it.
Plaintiff:	Why not?
Principal C:	She pointed out certain inaccuracies in the report which needed correction.

[3] The Defense Attorney in this case represents the Board of Education.
[4] The Co-defendant in this case is Teacher B.

Plaintiff:	This statement is contained in the report: "In my opinion, this teacher is incompetent and should not be rehired." Is this an inaccuracy which you intended to change?
Principal C:	No.
Plaintiff:	Then in your opinion, this teacher is incompetent?
Principal C:	At the time I wrote the report, I was of that opinion.
Plaintiff:	Are you not now of that opinion?
Principal C:	Since early December, we have had a reading specialist in the room to assist the teacher. Since that time, the room has been an adequate environment.
Plaintiff:	But at the time this suit was instigated, you had not changed your opinion concerning the question of teacher competence?
Principal:	No sir.
Plaintiff:	Your witness.
Defense:	No questions.
Co-defense:	Principal C, have you filed a complaint against this teacher?
Principal:	No.
Co-defense:	No further questions.
Plaintiff:	I call the Superintendent of Schools. [Excellent credentials.]
Plaintiff:	Superintendent, when were you first aware of the problem in this classroom?
Superintendent:	I met with a deputation of parents the day before I received a subpoena. It was a good meeting and I assured them that we would investigate the matter thoroughly.
Plaintiff:	Did they request that the teacher be relieved of responsibility?
Superintendent:	Yes.
Plaintiff:	And what did you respond?
Superintendent:	I told them that I was unable to do that. The teacher had the right to a full investigation.
Plaintiff:	Do you mean that the teacher's union would raise the devil unless you carried out a certain set of procedures?
Defense:	Objection. Calls for conjecture by the witness.
Judge:	Sustained.

Plaintiff:	Why did you not accede to the parents' wishes?
Superintendent:	The teacher had the right to a full investigation.
Plaintiff:	Your witness.
Defense:	When did you first learn of the classroom problem?
Superintendent:	December 3.
Defense:	And what did you do?
Superintendent:	I conferred with the principal and the Assistant Superintendent for Instruction. After that meeting, a reading specialist was assigned to help in that room.
Defense:	And when did that help begin?
Superintendent:	On the following Monday.
Defense:	No further questions.
Plaintiff:	I call Mrs. D. [Excellent credentials.]
Plaintiff:	Mrs. D, do you have a child who is assigned to the open classroom?
Mrs. D:	Yes.
Plaintiff:	And have you observed the room?
Mrs. D:	Yes, one morning a week for the first 6 weeks of school. Then I couldn't take it any more.
Plaintiff:	In what capacity were you observing?
Mrs. D:	Some of the mothers were supposed to take turns helping out.
Plaintiff:	You said you "couldn't take it any more." Will you explain that?
Mrs. D:	The room was awful, dirty, with empty cans and cereal boxes piled at one end. The kids were moving around constantly. I never saw the teacher give any instruction. And, when I was supposed to hear a child read, she told me to do it out in the hall. She didn't want me to see what was going on. One little boy asked her what he should do next. And all she said was, "You want to know what you should do next." She never told him what to do! And the instructional material! Faint little ditto sheets, and the workbook that goes with the reading series was awful. Some of the printing ran into the binding. I heard one boy say, "I won't do this stupid stuff!" When I complained about the lack of instruction, the teacher said that she was going to give instruction in using quotation marks that day. And that was pretty good—I guess.

Plaintiff:	You would say then that the learning situation was inadequate?
Defense:	Objection. The witness has not been qualified as to expertness on classroom learning.
Judge:	Sustained.
Plaintiff:	Let me ask the question this way. Will you allow your child to attend this class?
Mrs. D:	Not unless we get another teacher.
Plaintiff:	Your witness.
Defense:	Did you sign the petition asking for an open classroom?
Mrs. D:	Yes, but I never expected to have an incompetent teacher doing it. I don't think it's had a fair trial.
Defense:	Do you think things are better since the arrival of the reading specialist?
Mrs. D:	Yes, they're much better. It should have been done in September.
Defense:	No further questions.
Co-defense:	No questions.
Plaintiff:	No further witnesses at this time, your honor.
Judge:	Defense and Co-defense, do you wish to call witnesses?
Co-defense:	I call Ms. E, a reading specialist. [Excellent credentials.]
Co-defense:	How long have you assisted in Teacher B's room?
Reading Specialist:	Since December 11.
Co-defense:	Do you know Teacher B personally?
Reading Specialist:	I know her professionally.
Co-defense:	Is there a substantial testing program used in this classroom?
Reading Specialist:	Yes sir. All classes use the Gates–McGinnitie battery in the fall and spring and there are mastery tests for reading and math.
Co-defense:	Are the children in this room deficient in reading and math?
Reading Specialist:	No sir. The average achievement is about two grades above normal.
Co-defense:	What did you do in the 3 weeks you were there?
Reading Specialist:	I played the same role as the mothers and from time to time, gave small group instruction in reading.
Co-defense:	Have you taught in an open classroom before?
Reading Specialist:	Yes sir.

Co-defense:	In your opinion, was this classroom substantially different in adequacy from other classrooms?
Reading Specialist:	No sir.
Co-defense:	Do you think the teacher is incompetent?
Reading Specialist:	No sir. She is extremely aware of the children and their needs.
Co-defense:	Is your presence necessary in the room to maintain an adequate environment?
Reading Specialist:	No sir.
Co-defense:	Your witness.
Plaintiff:	No questions.
Co-defense:	I call Teacher B. [Excellent credentials; excellent evaluations in 7 years of teaching.]
Co-defense:	Are the children out of control?
Teacher B:	No sir.
Co-defense:	Do you have a substantial testing program?
Teacher B:	Yes.
Co-defense:	Are you incompetent?
Teacher B:	I didn't think so until I began to read the newspapers. I think I'm very competent.
Co-defense:	Your witness.
Plaintiff:	No questions.
Co-defense:	No further witnesses, Your Honor.
Plaintiff:	I call Dr. F. [Educational psychologist; excellent credentials.]
Plaintiff:	Will you tell the court whether you believe irreparable harm can be done to children due to inadequate education in Grades K–2?
Doctor:	The term *irreparable* is difficult to deal with. In many cases, their achievement deficiencies can be repaired. But the child's image of himself, as a winner or a loser in life, is largely determined by these first school experiences.
Plaintiff:	No further questions.
Co-defense:	Doctor, would you care to offer an opinion on the adequacy of this classroom?
Doctor:	No, since I haven't observed the room nor seen the achievement data. But I would like to discuss the open classroom concept briefly, if I may. The primary difference between open and traditional classrooms is the question, Who makes certain decisions? In the open classroom, children are given latitude in

deciding when and what they will do, within limits. The decisions and the planning are critical independence learnings. And both children and teacher have a difficult time for the first few months. It's unfortunate when outsiders witness the trauma and confusion. If left alone with the teacher, the children mature rapidly and enjoy the new responsibility greatly. A traditional classroom tends to be more smooth and orderly: Teachers make the decisions. In many places where open classrooms are attempted, parents complain, probably for two reasons: (*1*) The classroom looks different from what they remember (it's dirty and disorderly); (2) the children act independently at home. That can be a shocking experience for parents—but the long-term outcomes appear to justify it.

[The judge retires to prepare a decision.]

Opinion:

Children have rights—a day lost in the life of a child cannot be restored. The schools were notified of parent concerns in early September, several times in October, and several times in November (letters to principal). The argument that no written complaint was received until December is not correct. All parties agree that present classroom conditions (with a reading specialist in attendance and with **no** parents present) are adequate. (*Adequate* means "somewhat above a minimum level.") The status quo shall be continued until such time as the board presents an acceptable alternative plan.

The open classroom has great appeal for those who are concerned with maximum development of children's creativity and who view conventional classrooms as dull and stultifying. It certainly sounds exciting: Children self-select from numerous possible materials and activities, evaluate their own work, and call upon an expert resource as necessary. They govern themselves in both their academic and social behavior. These are the goals of the open classroom.

But let us not confuse the goals with the process:

• Children learn to make choices by starting in a limited way, choosing between two familiar activities, then three, then more.

- Children govern themselves when they are keenly aware of their current behavior and its likely consequences; months and sometimes years of feedback provided by adults and peers are necessary to learn self-management.
- When the teacher is required to provide an individualized program—somewhat different for every child—virtually all energy must be used for diagnosis; little or none is available for instruction. So materials must be outstanding.
- Virtually nothing can be learned in a noisy, disorderly environment.

A teacher must have superior classroom management skills, a wealth of carefully constructed, self-instructional materials, and a testing procedure that is virtually autonomous in order to succeed in an open classroom.

From the evidence provided in the transcript, we may infer that one or more of these requirements was missing. And concerned parents are justified in their complaint.

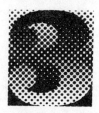

MEASURING GOALS AND
PRODUCING AN ENVIRONMENT

Six conditions required for an adaptive system have been specified: sub-routines, goals, materials, environment, self-evaluation, and practice to mastery.

I. Measuring Goals

In Kim's classroom, goals were provided weekly (a certain number of pages completed) and, in some subjects such as math, spelling, and handwriting, the goal was completion of a workbook. For most children, those goals will suffice. For a sizable minority, they will not. Certain goal-related questions were raised earlier: What **is** good reading? How many words must I be able to write? How legible is legible printing? How can I know if I comprehend text well enough? For this minority, such questions must be answered explicitly. Otherwise, declining motivation will sink the classroom. And those questions can be answered. A comprehensive set of criterion tests, graded in difficulty and defining goals in reading, writing, listening, and speaking, will provide goals understandable to the child. When his test results are compared with a standard, he will receive a clear feedback signal on the amount and nature of the learnings to be mastered. A record sheet for one such set of tests appears on the next five pages and will be referred to in later chapters.[1]

[1] Reproduced, with permission, from *Criterion-Referenced Tests for Reading and Writing*, by J. M. Smith, D. E. P. Smith, and J. R. Brink (New York: Academic Press, 1977).

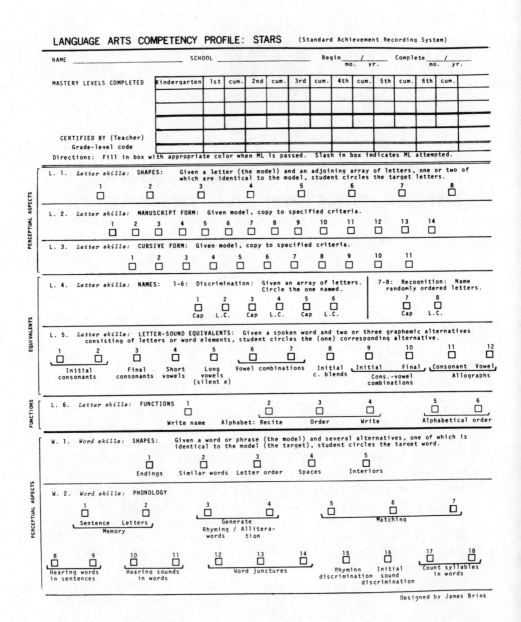

LANGUAGE ARTS COMPETENCY PROFILE: STARS   (Standard Achievement Recording System)

NAME _____ SCHOOL _____ Begin____/____ Complete____/____
                                                          mo.   yr.   mo.   yr.

MASTERY LEVELS COMPLETED	Kindergarten	1st	cum.	2nd	cum.	3rd	cum.	4th	cum.	5th	cum.	6th	cum.

CERTIFIED BY (Teacher)
Grade-level code
Directions: Fill in box with appropriate color when ML is passed. Slash in box indicates ML attempted.

PERCEPTUAL ASPECTS

L. 1. *Letter skills:* SHAPES: Given a letter (the model) and an adjoining array of letters, one or two of
        which are identical to the model, student circles the target letters.
        1   2   3   4   5   6   7   8
        □   □   □   □   □   □   □   □

L. 2. *Letter skills:* MANUSCRIPT FORM: Given model, copy to specified criteria.
        1 2 3 4 5 6 7 8 9 10 11 12 13 14
        □ □ □ □ □ □ □ □ □ □   □   □   □   □

L. 3. *Letter skills:* CURSIVE FORM: Given model, copy to specified criteria.
        1 2 3 4 5 6 7 8 9 10 11
        □ □ □ □ □ □ □ □ □ □   □

EQUIVALENTS

L. 4. *Letter skills:* NAMES: 1-6: Discrimination: Given an array of letters. | 7-8: Recognition: Name
                                      Circle the one named. | randomly ordered letters.
                        1   2   3   4   5   6 | 7   8
                        □   □   □   □   □   □ | □   □
                       Cap L.C. Cap L.C. Cap L.C. | Cap   L.C.

L. 5. *Letter skills:* LETTER-SOUND EQUIVALENTS: Given a spoken word and two or three graphemic alternatives
        consisting of letters or word elements, student circles the (one) corresponding alternative.
   1   2   3   4   5   6   7   8   9   10   11   12
   □   □   □   □   □   □   □   □   □   □   □   □
 Initial Final Short Long   Vowel combinations Initial Initial Final Consonant Vowel
consonants consonants vowels vowels   c. blends Cons.-vowel   Allographs
                          (silent e)   combinations

FUNCTIONS

L. 6. *Letter skills:* FUNCTIONS   1   2   3   4   5   6
                                    □   □   □   □   □   □
                              Write name   Alphabet: Recite   Order   Write   Alphabetical order

PERCEPTUAL ASPECTS

W. 1. *Word skills:* SHAPES: Given a word or phrase (the model) and several alternatives, one of which is
        identical to the model (the target), student circles the target word.
        1   2   3   4   5
        □   □   □   □   □
     Endings Similar words Letter order Spaces Interiors

W. 2. *Word skills:* PHONOLOGY
   1   2   3   4   5   6   7
   □   □   □   □   □   □   □
Sentence   Letters   Generate   Matching
    Memory   Rhyming / Allitera-
                           words   tion

 8   9   10   11   12   13   14   15   16   17   18
 □   □   □   □   □   □   □   □   □   □   □
Hearing words   Hearing sounds   Word junctures   Rhyming   Initial   Count syllables
in sentences   in words   discrimination sound   in words
                                                                      discrimination

Designed by James Brink

LANGUAGE ARTS COMPETENCY PROFILE: STARS   (Page 2)

EQUIVALENTS

W. 3. *Word skills:* WORD RECOGNITION: Given a printed sentence, and one or two spoken words, student circles named word(s). (Exceptions: ML's 4 and 8.)

MASTERY LEVELS	1	2	3	4	5	6	7	8	9	10	11
	☐	☐	☐	☐ Read sentence	☐	☐	☐	☐ Read phrase	☐	☐	☐

W. 4. *Word skills:* SPELLING: Given a word list of specified difficulty, approximately one third of which are misspelled, student marks the misspelled words.

MASTERY LEVELS	1	2	3	4	5
	☐ freq. 1-100	☐ freq. 1-300 Short words	☐ freq. 1-300 Long words	☐ freq. 301-600	☐ freq. 601-1000

GRAMMATICAL MEANING

W. 5. *Word skills:* VOCABULARY: SYNTACTIC FACTOR

1	Given sentence, select illustration.				Select words w/ similar meaning			Answer questions				Fill in blank
	2	3	4	5	6	7	8	9	10	11	12	13
☐ Sing/ Plur	☐ Action Actor Object	☐ Action	☐ Actor	☐ Object	☐ Tense	☐ Actor	☐ Object	☐ Scope	☐ Action	☐ N/V, V/mod NV, N/mod	☐	☐ Infl. cues

W. 6. *Word skills:* VOCABULARY RANGE: (Three range paradigms, 18 mastery levels.)

(A). Given an incomplete sentence and several alternatives which fulfill sentence conditions ("make sense in the sentence").

1	2	3	4
☐	☐	☐	☐

(B). Given a noun, determine appropriate:

5	6	7
☐ Class name	☐ Action	☐ Modifier

(C). Given incomplete sentences, choose appropriate completion word.

8	9	10	11	12	13	14	15	16	17	18	19	20
☐	☐	☐	☐	☐	☐	☐	☐	☐	☐	☐	☐	☐

REFERENTIAL MEANING

W. 7. *Word skills:* VOCABULARY: SEMANTIC FACTOR

Given sets of 3 sentences with the same word underlined, student marks the two sentences in which the underlined word has the same meaning.

1	2	3	4	5	6	7	8	9
☐ Noun: within class	☐ Noun: between classes		☐ Main verb/ auxiliary verb	☐ Verb within class	☐ Verb: between classes	☐ Modifier: within class	☐ Modifier: between classes	☐ Usage

W. 8. *Word skills:* VOCABULARY: CLASSIFICATION FACTOR: Given a word or a sentence, select another word having a specified relationship to the model.

1	2	3	4	5	6	7	8	9	10	11	12
☐ Syn	☐ Syn	☐ Ant	☐ Hom	☐ Syn	☐ Ant	☐ Class	☐ Class	☐ Syn	☐ Syn	☐ Emphasis	☐ Analogies

W. 9. *Word skills:* VOCABULARY FLUENCY

1	2	3	4	5	6	7
☐ Complete partial sentence	☐ Names of things	☐ Can do...	☐ Fill blank	☐ Words that start with... (letter)	☐ Words that end with... (sound)	☐ Words that start w/ (blend).

LANGUAGE ARTS COMPETENCY PROFILE: STARS   (Page 3)

S 1. *Sentence skills:* ORAL READING: Read sentences with appropriate intonation.

1	2	3
4-7 Words	8-14 Words/Quotes	15-24 Words/Dramatic

S 2. *Sentence skills:* SPACES BETWEEN WORDS: Recognize and produce spaces between words.

1

S 3. *Sentence skills:* SENTENCE MEMORY: Reproduce sentences of increasing complexity.

1	2
3-5 Words	5-8 Words

S 4. *Sentence skills:* DICTATION: Write dictated sentences.

1	2	3	4	5	6
		Frequencies 1-300		301-600	601-1000

S 5. *Sentence skills:* CAPITALIZATION: Use capitals correctly.

1	2	3	4	5	6	7	8	9	10
Initial Words Names	Place Names	Titles Initials	Time	Address Organization	Religious	Vehicles Plants Animals	Trade names	Quotes	Titles

S 6. *Sentence skills:* PUNCTUATION: Use punctuation marks correctly.

1	2	3	4	5	6	7
Marks						Direct quotes

8	9	10	11	12	13	14
Compound sentence	Series	Interjections	Appositive	Antithetical	Dates Places	Parenthetical elements

15	16	17	18	19	20	21
Mistaken junctions	Intro- clauses	Nonrestrictive	Sentence break	Series		Combination

S 7. *Sentence skills:* TRANSFORMATIONS: Rewrite sentences to fulfill grammatical constraints.

1	2	3	4	5	6	7	8
Singular	Plural	Negation	Pronoun	Pronoun	Tense: Present	Tense: Past	Tense: Future

9	10	11	12	13	14	15	16	17
Aux. have	Aux. be	Aux. be + have	Passive	Links	Links	Links	Links	Word order

S 8. *Sentence skills:* DIRECTIONS: Follow workbook and test directions.

1	2
Circle Underline Cross out	Draw Make Put

S 9. *Sentence skills:* QUESTIONS: Produce questions controlled by answers.

1	2	3	4	5	6
Who	What	Where	When	Why	How

S 10. *Sentence skills:* SENTENCE MEANING: Choose meanings which conform to particular constraints.

1	2	3
Picture constraint	Internal constraint (sense)	External constraint (paragraph)

S 11. *Sentence skills:* FIGURATIVE LANGUAGE: Recognize idioms and similes.

1	2	3	4
Recognize idioms	Recognize idioms	Recognize idioms	Interpret similes

PERCEPTUAL ASPECTS

GRAMMATICAL ASPECTS

REFERENTIAL ASPECTS

LANGUAGE ARTS COMPETENCY PROFILE: STARS (Page 4)

FORM

P 1. *Paragraph skills:* FORM CONVENTION: Recognize and produce indented form.

  1   2
□   □

P 2. *Paragraph skills:* GRAMMATICAL PATTERNS: Recognize and produce consistent tense, number and structure.

1	2	3	4
□	□	□	□
	Parallel structure	Tense	Number

P 3. *Paragraph skills:* PHONOLOGICAL PATTERNS: Recognize and produce rhyme, alliteration, rhythm (poetry).

1	2	3	4	5
□	□	□	□	□
Rhyme	Alliteration	Rhythm	Combined	Produce

CONTENT

P 4. *Paragraph skills:* UNIVERSE OF DISCOURSE: Recognize universe of discourse by vocabulary and style.

1	2
□	□
Topic	Genre

P 5. *Paragraph skills:* TOPIC: Identify topic by listening and reading; produce a paragraph orally.

1	2	3	4	5
□	□	□	□	□
Oral: Recognize topic	Oral composition	Read: Recognize topic	Part - Whole	Read: Name topic

P 6. *Paragraph skills:* PLOT: Recognize and produce 8 paragraph plots.

1	2	3	4	5	6	7	8
□	□	□	□	□	□	□	□
Similar-Different		Example-Reason		Space-Time		Restate-Cause	
Recognize-Produce		Recognize-Produce		Recognize-Produce		Recognize-Produce	

P 7. *Paragraph skills:* REFERENTIAL LINKS: Recognize and produce referential links.

1	2
□	□
Referential	
Recognize/Produce	

P 8. *Paragraph skills:* RELATIONAL LINKS: Recognize relational links and rewrite sentences adding links.

1	2	3	4	5	6
□	□	□	□	□	□
Recognize links	Recognize links	Recognize links	Produce links	Recognize links	Produce links

P 9. *Paragraph skills:* INFORMATION: Identify answers to information questions and produce questions.

1	2	3	4	5	6	7	8	9
□	□	□	□	□	□	□	□	□
	Who, What, Where, When, Why			Questions		Questions		Questions
	Recognize			Produce		Recognize-Produce		Recognize-Produce
				I		II		III

EQUIVALENTS

P 10. *Paragraph skills:* SUMMARIZATION: Recognize and produce summary statements outside and within paragraphs.

1	2	3	4	5
□	□	□	□	□
Recognize summary-statement		Recognize main idea in paragraph		Produce summary

P 11. *Paragraph skills:* INDUCTION (inference): Recognize and produce valid inductions.

1	2	3	4	5	6
□	□	□	□	□	□
Recognize inference		Recognize and produce		Infer reasons	Produce inference
		an inference			

P 12. *Paragraph skills:* DEDUCTION: Use syllogistic reasoning to draw conclusions.

1	2	3
□	□	□
Solve syllogism	Recognize logical conclusion	Produce logical conclusion

LANGUAGE ARTS COMPETENCY PROFILE: STARS (Page 5)

IMPACT

P 13. *Paragraph skills:* FOCUS: Identify focus (setting, topic, action, time, motive).

1	2	3	4	5
☐	☐	☐	☐	☐
Select focus	Recognize time & motive	Recognize setting description	Recognize topic description	Recognize action description

P 14. *Paragraph skills:* POINT OF VIEW: Recognize and produce paragraph reflecting point of view.

1	2	3	4
☐	☐	☐	☐
Recognize point of view (who)	Produce paragraph from a point of view	Recognize pro or con point of view	Produce pro or con point of view

P 15. *Paragraph skills:* MOOD: Recognize mood.

1	2	3
☐	☐	☐
Sad Happy	Mysterious Adventurous	Humorous Serious

P 16. *Paragraph skills:* ORAL READING:(dramatic): Read aloud with appropriate intonation.

1	2	3	4
☐	☐	☐	☐
Essay & Drama	Essay & Drama	Story	Poetry

B 1. *Book skills:* FICTION: Recognize and produce fictional works.

1	2	3	4	5	6	7
☐	☐	☐	☐	☐	☐	☐
Reference data	Genre	Book report	Write stories: Character	Write stories: Setting	Write stories: Action	Write stories: Motivation

B 2. *Book skills:* NONFICTION: Recognize and produce nonfictional works.

1	2	3	4	5
☐	☐	☐	☐	☐
Reference data	Genre	Research	Organize report	Produce report

B 3. *Book skills:* TEXTBOOKS: Use a textbook properly.

1	2	3	4	5	6	7
☐	☐	☐	☐	☐	☐	☐
Orientation	Reference data		Skimming	Formulate study questions	Answer study questions	Technical terms

B 4. *Book skills:* REFERENCE WORKS: Use appropriate reference works.

1	2	3	4	5	6	7	8	9
☐	☐	☐	☐	☐	☐	☐	☐	☐
Dictionary		Encyclopedia			Thesaurus	Almanac	Library	

B 5. *Book skills:* PERIODICALS: Find and use books and newspapers.

1	2	3	4	5
☐	☐	☐	☐	☐
Newspaper	Newspapers	Magazines	Newspapers	

B 6. *Book skills:* LETTERS: Identify letter format; write letters for differing purposes.

1	2	3	4	5	6
☐	☐	☐	☐	☐	☐
Recognize format	Produce format	Recognize format	Produce format	Produce letter of complaint	Respond to a survey

The Language Arts Competency Profile describes tests at the five levels of printed language: Letter, Word, Sentence, Paragraph, and Book. For example, Letter Skills includes Shapes, Manuscript Form, Cursive Form, Names (of letters), Letter–Sound Equivalents, and Functions. Each of these subsets includes a series of one-page tests, graded in difficulty.

Taken together, the 353 tests measure all, or virtually all, language arts competencies from kindergarten to Grade 6.

As noted, this record form, kept by the teacher, will be referred to in later chapters. Use of the tests, or of some equivalent set, makes possible a definition of goals sufficient to motivate the most laggard child.

* * * * *

But what if such tests are unavailable or inappropriate? To design your own goal measures and progress charts, complete Module 1, Designing and Using Feedback Forms.

MODULE 1
Designing and Using
Feedback Forms[2]

Purpose

This module is designed to teach you how to use student performance data to improve student performance.

Objectives

Reading teachers will

(1) Design forms to collect data on performance.
(2) Plot data.
(3) Analyze data and use them to make educational decisions.

[2] By Geraldine Markel and Daniel Wolter. Reprinted by arrangement with the authors.

Directions
(*1*) Find the sub-criterion test for Part I (p. 43).
(*2*) Read through the test. If you can complete it, do so and go on to Part II. If not, complete the Introduction and Part I.

Introduction

School personnel are responsible for making educational decisions that affect individuals and groups. If possible, such decisions should be based on objective, measurable, and communicable information about student performance. When such information on performance is collected and used to influence future performance, it is called **feedback**.

PROBLEM	**USE OF FEEDBACK**
Elementary-school students in a remedial reading class did little work on lessons, dawdled, daydreamed, rule tested, and so on.	Feedback consisted of charting tasks completed by the class. Amount of work increased and irrelevant behavior decreased; work behavior was maintained.

PROBLEM	**USE OF FEEDBACK**
A 9-year-old retarded girl worked reasonably hard, but her error rate indicated random responding.	Feedback consisted of charting correct responses. The number of incorrect responses declined to less than 3%.

Here are some other examples of school behaviors that have been modified using feedback procedures:

(*1*) Increased number of pages read per day
(*2*) Increased production on assignments in a self-directed learning packet
(*3*) Increased independence on starting work in a special reading class
(*4*) Increased number of words read correctly from 100 running words

To obtain and analyze information that will influence your decisions, and those of your students, you need to develop the following skills:

(*1*) Design forms to collect various types of information (Part I).

(*2*) Record and plot the information each time it occurs (Part II).

(*3*) Analyze and use the information to make educational decisions (Part III).

I. Designing Graphs and Forms

Several basic forms are used to collect information for decision making. The simplest are those designed for an individual pupil working on one subskill during a short period of time; more complex are those designed for classes of students working on a variety of objectives over a long time.

CRITICAL

> Those making decisions must help construct and then use the forms. Both teachers and students make decisions. Thus, both must help construct the forms.

The teacher or consultant uses the information to decide how to arrange environments, materials, and the sequence of instruction. The student uses the same form to observe the current level of his performance and to estimate his progress. Thus both teacher and student self-management are attainable. Relevant progress information is used to make decisions by both.

Initially, teacher, student, and parent need to observe the answer to the question, How much was produced? The question can be answered in terms of amount per minute, per day, per week; it is usually answered by some tally and/or graphic representation of response frequency.

The child should be able to explain the graph or tally form to you or to another student. This provides proof of understanding and shows what needs to be further illustrated.

SAMPLE

> Which one should the teacher say?
> a. You do understand it don't you?
> b. Will you show me how we're going to use this graph?

(The answer key to Part I is on p. 46.)

A. Bar Graphs

For the younger student, a bar graph drawn by or with the teacher is the simplest to construct and use. Initially the teacher models the recording process by helping the child to count responses and to plot his progress. For young students, a simple, concrete, visually appealing system is necessary.

The design of a bar graph is dependent on the entering skill level of the student. The first and simplest form has the actual responses recorded. Later, the child places on the graph a symbol that represents each response made. Finally, the pupil tallies the responses and plots the total number of responses on the graph.

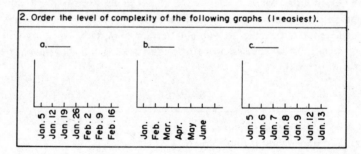

As student skill increases, more complex behaviors (in terms of length of time, number of responses, and units of performance) are recorded. Complexity is found not only in the kinds of response or performance but also in the time intervals used.

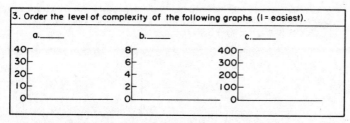

3. Order the level of complexity of the following graphs (1 = easiest).

    a._____   b._____   c._____

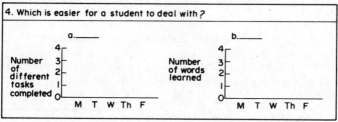

4. Which is easier for a student to deal with?

    a._____   b._____

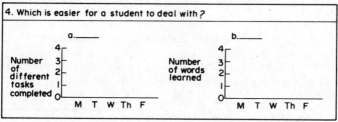

If a graph is designed wrong, problems result. These graphs are designed wrong. Redo them.

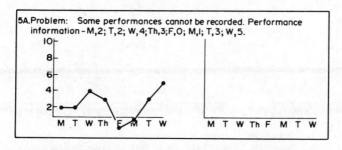

5A. Problem: Some performances cannot be recorded. Performance information – M,2; T,2; W,4; Th,3; F,O; M,I; T,3; W,5.

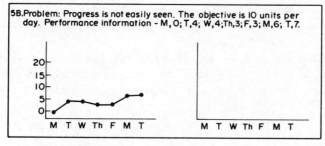

5B. Problem: Progress is not easily seen. The objective is 10 units per day. Performance information – M,O; T,4; W,4; Th,3; F,3; M,6; T,7.

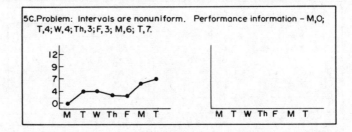

5C.Problem: Intervals are nonuniform. Performance information – M,O; T,4; W, 4; Th, 3; F, 3; M,6; T,7.

B. Frequency and Cumulative Graphs

A cumulative graph is used when a student is expected to maintain a constant rate of growth. Each day's progress is added to the previous total.

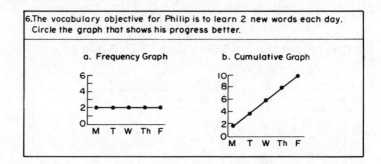

6.The vocabulary objective for Philip is to learn 2 new words each day. Circle the graph that shows his progress better.

a. Frequency Graph   b. Cumulative Graph

7.Circle the types of objective with which you would use a cumulative graph.

    a.   Completing 1 chapter each week.
    b.   Answering as many questions as possible in 10 minutes.
    c.   Answering 3 quiz questions each day.

Cumulative graphs are useful also when a student's performance is low and rate of increase is slow. In such cases, frequency graphs often do not provide sufficient positive feedback to result in increased performance.

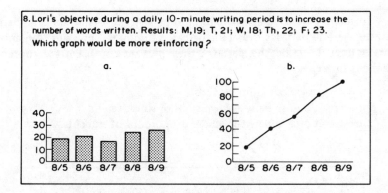

8. Lori's objective during a daily 10-minute writing period is to increase the number of words written. Results: M, 19; T, 21; W, 18; Th, 22; F, 23. Which graph would be more reinforcing?

Cumulative graphs should have a larger range of numbers indicating frequency than bar graphs since the number of responses will be continuously added to itself. Rough estimates of range are made by multiplying the expected response rate by the number of days. The intervals used on the left side are usually the expected daily rate.

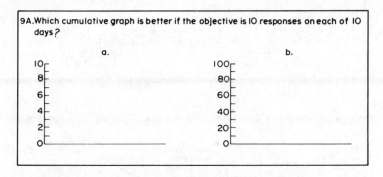

9A. Which cumulative graph is better if the objective is 10 responses on each of 10 days?

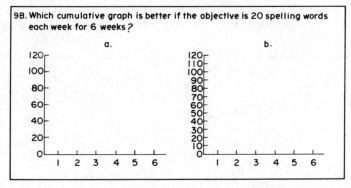

9B. Which cumulative graph is better if the objective is 20 spelling words each week for 6 weeks?

It is often useful to graph two or more progress trends on one graph to illustrate learning patterns over time or between groups and skills. A number of graphs follow. Describe the patterns they illustrate by using the appropriate letter next to each graph:

(*a*) Shows a pattern over time periods
(*b*) Shows relationship between two skills or subskills
(*c*) Shows relationship between students or groups of students

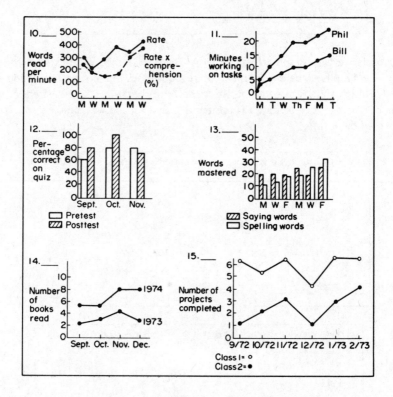

C. Forms

A record form should be specific to the kind of decision to be made. Initially a reading teacher might have a card or page for each child and each skill. This could be used with the child and parent for individual programming. Later, various skills should be combined to view the child's total growth in several areas over an extended period of time. Information from the forms are used to construct graphs.

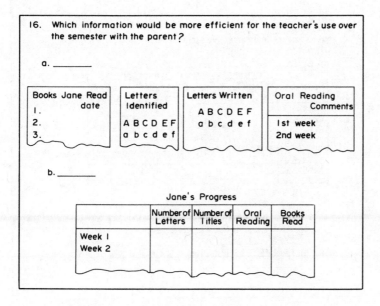

16. Which information would be more efficient for the teacher's use over the semester with the parent?

a. _____

Books Jane Read date	Letters Identified	Letters Written	Oral Reading Comments
1.		A B C D E F	
2.	A B C D E F	a b c d e f	1st week
3.	a b c d e f		2nd week

b. _____

Jane's Progress

	Number of Letters	Number of Titles	Oral Reading	Books Read
Week 1				
Week 2				

For effective instructional programming it is necessary to see the progress trends of students over long periods of time.

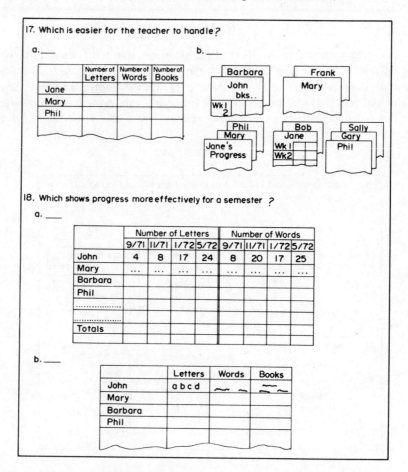

Record forms are commonly designed for long-term pretest and posttest scores. One paper should contain (*1*) all scores, (*2*) differences between scores for each subtest, and (*3*) differences between the total scores.

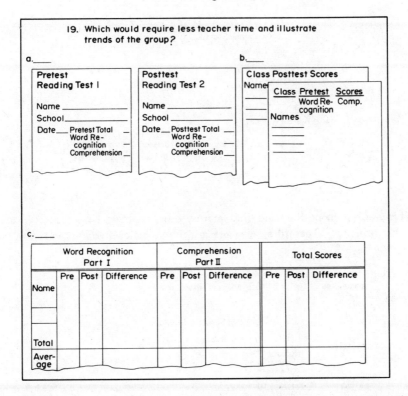

19. Which would require less teacher time and illustrate trends of the group?

a.____

Pretest
Reading Test I

Name _____
School _____
Date___ Pretest Total __
    Word Re- __
      cognition
    Comprehension __

Posttest
Reading Test 2

Name _____
School _____
Date___ Posttest Total __
    Word Re- __
      cognition
    Comprehension __

b.____

Class Posttest Scores
Name

Class Pretest Scores
    Word Re- Comp.
    cognition
Names

c.____

Name	Word Recognition Part I			Comprehension Part II			Total Scores		
	Pre	Post	Difference	Pre	Post	Difference	Pre	Post	Difference
Total									
Average									

The amount of information required by your design depends on the person who will use it for making decisions.

If one student uses the form by himself, he will need answers to these questions:

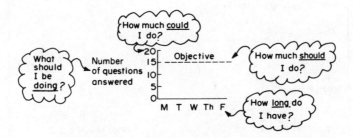

If students are working on individual assignments, more specificity may be required:

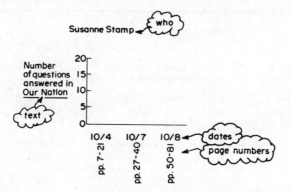

This graph is to be filed and used later by other teachers, parents, consultants, or the principal. Therefore, answers to the questions *where* and *how* are included.

If this graph were to be filed and later used by other teachers, parents, consultants or the principal, answer "where" and "how".

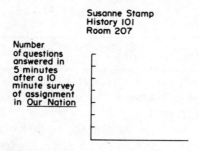

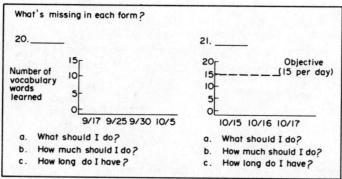

What's missing in each form?

20. _____

Number of vocabulary words learned

9/17 9/25 9/30 10/5

a. What should I do?
b. How much should I do?
c. How long do I have?

21. _____

Objective (15 per day)

10/15 10/16 10/17

a. What should I do?
b. How much should I do?
c. How long do I have?

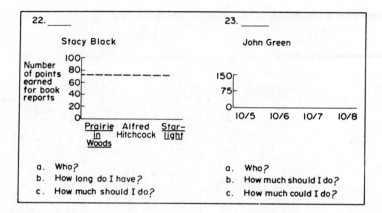

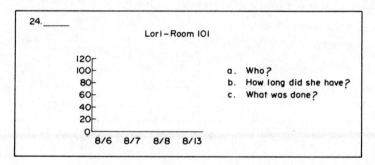

The following form will be used with parents or the principal. What's missing?

Record forms and tally sheets should provide the same information as a graph. In order to use information, we must know how good performance is in relation to an objective and the dates of performance. If this is lacking, our decision-making capacity is reduced.

On the following pages are feedback forms for surveying and oral reading that will be used by a teacher. Decide what is missing for each one.

25. _____ This form will be used by the teacher. What is missing?

    a. Who did it?

    b. What was done?

    c. When was it done?

B-83 Basic Instructions: Set objectives or an increase in one or more of the steps, survey, summary, etc.

Bonus Points   *Larry*

+1 - Each word in summary

+1 - Each (wₐh) word

+1 - Question

SURVEY FEEDBACK AND PLANNING

Objective	Text Time	Survey No. Pages	Summary No. Words	Questions Pred.	Answers Pred.	Answers Confirmed	Total Points
1. Pre Test shaving commerc.	Picture 1 min.	Picture	2	2	2	—	7
2. Picture history book	Picture 1 min.	2 pts Picture	3	3	3	3	14
3. Inc. summary to 5 w.	Picture sc. book	Picture 5	5	3	3	3	16
4. Inc. # of quest. pred.	Picture	Picture	6	4	3	3	17
5. write two questions using (w,w,w,w,w, H)	1 min Picture	Picture	6	3	3	3	17
6. Write 3 questions	Pict.		3	4	3	3	13
7. write 3 quest.	Pict.	Pict.	3	8	4	4	19
8. write 3 quest.	Pict.	Pict.	5	8	4	4	21
9.							
10.							

26. ____ What is missing?
    a. Who did it?
    b. What was done?
    c. How much should be done?

ORAL READING	Name: *Eric*
	Date: *July 29 F*
	Material: *SRA Lab*
	Level: *Purple*
	Time: 5 minutes

Number Correct	
1st minute	
~~|||| |||| |||| |||| |||~~	*23*
2nd minute	
~~|||| |||| |||| |||| |||| |||| |||| |||| ||||~~	*45*
3rd minute	
~~|||| |||| |||| |||| |||| |||| |||| ||||~~	*45*
4th minute	
~~|||| |||| |||| |||| |||| |||| |||| |||| ||||~~ *||||*	*54*
5th minute	
~~|||| |||| |||| |||| |||| |||| |||| |||| ||||~~ *|||||*	*50*
Comments - types of errors etc.	*217*

Point System *1 pt. for each word*

Points Earned ___ *217*

27. ___ This form will be used by other teachers or
       consultants. What's missing?

   a. What was done?
   b. How much should be done?
   c. How much could be done?

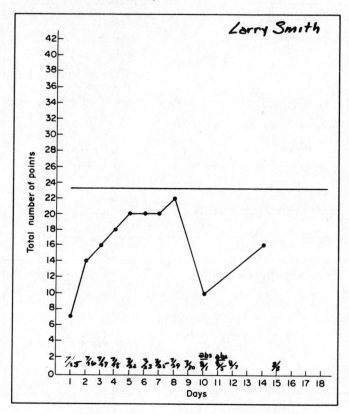

It is often necessary to design one form for students to record daily performance and another form to track total class progress. The teacher "chunks" information into larger sections since the decisions to be made cover more time and a number of pupils.

For example:

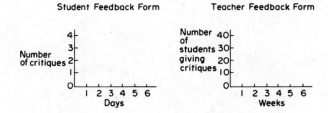

Objective: Students will give spontaneous critiques of books.

Student Feedback Form   Teacher Feedback Form

SUB-CRITERION TEST

28. Draw student and teacher graphs for the following objective.

Objective: Students will attain 100% mastery on daily unit tests.

Student   Teacher

29. Below is a form used by a first grade student to illustrate the number of problems correct on daily quizzes in May.
Draw a class record form for the teacher for the month.

Make Oscar's home colorful (_____)
name

Student
Form

May
1 2 3 4 5

Problem
% correct

10
9
8
7
6
5

May
8 9 10 11 12

10
9
8

May
15 16 17 18 19

10
9
8
7

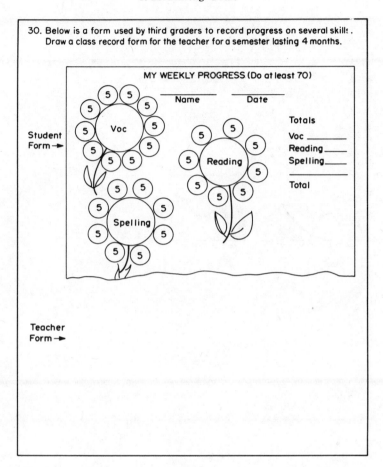

30. Below is a form used by third graders to record progress on several skills. Draw a class record form for the teacher for a semester lasting 4 months.

Summary

Part I has provided examples and exercises to increase your skill in designing feedback forms.

The frequency graphs and record forms for individuals or classes provide a structure for collecting and recording performance information. This design process often helps the teacher to focus on objectives, criteria, and the information that will be necessary for decision making throughout the instructional process.

Even more, it has a powerful motivating effect on students.

Answer Key for Part I

Sample: b

1.	a. 3	b. 1	c. 2
2.	a. 2	b. 3	c. 1
3.	a. 2	b. 1	c. 3
4.	b		

5. A.   B, C.

6. b

7. a, c

8. b

9. A. b   B. a

10. b

11. c

12. a

13. b

14. a

15. c

16. b

17. a

18. a

19. c

20. b

21. a

22. b

23. b

24. c

25. c

26. c

27. a

28.

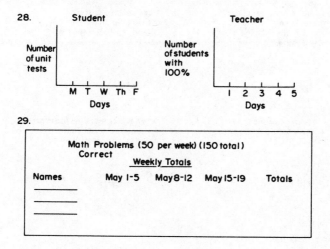

29.

```
┌─────────────────────────────────────────────────────────────────┐
│      Math Problems (50 per week) (150 total)                      │
│      Correct                                                      │
│                        Weekly Totals                              │
│                                                                   │
│   Names          May 1-5    May 8-12   May 15-19     Totals       │
│   ─────────                                                       │
│   ─────────                                                       │
│   ─────────                                                       │
│                                                                   │
└─────────────────────────────────────────────────────────────────┘
```

30.

```
┌───────────────────────────────────────────────────────────────────────────────┐
│                          Progress Points                                        │
│                   Monthly and Semester Totals                                   │
│                                                                                 │
│   Names        Vocabulary            Reading              Spelling              │
│              S*│O│N│D│Total││    S│O│N│D│Total││    S│O│N│D│Total││             │
│   ────────    │ │ │ │      ││     │ │ │ │     ││     │ │ │ │     ││             │
│   ────────    │ │ │ │      ││     │ │ │ │     ││     │ │ │ │     ││             │
│               │ │ │ │      ││     │ │ │ │     ││     │ │ │ │     ││             │
└───────────────────────────────────────────────────────────────────────────────┘
```

*S = September, O = October, etc.

II. Recording Information

After you design a graph or tally form, the information should be accurately recorded and summarized for decision making.

a. To plot scores on a line
    graph, begin on the
    bottom line with the
    day or date.

    M T W
     9/17

b. Move up until you reach
    the number on the left
    side which indicates the
    score.

      M
     9/17

c. Place a dot at the point
    where the date and score
    cross.

      M
     9/17

d. When two or more performances
    are being recorded, a line
    is drawn to connect them.

    M T W Th
     9/17

(The answer key is on p. 56.)

---

1. A class is earning points toward a weekly party. The objective
   is to earn 75-85 points per day. Plot their daily totals: M, 15;
   T, 40; W, 70; Th, 50; F, 75.

During instruction, information for a graph is tallied from the student's
worksheet and then recorded on a graph.

---

2. The objective for Henry is to increase by 100% the number of
   words written about a picture in 10 minutes. He earns one
   point per word. His work is displayed on the next page. Tally
   each writing task and plot the scores on a frequency graph.

I-II
WRITING BASELINE

NAME *Henry*

DATE 7/21

MATERIAL *Magazine Picture*

TIME 10 minutes

Topic *picture*

Answer some questions like who? where? when? how? why?

A boy looking at that ski, and sheep's were around hem. Number of Points —

7/29

Magazine Picture

Henry

Three guys eating orange. one lady and tour mans. the right man tast so will, the left man tast tour sour tu.

Number of Points —

7/30

Number of points —

Henry

the indian is talking to was un the microphone becuas he is a indian news man. hes hat is mes he is a indian king.

Often several trends are recorded on the same page. Different activities are symbolized by different kinds of dots or shapes, as shown in question 3.

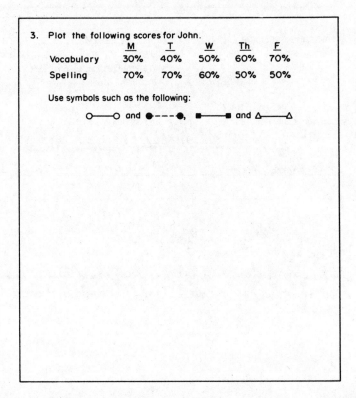

3. Plot the following scores for John.

	M	T	W	Th	F
Vocabulary	30%	40%	50%	60%	70%
Spelling	70%	70%	60%	50%	50%

Use symbols such as the following:

○———○ and ●----●, ■———■ and △———△

Sometimes one graph is placed above another so that trends can be compared. For example, reading efficiency classes plot progress for rate, comprehension, and a combined score:

Session	Rate (words per minute) X	Comprehension (%) =	Reading efficiency (R/C) (rate X % comprehension)
1	273	70%	191
2	506	50%	253
3	384	80%	307
4	675	80%	540

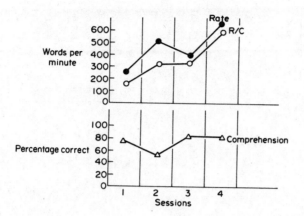

4. On the next page is a reading efficiency tally form for class I. Plot the average scores in rate, comprehension, and R/C for the 1st, 4th, and 9th exercises.

Class I (M–W 10–11)

READING EFFICIENCY TALLY FORM

Students	First Exercise			Fourth Exercise			Ninth Exercise		
	Rate	× Comp. (%) =	R/C	Rate	× Comp. (%) =	R/C	Rate	× Comp. (%) =	R/C
1	331	85	281.35	538	100	538.00	1257	100	1257.00
2	279	88	245.52	309	100	309.00	460	100	460.00
3	280	100	280.00	333	89	296.37	265	65	172.25
4	200	75	150.00	213	60	127.80	274	100	274.00
5	220	100	220.00	272	100	272.00	392	70	274.40
6	250	68	170.00	420	100	420.00	220	100	220.00
7	260	54	140.40	200	75	150.00	320	65	208.00
8	330	85	280.50	355	100	355.00	440	100	440.00
9	350	100	350.00	376	100	376.00	190	95	180.50
10	224	100	224.00	276	85	234.60	194	100	194.00
11	194	60	116.40	234	100	234.00	376	90	338.40
12	216	100	216.00	194	100	194.00	270	100	270.00
13	190	90	171.00	292	50	146.00	356	100	356.00
14	317	95	301.15	336	95	319.20	244	100	244.00
15	285	90	256.50	245	100	245.00	262	100	262.00
16	308	95	292.60	334	100	334.00	510	100	510.00
17	320	100	320.00	420	100	420.00	393	100	393.00
18	330	100	330.00	358	100	358.00	372	100	372.00
19	380	100	380.00	385	89	342.65	270	72	194.40
20	270	86	232.20	252	72	181.44			
	5534	1771	4958	6342	1815	5853	7065	1757	6619.9
Average	276.7	88.6	247.9	317.1	90.8	292.6	371.8	92.5	330.9

5. Sally's task is to look at a picture and write the answer to some
    questions like who?, where?, when? She is allowed 10 minutes
    and earns 1 point per word written. The objective for the first
    week is to increase fluency and write between 45-50 words.

    Tally these writing tasks on the next 2 pages and fill informa-
    tion on the tally form below.

Day	Date	Goal	Number of words written

Sally   Writing   Monday 10/14   10 min

Kooking, art, a new bike,
a pretty dress, play piano,
singing, dansing, play game,
reading, make a doll, weaving,
go to shoping with mother,
friends, camping, chuing gom,
make things.

_____

Sally   wednesday 10/16

I like to go camping in the tent,
it was so fun we cook by au slef,
some time we eat cans, It was
fun when we sleep in the tent, but
we have to get some light, to
see the dark, I like to camping
with many peoples, we can
do many things togather,
and play together like go to
woo or ..

Room 104

Writing Dictionary (10 min)   Sally
                                   Friday 10/18

I like pets My father pet is dog or
cat, I have a cat but I didn't get a
dog yet. My cats name TieTa
She's a nice cat, she is 5 years
old . She likes to sleep with poepel
she like to set on your two nees,
my brother likes to play with
her but not very nice, some
time he sger her, when Tieta get
sger she always hide.

Sally   Monday 10/21
Three little boy and a old men and
a dog and a cat .
    the old men give come can of food
for three boys and the cat look out
for the can the boy was eating.
    beacause the cat wont to eat
it .
    Theye were at the back gard of
old mens house.
    the can was very good .
when a boy set on a doghouse, when
the old men was give the can to
the boys, when

Answer Key for Part II

1.

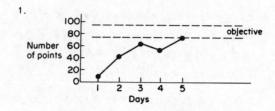

2.

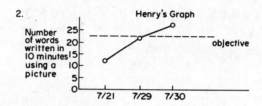

3.

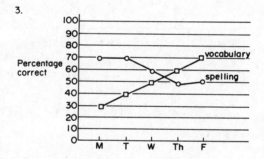

4.

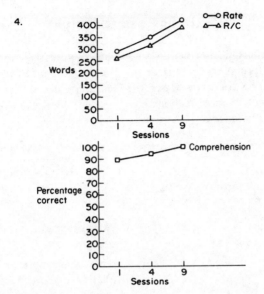

5.

Sally

Day	Date	Goal	Number of words written
M	10/14	45–50	30
W	10/16		62
F	10/18		72
M	10/21		78

III. Using Feedback Forms

Once having collected information on student performance, the teacher's task is to use that information for instructional or environmental decision making. The information on the form is summarized and analyzed so that trends or patterns are evident. If modifications are indicated, the teacher then determines which changes are necessary.

Steps to use feedback forms:	Questions to ask:
(1) Summarize:	What progress toward the objective is evident?
(2) Analyze:	What trends, patterns, or relationships are there?
(3) Decide:	Should revision be made? What revisions should be tried?

Revisions should be tried if the trend of progress or performance is low or decreasing.

(The answer key is on p. 62.)

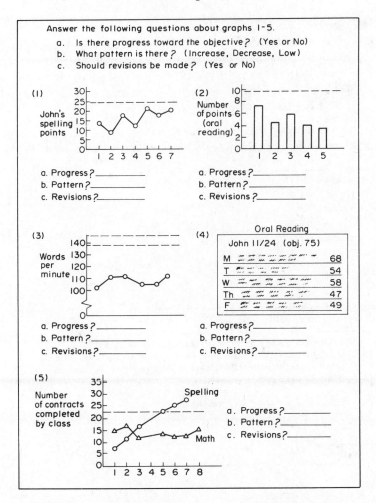

Answer the following questions about graphs 1-5.
  a. Is there progress toward the objective? (Yes or No)
  b. What pattern is there? (Increase, Decrease, Low)
  c. Should revisions be made? (Yes or No)

(1) John's spelling points

a. Progress?_____
b. Pattern?_____
c. Revisions?_____

(2) Number of points (oral reading)

a. Progress?_____
b. Pattern?_____
c. Revisions?_____

(3) Words per minute

a. Progress?_____
b. Pattern?_____
c. Revisions?_____

(4) Oral Reading
John 11/24 (obj. 75)

M		68
T		54
W		58
Th		47
F		49

a. Progress?_____
b. Pattern?_____
c. Revisions?_____

(5) Number of contracts completed by class
Spelling
Math

a. Progress?_____
b. Pattern?_____
c. Revisions?_____

Which revisions are tried depend on the performance patterns and relationships among factors within the environment. Analysis of these trends helps the teacher to decide whether to modify (*1*) instructional procedures or (*2*) management strategies.

(*1*) Instructional procedures can include
   (*a*) Type of task: content area, subskill
   (*b*) Level of objective: realistic aims
   (*c*) Type of material: relevancy; magazines, programmed texts, short books, machines
   (*d*) Level of material: format, grammatical structure, vocabulary

(2) Management strategies can include

    (a) Type of environment: movement opportunities, location of seat, room, noise, time of doing, length of instructional period

    (b) Type of interactions: 1 : 1, small group, large group, teachers/aides

    (c) Type of frequency of consequence system: rules of class, tokens, praise, feedback methods.

If the teacher decides that instructional revisions are indicated, the performance patterns are again reviewed to decide exactly what to revise.

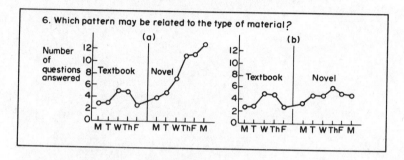

6. Which pattern may be related to the type of material?

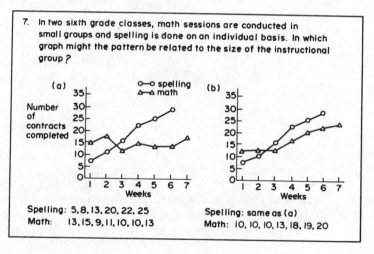

7. In two sixth grade classes, math sessions are conducted in small groups and spelling is done on an individual basis. In which graph might the pattern be related to the size of the instructional group?

Spelling: 5, 8, 13, 20, 22, 25
Math: 13, 15, 9, 11, 10, 10, 13

Spelling: same as (a)
Math: 10, 10, 10, 13, 18, 19, 20

8. In an elementary resource room, two student aides assist the teacher on alternate days. Which student's pattern might be related to the presence of different aides ?

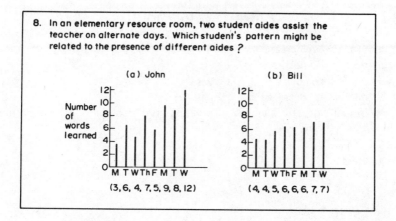

(a) John

(3, 6, 4, 7, 5, 9, 8, 12)

(b) Bill

(4, 4, 5, 6, 6, 6, 7, 7)

Performance patterns that are erratic, or that drop off suddenly, often indicate a need for management revisions.

9. Which pattern of performance indicates a management revision ?

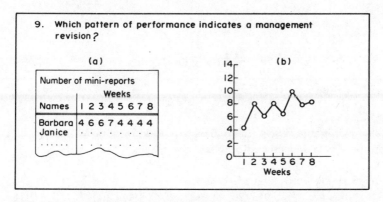

(a)

Number of mini-reports

Names	Weeks							
	1	2	3	4	5	6	7	8
Barbara	4	6	6	7	4	4	4	4
Janice	.	.	.	.	.	.	.	.

(b)

Weeks

10. Which performance pattern indicates a management revision?

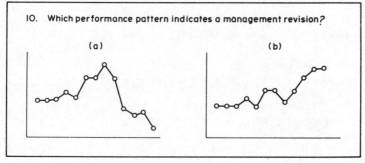

(a)

(b)

Answer Key for Part III

1. a. yes   b. increase   c. no
2. a. no   b. decrease   c. yes
3. a. no   b. low   c. yes
4. a. no   b. decrease   c. yes
5. a. in spelling   b. spelling increase and math decrease   c. yes—in math
6. a
7. a
8. a. John
9. a
10. a

The criterion test follows.

Criterion Test

Given the following performance information, complete tasks 1, 2, and 3:

Third Grade Class

Spelling—Initial objective: Learn **5** words/week.
Reading—Initial objective: Complete **1** unit/week.

John Spelling words learned—
Week of: 9/13, 4; 9/20, 8; 9/27, 10; 10/4, 12; 10/11, 9; 10/18, 3.

Reading units completed—
Week of: 9/13, 0; 9/20, 1; 9/27, 2; 10/4, 3; 10/11, 2; 10/18, 1.

Paul Spelling words learned—
Week of: 9/13, 2; 9/20, 4; 9/27, 4; 10/4, 4; 10/11, 2; 10/18, 1.

Reading units completed—
Week of: 9/13, 0; 9/20, 0; 9/27, 1; 10/4, 2; 10/11, 0; 10/18, 0.

---

1. Design record forms for
   a. Student use

b. Parent use

c. Teacher use

2. Record the information on the forms you designed.

3. Use this information to answer the following questions for each student:
   a. Is progress being made?
      John_____
      Paul_____
   b. What performance pattern/trends are revealed?
      John_____
      Paul_____
   c. Should any revisions in the instruction be made?
      John_____
      Paul_____
   d. What revisions might be indicated?
      John_____
      Paul_____

II. Producing a Learning Environment

Let us assume that goals are clear and progress measures are available. Next, we need competencies for managing a learning environment: room arrangement and materials, of course, but even more important, ways of interacting with children.

Several years of studying learning environments and of operating experimental classrooms have made one fact abundantly clear to us: Children are neither happy nor productive unless the classroom environment is conducive to work. And the conditions that make children comfortable are not what most teachers would predict.

The following sections on learning environments (pp. 64–87) are taken verbatim from the book *Classroom Management*.[3] Read them to find out how to establish a comfortable, productive classroom.

[3] Reprinted, with permission, from *Classroom Management*, by J. M. Smith and D. E. P. Smith (New York: Random House, 1975). © 1970 by Donald E. P. Smith.

A STABLE ENVIRONMENT

A stable environment is a predictable one. It contains rules that are clearly defined and consistently enforced. The behavior of the authority figure (the teacher) is consistent and predictable. The daily routine, and even the appearance of the room, are never changed capriciously. A child who has spent a week in this room feels safe here, for he knows what to expect. His feelings of uncertainty are concentrated on the learning tasks he faces.

This description is somewhat different from the usual picture of an ideal classroom. There is no mention of the patient, loving teacher. There is no mention of concern and tolerance for individual differences. It is not that these qualities are absent from stable classrooms. The patience, love, and concern are present—but they may be present in unstable classrooms, too. Stability is not automatically a product of love and concern. It requires specific action by the teacher to increase predictability. The stability that is achieved makes efficient learning possible.

But why is stability so important to learning? It is hard for most adults to remember the panic and anxiety of the first day of the school year, faced with a teacher you did not know, new classmates, a new room, new books. It is not surprising that some children become physically ill. The first few days are spent getting to know the teacher, the room, the books, and the other children. Little skill training is achieved. The children are too concerned with such questions as, "What makes the teacher mad? What pleases him? What will he say (in various circumstances)? Where is the pencil sharpener, the clock, my chair, the class library? Which is the reading book? How hard is it? Who is the smartest kid? Who is nice and who is mean? How do I compare?"

The overwhelming uncertainty that the child feels is reduced a little every time he discovers the answer to one of these questions. When uncertainty is reduced to a manageable level, he can begin to concentrate on learning tasks. Children differ greatly in the level of uncertainty that they can tolerate and in the skills for reducing it.

Anything a teacher can do to increase the predictability of the environment makes the child's orientation easier and increases his chance for academic success. A few clearly defined rules, a consistent policy of enforcement, a dependable class routine, even the physical arrangement of the room, can greatly increase children's success.

It is impossible to eliminate completely the uncertainty arising from the environment. For one thing, the child himself is changing. Things look different each day. Even if everything in the classroom were to remain exactly the same, his perceptions of them would change. But, of course, they do not remain the same. Even when the teacher is doing everything in his power to maintain stability, some things will change. The lessons are different. The children grow older and act differently. The teacher, alas, grows older too. New books become worn, floors become scuffed, windows get dirty. The child responds to each change—both internal and external—with an increase in uncertainty. But most changes are superficial. Essentially the class remains the same. It is this phenomenon of change within a stable environment which leads to "rule-testing."

Having once discovered the "rules" of the environment, natural and man-made, the learner has a quick easy way of reducing his uncertainty. He simply "tests" a few rules to see if things are really the same. If they are, he can relax.

Watch a youngster as he enters the classroom. He flicks the light switch. Yes, the lights still go on. He walks to his seat. It is still there. A classmate walks by. He punches him on the arm and receives a kick in the shins. Same old Joe! The teacher asks for attention. He whispers to the girl in the next seat. The teacher says, "The rule is no talking." Same old teacher! Now he starts to work.

Rule-testing can be an efficient, reliable way of reducing uncertainty. In that sense, rules were made to be tested. In a stable, relatively unchanging environment, rule-testing is common, but the tests are predictable and minor. In an unstable classroom, rule-testing occupies more time and energy than any other activity. Faced with an unstable environment, the child must test every aspect of it. Since responses to his rule-testing are not consistent, the child's uncertainty is never really reduced. His tests become more frequent and more extreme. He usually has little energy left for academic work.

How a Stable Environment
Can Be Achieved in an Average Classroom

Some of the ways a teacher can increase stability have already been mentioned. The first step is a regular daily schedule of activities (math at 9, reading at 10, recess at 10:30, etc.). An opening ritual, such as the salute to the flag, a song, or the school news report, is another helpful procedure. Maintaining a consistent room arrangement—seats in the same places, children in the same seats—is also important. But the basic difference between a stable classroom and an unstable classroom lies in the rules and their enforcement. A stable classroom has a few rules that are always enforced. An unstable classroom usually has many rules, **some** of which are **sometimes** enforced.

The rules that the authors recommend for use with the MICHIGAN LANGUAGE PROGRAM (hereafter, the MLP) and the methods of enforcement are described below.[4]

---

[4] For a complete discussion of rules and consistency, see D. E. P. Smith and J. M. Smith (1976).

1. GAINING ATTENTION

a. Regular Procedure. To begin a new activity, say, "Sit quietly and fold your hands."

Then wait, in a neutral attitude, for as long as two minutes while learners comply. (Use a stopwatch, timer, or clock with a second hand to ensure a two-minute interval.) As soon as all learners have folded their hands, or at the end of two minutes, count aloud "5-4-3-2-1-0."

If any students have not complied, enforce the procedure by saying, "Johnny and Mary, you did not fold your hands. We will begin now." Then go on with the activity.

It is not necessary that Johnny and Mary actually fold their hands after the enforcement, although they probably will. The word enforcement does not mean "punishment" or "forced compliance" in this program. An enforcement is an established routine that occurs whenever a rule is tested and that tells the learner that his rule-testing was observed and noted by the teacher. Further action is necessary only in the case of repeated rule-testing by a single student.

If any learner is not attending to the teacher following the enforcement, it may be assumed that he is unable to do so. Move him to a seat where he will be less distracted and more secure.

Test your knowledge of the regular procedure for gaining attention.

1. At the beginning of a new activity you will say,
- ☐ *a.* *"Sit quietly and fold your hands."*
- ☐ *b.* *"Get ready to begin the new activity."*

2. While learners get ready, you will wait as long as
- ☐ *a.* *5 minutes.*
- ☐ *b.* *2 minutes.*

3. After waiting, you will,
- ☐ *a.* *begin immediately.*
- ☐ *b.* *countdown, "5-4-3-2-1-0."*

4. If any learners do not comply, you will
- ☐ *a.* *tell each one that he did not comply.*
- ☐ *b.* *require each one to stay after school 2 minutes.*

5. If a learner is still not attending after enforcement, you know that
- ☐ *a.* *he is not able to attend, and needs a better place to work.*
- ☐ *b.* *he should be informed of the need to follow class rules.*

6. This procedure is "enforced" by
- ☐ *a.* *punishing a rule-tester.*
- ☐ *b.* *giving the learner information about the rule and his behavior.*
- ☐ *c.* *forcibly folding his hands.*

After the students have become familiar with the gaining attention procedure, it is a source of comfort—a completely predictable event. They cherish it and explain it to a substitute teacher. But, at first, students are not accustomed to a teacher who means precisely what he says. You may expect them to "test" the rule in many ways. For the procedure to be completely effective, the following conditions should be met.

(1) Stand (or sit) in the same place every time you gain attention.

(2) Adopt a calm, neutral tone of voice.

(3) Fold your own hands while making the statement.

(4) The first week, you may repeat the statement 30 seconds after you first make it, if you think it necessary. After the first week, do not repeat the statement. Say it only once.

(5) **Never** use the procedure as punishment.

(6) Decide ahead of time what you mean by "fold your hands." It does not matter what your definition is, as long as you abide by it.

(7) Use the procedure consistently, i.e., it should **always** be used before certain activities.

(8) Begin using the procedure as early as possible in the formation of the group.

(9) Enforce **every** infraction of the rule. Under no circumstances should the teacher ignore a student who has not complied with the request.

Test your knowledge: Which of the following situations will enable the teacher to gain attention effectively?

1. ☐ a. *On the first day of school, as soon as the seats have been assigned, the teacher says, "Sit quietly and fold your hands."*

   ☐ b. *On the third day of school, the children are becoming unruly. The teacher says, "Sit quietly and fold your hands."*

2. ☐ a. *The children were very noisy when the teacher was out of the room for a minute. When she returns, she says, "Sit quietly and fold your hands."*

   ☐ b. *After hearing a story, and before beginning the listening lesson, the teacher says, "Sit quietly and fold your hands."*

3. ☐ a. *The teacher says, "Sit quietly and fold your hands," whenever it is time for reading or arithmetic activities. She starts this practice on the first day.*

   ☐ b. *The teacher says, "Sit quietly and fold your hands," three or four times the first week. She plans to increase the use of this procedure as weeks go by and the children are more familiar with the class.*

4. ☐ a. *It is time for reading. The teacher says, "Sit quietly and fold your hands." One boy does not comply. In two minutes she says, "George, you did not fold your hands."*

   ☐ b. *It is time for reading. The teacher says, "Sit quietly and fold your hands." One boy does not comply. The teacher knows he is upset because he missed the bus and was late. Not wanting to embarrass him further, she begins the lesson.*

5. □ a. *The first time the teacher uses the gaining attention procedure he is sitting at his desk. The next time he is sitting on his desk. The next time he is standing by the blackboard.*

    □ b. *The teacher always stands in the right front corner of the room, under the clock, whenever he uses the gaining attention procedure.*

6. □ a. *9:41 a.m.: "Sit quietly and fold your hands."*
        9:42 a.m.: "I told you to fold your hands."
        9:42' 15" a.m.: "I'm getting tired of waiting."
        9:42' 30" a.m.: "Jimmy, sit quietly, I said."
        9:43 a.m.: "I'm ready to begin, but you aren't."

    □ b. *9:41 a.m.: 'Sit quietly and fold your hands."*
        9:43 a.m.: "5-4-3-2-1-0, Jimmy, you did not fold your hands. We will begin."

b. Alternative Procedures. The regular procedure for gaining attention has been extensively used and has proved uniformly successful. The important elements of the procedure are these:

(1) Learners are required to do some observable action to demonstrate attention.

(2) The teacher waits a uniform, reasonable length of time for learners to come to attention.

(3) The teacher enforces the procedure with a simple, predictable routine.

Any procedure that has these elements will work as effectively to gain attention. Two possible alternative procedures are suggested here.

Alternative 1.

Cut a circle from cardboard, and color one side green and the other side red. Attach the circle to a sturdy string. Prepare one such "attention disc" for each learner. Attach the string to a corner of the desk (securely). [See the following figure.]

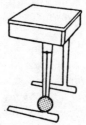

To gain attention, say, "Put the circle on your desk, green side up, and wait quietly to begin." Wait two minutes while learners comply, as you would do for the regular procedure. Enforce by saying, "Johnny and Mary, your green circles are not up." (The red side can be used when gaining attention before leaving the room, as for recess, lunch, or at the end of the day.)

Alternative 2.

To gain attention say, "Clear your desks and wait quietly." Wait 2 minutes while learners comply, as for the regular procedure. Enforce by saying, "Johnny and Mary, your desks are not clear."

2. THE "ONE AT A TIME" RULE

This rule is used whenever an activity involves individual oral responses by learners. It is certainly reasonable and necessary for conversation that one does not interrupt and waits his turn to speak. Such patience is not easily learned, as many leaders of adult discussion groups can testify. But it is possible even for first graders to learn to converse in a spontaneous, yet orderly way, if the teacher is diligent in enforcing the "one at a time" rule.

Definition: "One at a time may speak" is the full statement of the rule. It means that a student may not interrupt another who is speaking; a student may not make extraneous comments to his neighbors while another student is speaking; and a student may not talk while the teacher is talking.

Enforcement: Whenever a learner talks while some other student is speaking, say, "One at a time, **learner's name.**" At first, rule infractions will be numerous. They will gradually decrease if you are diligent in enforcing after **every** rule infraction. For feedback on the effectiveness of this procedure, keep a tally of every rule enforcement you make during a particular oral activity. Then you will be able to see progress even though you must still enforce the rule often.

3. THE "NO TALKING" RULE

The "no talking" rule is used whenever students are working independently. It is a reasonable rule for those periods, since talking is inevitably distracting to nearby students who are trying to work. The reasonableness of the rule is not its main advantage, however. It provides a clear, easily enforceable limit for work periods. When students are faced with learning tasks, they feel somewhat uncertain and anxious. It is desirable that they reduce this uncertainty by attacking the tasks in front of them, rather than by attacking the teacher or each other. If they must engage in rule-testing, having a simple, easily enforceable rule to test allows students to turn more quickly to tasks. The "no talking" rule is such a rule.[5]

Definition: Students will not talk aloud to classmates, the teacher, or themselves. This includes whispering and any other vocal sound. The teacher must decide for himself whether it includes lip-smacking, whistling, clucking, and any other borderline sounds that children will make. Once you make a decision, stick to it. If you classify a sound as talking on Monday, it must be handled in the same way on Tuesday.

Which of these child behaviors would you classify as "talking"?

- ☐ *a.* saying, "I lost my pencil"
- ☐ *b.* singing a popular song
- ☐ *c.* humming
- ☐ *d.* tongue-clicking
- ☐ *e.* loud nose-blowing
- ☐ *f.* whispering to neighbor
- ☐ *g.* grinding teeth
- ☐ *h.* whistling
- ☐ *i.* making popping sound by emitting air from cheek
- ☐ *j.* sniffling
- ☐ *k.* hiccupping

Enforcement: The rule is enforced by the teacher. Whenever talking occurs, the teacher says, "The rule is 'no talking.' " An equivalent phrase can be used, such as "do not talk," "no talking, please," and so on. Use the **same** phrase every time and say it in a neutral voice, with no special emphasis, the same way each time. To be effective, the phrase must be directed, *by name,* to the individual who tested the rule. If you are uncertain who was responsible, direct the phrase to the vicinity of the talking.

Consistency: It is **absolutely essential** that the rule be enforced **every time** it is broken. At some time after this routine has been instituted, you will find that you want to overlook minor infractions of the rule. This is particularly true in the case of problem children who have just begun to succeed. You may be afraid to "rock the boat" by enforcing the rule. It is very important that you resist the urge to overlook rule-testing. The children who seem to demand exceptions are precisely the ones who need consistency the most. They need a dependable, predictable authority if they are to feel safe.

Punishment: The only enforcement procedure that is used is the repetition of

---

[5] This technique is used for independent work periods, that is, times at which children are expected to work alone. That might be as little as 10 minutes per day and probably not more than two 20-minute periods per day. (Alone means **alone**.)

an enforcing phrase, such as, "The rule is 'no talking.' " No punishment or threats are given. They are unnecessary in this classroom system. Rules are instituted so that children can test them. On days when their uncertainty is high, rule-testing is a shortcut method for ascertaining that the world is still dependable. The purpose of the rule is not to eliminate all instances of talking. However, after it has been in force for a while, instances of rule-testing (talking) will be rare.

At first, enforcement of the rule causes a few children to be highly embarrassed by the public acknowledgement of their rule-testing. In extreme cases, tears, tantrums, and sullen withdrawal will mark their behavior when you enforce the rule. These behaviors are normal, angry responses. They occur whenever a prediction is unfulfilled. When a child talks, he may have predicted, on the basis of past experience, that you would **not** enforce the rule. When his prediction proves wrong, he becomes angry. Tears or withdrawal are the most common expressions of anger, but an angry verbal outburst or tantrum also occurs occasionally. All such behaviors (tears, tantrums, withdrawal) are irrelevant behaviors and should be ignored.

Irrelevant Behaviors: While children are working independently, they will behave in a number of ways that are irrelevant to the learning tasks, but that cannot be classified as talking. These irrelevant behaviors include taking peculiar postures; dropping pencils and books; daydreaming; shaking and waving hands, legs, and head; and many other actions.

Irrelevant behaviors should be ignored unless they disturb other learners. . . . If the behavior is directed at the teacher, it will disappear when he does not respond. Some strange behaviors, especially postures, are annoying to teachers but are helpful to a tense child who is trying to maintain attention. These behaviors may not disappear until much later when the child is more relaxed in the classroom. As long as the behavior is not disturbing to other learners, it should be ignored.

Which behavior requires that the "no talking" rule be enforced?

1. ☐ *a. Cheryl stands up while working.*
   ☐ *b. Russell boisterously challenges others to work as fast as he does.*
2. ☐ *a. John scribbles violently.*
   ☐ *b. Steven walks around the room, whispering to some of the children.*
3. ☐ *a. Marie is reciting "The Three Little Kittens."*
   ☐ *b. Randy has been staring out of the window for fifteen minutes.*
4. ☐ *a. Don asks his neighbor if he has finished yet.*
   ☐ *b. Mark is obviously copying from Frank.*
5. ☐ *a. Mabel looks very puzzled and does not seem to know what to do.*
   ☐ *b. Barbara is explaining directions to Gloria.*

6. ☐ a.   Violet has a habit of tapping her fingers on her desk while working.
   ☐ b.   Bob is reading aloud.
7. ☐ a.   Sheila makes many trips to the drinking fountain and lavatory.
   ☐ b.   James asks if he can help with the milk today.
8. ☐ a.   Mike is crying.
   ☐ b.   Jeff is telling Joe what he missed when he was absent.

How to Ignore a Behavior: Ignoring an obvious behavior is sometimes difficult, particularly if it evokes an emotional response in the teacher. To ignore the behavior requires that the teacher determine exactly what he was doing when the behavior occurred—and then to carry on as though the behavior were not an abnormal or unusual thing. The teacher may *see* the behavior, but not respond to it, either positively or negatively.

In each case below, how should the teacher respond?

1. Child waves his hand repeatedly. Teacher is observing leg kicking and other signs of tension.
   ☐ a.   *"I told you to do it by yourself."*
   ☐ b.   *Teacher's eyes pass over child as he continues observing tension signs.*
2. Child falls out of his chair. Teacher was studying children's drawings in rear of room.
   ☐ a.   *Continues studying drawings. Remains expressionless.*
   ☐ b.   *Teacher smiles. "Did you hurt yourself?"*
3. Child drops his books. Teacher was, at that moment, looking at **that** child.
   ☐ a.   *Quickly looks away.*
   ☐ b.   *Continues to look at child, then moves attention elsewhere.*
4. Child pages through book and says, "I can't find my place." Teacher is recording attendance.
   ☐ a.   *Continues to record attendance.*
   ☐ b.   *"The rule is no talking."*

4. THE "DO NOT DISTURB OTHERS" RULE

This rule is used whenever group learning activities are carried out, whether they involve independent work or class participation. It is **not** appropriate when learners are interacting socially, such as recess or the lunch hour. At those times, students are learning how to deal with one another as peers. If a student desires privacy at such a time, he must learn to maintain it himself. If a teacher intervenes to protect a student from others who are "disturbing" him, the result will be a child who becomes dependent on the teacher and alienated from the other students.

Learning activities, however, are quite different from social activities. To enable a learner to devote his total energy to the learning tasks in front of him, the teacher protects him from distractions and interruptions.

Definition: Whenever a student's behavior is disturbing to other learners, invoke the "do not disturb others" rule. "Disturbance" is defined as any noise or activity that results in distraction of another student. Such distraction will be apparent as soon as another student shifts his attention to the distracting student. As soon as the teacher sees evidence of distraction, the rule must be enforced.

Note that "others" refers to other learners, not the teacher. If the other learners ignore a behavior, the teacher also ignores it, no matter how annoying it may be to him. Similarly, if any class member is disturbed, the rule must be invoked, no matter how insignificant the disturbance appears to be. Evidence of distraction may be: looking at the disturbing student, laughing at him, glaring at him, talking to him. Or, it may be a frown, a sign of disgust, or an obvious inability to concentrate, which you attribute to the other student's behavior.

The motive that prompted the behavior is irrelevant in determining whether a disturbance has occurred. A student may be (or seem to be) unaware that he has done anything to disturb another student. The behavior may simply be a "nervous habit" over which he has little control. If it is disturbing to other learners, however, the rule must be enforced.

Usually classrooms have some limit similar to the one described here. The difference lies in the rigidity of the definition and enforcement. It leaves much less to the judgment and discretion of the teacher. He must act only on the basis of evidence. Rule enforcement depends on what he sees and hears, not on how he feels about it. Once he has decided to act, the routine is automatic. This is necessary if rule enforcement is to be predictable and reliable.

In most classrooms, rule enforcement is dependent on the physical and emotional state of the teacher. On Monday he can tolerate 80 decibels of noise. On Wednesday he "cracks down" when the noise level reaches 60 decibels. A week later, after a night on the town—or a colicky baby—he can tolerate only 10 decibels. The stated rules may be the same every day, but enforcement varies greatly. The rules becomes a **source** of uncertainty rather than a means to reduce it.

Which behavior requires enforcement of the "do not disturb others" rule?

1. ☐ a. *Bill has dropped his pencil three times in three minutes. No one pays any attention.*
   ☐ b. *Judy sings while working. The other children tell her to be quiet.*
2. ☐ a. *James fidgets and swings his legs, occasionally kicking the chair.*
   ☐ b. *Warren shoves and hits children within his reach.*
3. ☐ a. *Linda emits loud shrieks of laughter for no apparent reason. Other children are startled and jump when this happens.*

☐ *b.   Andrea is laughing. No one seems to notice.*
4. ☐ *a.   Louis is copying Carl's answers. Carl makes no attempt to cover his work.*
☐ *b.   Philip grabs Doug's book as soon as Doug opens it to work.*
5. ☐ *a.   Dana is scratching her fingernail across the desk. Julie covers her ears.*
☐ *b.   Kenneth is tapping the shoulder of the girl in front of him. She does not respond.*

Enforcement: The "do not disturb" rule is enforced in three steps.

Step 1. Restate the rule. Direct it to the student by name, describing his behavior as clearly as possible. E.g., "Robert, your foot tapping is disturbing others." Or, "Clare, you are disturbing others by poking them."

Step 2. If a learner disturbs others again in the course of the same time segment (reading lesson, arithmetic, etc.), he must be moved to a different spot for the remainder of the class period. If the learner is usually easily distracted, move him immediately to the special work corner. . . . If you predict that a lesser change is necessary, simply move his chair away from the group, or place him in a different seat elsewhere in the group. It is always better to be pessimistic in your assessment of his state of mind. It is easier (on both of you) to place a student in the special work corner the first time you move him, rather than find you must place him there after another disturbance. Your goal is to ensure that he can concentrate successfully on his schookwork, not to give him a chance to "prove" himself in what is, for him, a difficult situation.

Step 3. Occasionally a child will have lost control to such an extent that the disturbing behavior continues in the special work corner. If it continues to provoke a response from the group, the child must be excluded from the room. He cannot, of course, be left unsupervised. Here are several alternatives:

(*1*) The child may be supervised by another teacher along with that teacher's regular group. Provide books and drawing paper for the excluded child. This can easily be a reciprocal arrangement.

(*2*) The child may be supervised by the gym teacher along with a regular class. Participation with the class may be possible, making books and paper unnecessary.

(*3*) Sometimes a counselor, crisis teacher, or a similar staff member is available to supervise "problem children." The conditions here, however, are different than in most cases of exclusion. This is not a recommended time for therapy. The child needs the controlling presence of an adult, but not supportive counselling. Books and paper should be provided.

(*4*) The child may be supervised by the principal or office staff. Provide books and paper.

(*5*) The child may be dismissed early and told to return to his home. Schools usually have their own regulations regarding such dismissal.

(6) If the class is a special class, such as remedial reading, the child may be returned to his regular class.[6]

This rule is extremely difficult for most teachers to enforce consistently. It is normal for teachers to feel guilty about excluding a child for a relatively minor offense. The temptation to overlook disturbing behavior is very strong, especially if a child is just beginning to succeed in the class. Indeed, the trauma is often greater for the teacher than for the child.

The problem is that the teacher looks upon the enforcement as a punishment— even more so than in the case of the "no talking" rule. There is a difference between enforcing a limit and imposing a punishment, but the difference is mostly in the mind of the enforcer. The action taken might be exactly the same.

The child also may regard enforcement as punishment, especially if he senses the teacher's anger. Some children react with extreme anger themselves. Crying is a common expression of such anger. So also is arguing, cursing, threatening, and other verbal abuse. These behaviors are irrelevant and should be ignored. A teacher often feels a need to explain, defend, or console, when faced with such a tantrum. However, defensiveness on the part of the teacher only prolongs the tantrum and confuses the issue. The child is undoubtedly embarrassed by his own behavior, and will be greatly relieved if the teacher can treat the outburst as a routine event.

If a child refuses to leave the room after being told to do so, the teacher should follow these steps:

Step 1. Wait at least 30 seconds. Then repeat the directive in a calm, neutral voice. Repeat again if necessary.

Step 2. If, after 3 to 5 minutes, the child has not left voluntarily, he will have to be removed forcibly. It is best if another teacher or the principal can perform this action. The measure is extreme, and it is unusual to resort to it. If, however, a teacher knows that any child has a history of extreme behavior problems, it is wise to make arrangements in advance with some staff member to perform this function, should it become necessary.

Consider that the child does know the rules of the room. By creating a disturbance, he is telling the teacher that his uncertainty is very high, and cannot be sufficiently reduced in the usual ways. He may, in fact, be out of control. This is the case when exclusion from the room is necessary. When he is in such a state, he is incapable of working just as he would be if he had a temperature of $104°$ F. and red spots on his body. In the latter case, as in the former, you must exclude him from the class for his own protection as well as for the protection of other learners. The symptoms in the case of "high uncertainty illness" are not

---

[6] Step 3 arouses great interest and debate. The child's behavior should be interpreted as follows: He is unable to tolerate **this environment on this day**. A nonpunitive alternative must be found. More discussion follows.

so dramatic as they are for measles. It may be merely an inability to refrain from throwing spitballs. The incapacitation, however, is just as great.

The teacher often has an uncomfortable feeling that, by excluding a child, he is admitting failure. (Unfortunately, some administrators support this conclusion.) But if the teacher is conducting his class in accordance with the principles discussed in this manual, he can be sure that he is not responsible for the child's emotional state. The teacher can intensify the condition by vacillating, or he can contribute to regaining equilibrium by behaving consistently, i.e., enforcing the rule.

What to Expect. If the rules are established in the manner described previously, the behavior of the children will follow a predictable course.

Usually there is an initial "honeymoon" phase, during which time rule-testing is infrequent. This may last for one class session or for several. The next phase is the "testing" phase. Rule-testing increases in frequency and in intensity. The more disturbed children may cry or have a tantrum when the rule is enforced. Usually, this period of frequent testing lasts from two to four sessions, but it may continue for as long as two weeks. The next phase is an "extinction" phase, during which time the rule-testing and irrelevant behaviors diminish. The extinction may require several sessions.

Now a new cycle begins, with a longer honeymoon phase, a less intense testing phase, and a brief extinction phase. The cycle will continue to repeat itself as children grow and change, but each time the "good" periods will grow longer and the difficult periods will be less extreme.

If you were to chart instances of rule-testing by an individual or by the class, you would see clear evidence of this cycle. It might look like the following figure.

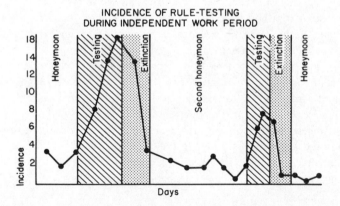

INCIDENCE OF RULE-TESTING
DURING INDEPENDENT WORK PERIOD

Which of these charts indicates that the teacher is responding in accordance with this program?

INCIDENCE OF TALKING DURING INDEPENDENT WORK

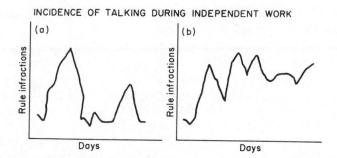

The teacher must be aware of these cycles to maintain the procedure long enough for extinction to occur. The initial establishment of the rules is the easiest part of the routine. The honeymoon phase lulls the teacher into a false confidence. The teacher predicts that everything will remain smooth and easy. Typically, then, when the testing phase begins, the teacher panics. He ignores infractions of the rule, as if to say, "If I don't see the rule-testing, maybe it will go away." When it becomes impossible to ignore the testing, the teacher abandons the established enforcement routine for a punitive one. He feels, perhaps, that only extreme measures can save the situation. He says, in effect, "I tried it, but it just doesn't work with my kids." As a result of these inconsistent teacher behaviors, the extinction phase never takes place. Rule-testing may cease temporarily if the punishing measures are frightening enough. It will reappear, however, whenever uncertainty becomes high. The inconsistent behavior of the teacher insures that the uncertainty will often be high, and each time a more frightening punishment must be used. In extreme instances, police must patrol school corridors.

The preceding dynamics can be avoided if the teacher realizes that intense rule-testing is a normal, natural phase in the procedure. He can be assured that if he behaves consistently, rule-testing **will** drop to a low level. Furthermore, the enforcement procedures described are entirely adequate to maintain control even with classes of "incorrigibles." When the teacher has ignored rule-testing to such an extent that it has become extreme, he can reestablish control through the enforcement procedures described, and if he behaves consistently from then on, extinction of irrelevant behaviors will occur.

Perhaps the most encouraging thing about this procedure is that it can be applied to a classroom even after a pattern of frequent rule-testing has been established. The initial testing phase may be more extreme than in a "virgin" classroom, the extinction may take longer, but it **will** occur. Furthermore, even though a teacher "backslides" from time to time, he can reestablish consistency by adhering to the procedure once more.

One caution must be added. These rules and procedures work effectively during any independent work period, whether or not learners are using the MLP.

But the teacher must provide learning tasks on which learners can succeed. If a child's work leads to frustration or boredom, he has no way to reduce his uncertainty except through rule-testing (misbehavior) or withdrawal (daydreaming). In other words, it is impossible to create a stable, productive classroom if ineffective learning materials are used.

Variety, the Spice of Life. The preceding discussion on maintaining stability may lead the reader to suppose that an ideal classroom is a bare room where nothing ever happens. This is certainly not the case. It is true that the teacher attempts to reduce uncertainty. It is true that anything new arouses uncertainty, but a manageable uncertainty is a prerequisite for learning. Another name for controlled uncertainty is "curiosity" or "interest." In a stable classroom, with a predictable routine and a dependable teacher, new objects and activities are maximally effective. A child's uncertainty is reduced by mastering the tasks he encounters, by perfecting skills, by finding out about everything he sees and hears.

The most interesting, creative, "enriched" classroom is sterile to the child who cannot look at the world around him. His neurotic attempts to manipulate the teacher and his classmates to reduce his uncertainty leave him no energy to cope with anything else.

In a stable classroom, the teacher is free to introduce any change in routine, or any new experience, knowing that most children will react with interest and enthusiasm, that a few will react with a temporary overload of uncertainty (routine rule-testing), but that **all** children will be able to cope with and to benefit from the experience.

SELF-SELECTION

In a self-selective classroom, students are free to choose what work they will do and how long they will work on the material. The classroom of the future may include a complex machine capable of presenting learning programs for a variety of skills, and responding immediately to the demands of the learner. Until such time, however, today's teacher can approximate the self-selective ideal within the constraints of an average classroom by providing learners with a choice of appropriate learning materials and time when they can pursue their own interests.

Which classroom in each pair could be described as "self-selective?"

1. ☐ a.   *Mary is reading a library book. Lewis is drawing. Joyce is working on Book 3. John is working on Book 5.*

☐ *b.* *Mary, Lewis, Joyce, and John each has a workbook on his desk. Each is opened to page 23. Mary has completed the page. Lewis is half through. Joyce and John have not yet started and are staring into space.*

2. ☐ *a.* *The teacher passes out library books, carefully choosing easy books for the poor readers and harder books for the good readers.*

☐ *b.* *The teacher puts library books on a table and invites children to come individually and choose one.*

3. ☐ *a.* *The teacher says, "Take out your reading books. Turn to page 82. Read the story and answer the questions."*

☐ *b.* *The teacher requires oral reports on a book chosen by the child from the class library.*

Why Self-Selection Is Necessary

All children in the first grade are expected to master the same basic content by the end of the year. Some, of course, are capable of learning much more in that period of time. A few will not finish the usual first grade curriculum. Their learning rates and learning styles are quite different. Some children make many discriminations spontaneously. Others require carefully designed tasks at every step along the way. Some children are able to concentrate on a single task for a long period of time. Others can maintain attention for only a few minutes. Typical classroom procedures cannot meet the requirements of all these children. The teacher usually tries to gear the class to the "average," although there are no more average children than there are "bright" or "slow" children in a classroom. A procedure that allows children to work at their own rates is appropriate for **all** the children.

The differences between children is not the only justification for a self-selective classroom. The first step in the design of effective learning programs is a thorough analysis of all skills required. In reading, for example, we isolate skills such as letter discrimination (visual), phoneme discrimination (aural), word discrimination, word naming, word analysis, spelling, and so on. But which skill comes first? It is likely that training in one skill is necessary for successful training in another. But advanced training in primary skills is facilitated by competence in a secondary skill. Further complicating the situation, children come to us with different levels of skill due to prior training. Self-selection is the only procedure that can accommodate these complexities.

How can one be sure that, when given the opportunity to choose, a learner will choose wisely? The so-called "wisdom of the body" has been the subject of a number of experiments. There is no conclusive answer. We have found that, under optimal classroom conditions, self-selection operates to produce an extremely high rate of response, resulting in rapid skill acquisition.[7] Argumentation, however, is unlikely to convince anyone of this likelihood if he has serious doubts. One must try it and see for oneself.

How Self-Selection Can Be Implemented in an Average Classroom

The principle of self-selection might be stated this way: "In an average classroom, with adequate feedback provisions, the learner probably knows what activities are best for him. Therefore, he should be allowed to make his own decisions whenever possible."

Thus, learners are always allowed to choose whether or not they will participate in an activity. Whenever it is feasible, they will be given a choice of learning tasks. Learners will always be allowed to complete materials at their own rate.

At one time it was assumed that self-selection required vast numbers of books and workbooks to serve all children. A good library of books is always highly desirable. Games, educational toys, crayons, drawing paper, clay, and other materials are necessary to provide a variety of activity choices. But a teacher can implement self-selection without the benefit of these items. He can arrange study times throughout the day when learners may work independently and choose which material they will complete. During such a time, a student may try arithmetic problems for a while, look at a picture book, complete a half-finished lesson, and "twiddle his thumbs" for the last 5 minutes.

Although attempts to use self-selection in classrooms have not been uniformly successful, some of the problems that arise can now be solved.

1. CLASSROOM CONTROL

A classroom must be reasonably quiet and orderly. Neither the teacher nor the learner benefits from chaos. Self-selection is not equivalent to anarchy. While students are always free to test rules, the teacher is always obliged to enforce them. Self-selection can operate effectively only if the environment is stable. . . .

2. ADEQUATE FEEDBACK

The feedback problem has two sides. First, if children are doing different things, how can the teacher keep track of the progress of each one? Second, learners cannot choose wisely among learning tasks if they do not know the consequences of their choices. If you were asked to choose among three brightly

[7] See D. E. P. Smith, D. Brethower, and R. Cabot (1969).

colored boxes, you might choose on the basis of shape, color, weight, or some similar criterion. But if you were told that the green box contained $100, the red box $50, and the yellow box $2, that knowledge would probably affect your choice. Students must have some way of knowing the value of the choices they are given. This value is reflected in a comprehensive feedback system. . . .

In a self-selective system with adequate feedback, learners will often choose activities that have a low payoff in terms of points, stars, or some other indicator. They make such a choice because they enjoy the activity greatly. But they will also choose tasks that are more difficult for them and that require more effort, because they have a relatively high payoff in progress toward a goal.

3. ADEQUATE MATERIALS

The self-selection strategy provides an exacting test for the effectiveness of materials. Any material used in such a system must pass this crucial test, i.e., do the learners use the materials? In the past, self-selection has often faltered because learners refused to use the materials. It is tempting to blame the learners, but . . . should we not criticize the instruction? Many materials that are attractive to adults are boring to children, hard to read, and hard to understand. Conversely, some materials that appear unattractive to adults are fascinating to children. Fortunately, many materials *are* available that please both students and teachers and these are the ones that must be used in a self-selective classroom.

4. ADEQUATE TRAINING

A student who is used to having adults make the majority of decisions concerning his welfare is not prepared to work well immediately in a completely self-selective classroom. It is the teacher's responsibility to train him to make choices wisely. Self-selection does not mean unlimited choice of activity. At first, the choice may be merely to participate. Or the student may be given a choice of two or three learning tasks he may complete at a certain time. As the learner grows in competence and independence, he is given more choice of activity.

INDEPENDENT WORK

Independent work means solving problems by yourself. To a child, it means finding his own place by himself, picking up his pencil, writing an answer, and knowing it is right without asking. A few students learn to work independently without any special instruction. Most do not. Many college students remain unable to work except under the pressure of threats or deadlines. They are often unable to evaluate the work they do. An educational system in which students are seldom required to make decisions for themselves and evaluation is an arbitrary process carried out by the teacher contributes to the problem.

Children can be trained to work independently, but it requires that a teacher set aside times when this important skill can be learned. He must also abstain from behaviors that tend to make children dependent. He must never solve problems for learners which they can solve for themselves.

Which teacher in each of the following situations is encouraging independent work?

1. Mary can't find her book.
   - ☐ *a.* *The teacher goes on with the lesson while Mary searches.*
   - ☐ *b.* *The teacher pauses briefly, searches, and finds the book.*
2. Joe says, "How do I do this page?"
   - ☐ *a.* *Teacher replies, "Do it by yourself."*
   - ☐ *b.* *Teacher replies, "I will explain it again."*
3. Sheila forgot her pencil.
   - ☐ *a.* *The teacher lends her a pencil.*
   - ☐ *b.* *The teacher refuses to lend her one. Sheila finds a crayon to use.*

Why Independent Work Is Necessary

Often the most efficient way to solve a problem is to ask someone else to solve it for you. If he does, you learn something. You learn to ask someone for help. On the other hand, if he refuses, you learn strategies for solving it yourself. Such strategies will be useful to you any time you are faced with a similar problem. Helpful friends are not always available.

A child who can learn only in the presence of a benevolent, help-giving adult is nearly as handicapped as a child who cannot learn at all. Children can be trained, under conditions described below, to work independently and to develop their own evaluative skills to monitor their work.

How Independent Work Can Be Developed in an Average Classroom

The procedure for developing independence is not complicated. The teacher sets aside certain times during the day for independent work. He sees that appropriate materials are available for work during that time. (He allows learners to employ self-selection of activities. . . .) During the independent work time he refrains from answering questions and giving help of any kind. At other times during the day, he encourages independence by allowing learners to solve problems for themselves, and he refrains from any behaviors that may tend to make learners dependent.

Just as self-selection requires effective materials, feedback, a stable classroom and independent work, this last condition depends on the presence of the other conditions to be effective. In addition, specific training in working independently is necessary, since most learners are unskilled in this area.

1. THE LEARNING MATERIALS

As long as children are faced with tasks that they cannot do by themselves, a teacher's help is necessary.

A learning program such as the MLP is constructed so that learners *can* do the tasks. Every task has been tried out, revised if necessary and tried again, until an accuracy rate of 95% is achieved. In such a program, differences in IQ are reflected in the rate of work and in the provision for skipping some portions of the program but never in decreased accuracy. Some learning programs are constructed with other standards of accuracy, however, and with non-programmed materials only an estimate of success is possible. Materials will have to be evaluated while in use.

2. ADEQUATE FEEDBACK

The crucial self-evaluation phase of independent work is possible only if a highly predictable feedback system is employed, one that is based mainly on objective criteria. Then learners can begin to predict successfully whether or not their work meets standards, a necessary condition for self-evaluation.

3. A STABLE CLASSROOM

Stability in the classroom is critical for the development of independence. In a stable classroom, learners are able to take on problems that would be too complex in more confused surroundings. And, of course, the teacher's consistency and predictability makes it possible for students to abandon attempts to manipulate him and to concentrate on the tasks facing them. If a teacher is consistent at other times, students will believe him when he refuses to help and will attempt to solve problems independently.

4. TRAINING

Independence training requires teachers to change their methods of answering questions and giving directions.

a. Questions.   During the independent work period, a teacher may not answer any questions. This includes questions such as: "Where do we start?" "Is this one right?" "What did you say?" "Did I do it right?" Since a "no talking" rule is usually in effect during independent work periods, **not** answering questions is relatively easy. The learners may not talk to themselves, to fellow students, or to the teacher. Therefore, the teacher's reply to any question is, "The rule is no talking."

At first, most teachers may find this behavior very difficult to accept. They believe, with some justification, that many learners will fail if they refuse to help. They are not aware that many students will fail **if** teachers help. Usually the teacher has no way of knowing whether he can reasonably expect success by all learners. If a child asks for help, the teacher assumes help is necessary. Actually, there are many other reasons why a student may ask for help.

When a learner faces a learning task, even one which he is capable of doing, he experiences a rise in uncertainty and feels anxious or tense. He looks for a quick way to reduce that uncertainty. He could reduce it by doing the task in front of him, i.e., by solving the problem himself. But he may have found that it is easier and more dependable to ask other people to solve the problem. This is particularly true if he has experienced failure in problem solving experiences in the past. He may have also discovered that asking people for help is flattering to them and makes them feel sympathetic toward him. Thus, even though he could easily do the task by himself, it is more rewarding for such a learner to ask for help.

When a student has had a number of experiences like the ones above, he comes to believe that he really is incapable of independent problem solving. It will not be a painless experience for him to change such a self-concept. A pattern of dependency has many benefits for a child. The disadvantages of the pattern are serious distortions of the student's learning behaviors, but these are not apparent to the student himself. It is up to the teacher to provide the conditions under which he can develop independence and self-reliance.

The teacher does not answer questions during work periods because it is not necessary to do so. Children can almost always find answers from sources other than the teacher. Answering a question will certainly lead the learner to ask more and more questions. Not answering them will lead him to develop independent work habits.

But what about other times, when the "no talking" rule is not in effect, when the lesson is less structured? Some questions are appropriate in these situations. In fact, we must consciously develop the ability to ask task-relevant questions.

In such a situation, an excellent technique is to acknowledge the question by restating it. Then ask the learner himself—or the class—to answer the question.

For example, "You are asking what the name of this letter is. Do you know it? Does anyone in class know it?"

Or, "You are asking what kind of cat this is. Do you know? Does anyone know?"

If no one answers the question, you may answer it yourself, or you may choose to leave it unanswered so that the learners may discover the answer for themselves at a later time.

Some questions, of course, are not task-relevant. When the learner hears the restatement of his question, he will recognize some incongruity with the subject under discussion: "You are asking if it is milk money day. Do you know?" In the middle of a discussion of cats, this question stands out as inappropriate. But the learner may not know this until he **hears** the question he has asked. The learner may answer his own question, or another in the group may answer it, but the teacher should refrain from answering irrelevant questions.

Which response is appropriate in each of the following situations?

1. Situation: It is an *independent work period.* Sally has finished a page and brings it to the desk. She says, "What do I do now?"
   - ☐ a. *"The rule is no talking."*
   - ☐ b. *"Go right on to the next page."*

2. Situation: It is a *class discussion period.* The group is discussing a picture. Jerry says, "What is that thing growing out of the roof?"
   - ☐ a. *"That's a chimney."*
   - ☐ b. *"You are asking what the pipe on the roof is called. Do you know?"*

3. Situation: It is a **class discussion period.** The group is discussing words that start with *b.* Marlene says, "How come Jo Ann isn't here today?"
   - ☐ a. *"You are asking why Jo Ann is absent. Do you know?"*
   - ☐ b. *"We aren't discussing Jo Ann. We are discussing things that start with b."*

4. Situation: It is an **independent study period.** Brian says, "What is this word? I can't remember it."
   - ☐ a. *"You are asking what this word is called. Do you know?"*
   - ☐ b. *"The rule is no talking."*

b. Directions. A second required change in teacher behavior concerns giving directions for learning tasks. Directions should be clear and concise and should be given only **once.** The only exception to this rule is that during the first week of school, the teacher may repeat directions 30 seconds after giving them. Only one repetition is recommended, however, even at this early time in the training period.

What often appears to be inability to perform a task is really inability to follow directions. A child may be able to read a question on a test but be unable to figure out where he should record his answer. Adults have nearly as much trouble as children in understanding verbal directions.

The problem is, first of all, the complexity of verbal directions. For this reason, directions in the MLP are very carefullly designed. The learner is "walked through" each step in making a response. A script is provided for the teacher. The pages in the student's book are coordinated with the script. The teacher may not improvise with these directions. They have been tried, revised, and retested, as were the tasks in the program.

Inadequate directions are sometimes found in educational materials. If you suspect that this is true of the materials you are using, you may be able to correct the problem by rewriting the directions. One formula for writing effective directions has three steps:

(*1*) Simplify

(*2*) Step-by-step

(*3*) Standardize

(*1*) Short, simple sentences are necessary. (*2*) Instruction is given for each step required for making an adequate response. (*3*) When students have learned to respond to one set of directions, use the same ones whenever you require the same kind of response. Such standardization of directions is efficient; it also permits you to shorten directions gradually, by leaving out parts that learners can already predict.

Students easily learn directions like those described above. Soon, learners begin saying them with you. "Which one is the same." "Go on by yourself." "Draw a circle around it." "The rule is no talking." The same technique can be applied to giving directions for nonacademic tasks. When it is time to clean up, the teacher always says, for example, "It's clean-up time. Put away your things. When you have finished, fold your hands and sit quietly." The teacher gives the directions word for word and the same every time. He gives them only once.

The second problem with directions is the inability of the learner to attend. Children, as well as adults, hear only a portion of what is said to them. Some figure out for themselves what is required. Others rely on a repetition of directions. They hear a little the first time, a little more the second time—and by the tenth repetition they know what to do. This procedure is inefficient for the teacher as well as for the learner. And it is unnecessary. Learners can be trained to listen to directions. It requires only that directions be clear (as described above) and that the teacher **refuse** to repeat them.

With certain exceptions in the early training period, directions for tasks should be given only once. If a learner is not attending when directions are given, he must solve the problems himself. He might remember a similar task and use it as a model. He might look at a classmate's work. He might put his book away in frustration. But tomorrow, when directions are given, he will be listening.

Which teacher is training children to listen to directions?

☐ *a.* *Teacher: "Take out your books. Turn to page 10." Learners do not immediately comply. Teacher: "I told you to take out your books right now." All but two children comply. Teacher: "John and Mark where are your books?"*

☐ *b.* *Teacher: "Take out your books. Turn to page 10." Learners do not immediately comply. Teacher waits until all have done so. This takes two minutes. Teacher: "Find a box at the top of the page. Point to it."*

Summary

We have been concerned with defining an adaptive or self-modifying classroom and with developing knowledge and skills needed to operate such a room. Defining characteristics of an adaptive classroom are as follows:

(*1*) Subroutines: These are also called **prerequisite skills**. They will be described later. For now, reference to the initial tests of the *STARS* series (Volume 2) will provide a survey of subroutines.

(*2*) Clear goals: These provide learning targets for children. If comprehensive, criterion-referenced measures are used, learners are in a position to become responsible for their own achievements.

(*3*) Materials: These have been mentioned in passing and will receive more attention in the light of skills and methods.

(*4*) Environment: Methods for establishing a comfortable environment include consistent behavior by the teacher, independence training, and doable materials.

(*5*) Self-evaluation: This is virtually absent at all levels of education except that of the preschooler. Young children teach themselves and evaluate their efforts. Once they are in school, that function is taken away. In the adaptive classroom, children compare their scores on criterion tests to the standard, identify deficits, and achieve mastery.

(*6*) Practice to mastery: Children are usually given only one chance to succeed, thus many fail. Ideally, the child has not completed his work until he has reached mastery. Therefore, opportunity to perfect skills must be afforded the learner.

Given an adequate environment, what competencies must children develop? Although skills are outlined in the Language Arts Competency Profile, each language component will be examined in the chapters of Part II of this book and a case will be made for teaching it.

* * * * *

To determine whether a given classroom is a productive environment, complete Module 2, Evaluating Classroom Effectiveness.

MODULE 2
Evaluating Classroom Effectiveness

Purpose

This module is designed to provide practice in three ways of estimating the productivity of classrooms.

Objective

Reading teachers will assess classroom productivity by using one of three procedures, as appropriate:

(1) The *P* Ratio Grid
(2) Rate of rule testing and enforcement
(3) Class Productivity Index

Directions

(1) Work through the module completely before arranging observations.
(2) Arrange for classroom observations as directed.
(3) Complete observations and make assessments.
(4) Complete the criterion test provided at the end of the module.

I. The Effective Classroom

Let us begin by agreeing on the **product** of our classrooms: boys and girls who are more competent in personal, social, and academic skills when they leave us than when they arrived.

That goal, increased competence in personal, social, and academic skills, may be translated in a number of ways: better self-image, mastery of the three Rs, improved confidence and self-awareness, better citizenship, greater self-actualization, greater rationality and sensitivity to others, and so on.

However, **one's definition is made concrete by what one measures.** It does little good to say, "But what I'm nurturing is not measurable." Even if that were true, in the absence of measures, the culture will apply **its** own yardstick. Schools will use standardized tests, parents will assess handwriting and spelling skills, employers will assess employee effectiveness, colleges will use aptitude measures. And teachers and schools will be judged by the child's competency on those measures.

How much better to make explicit what we hope to achieve, to measure it by some means (however subjective), and to have evidence that we are, in fact, achieving our goals.

*   *   *   *   *

If you cannot, in good conscience, agree that goals must be stated in measurable terms, do not complete this module. However, if you do agree that goals must be stated in measurable terms, go on to Part II.

II. Measures of Effectiveness

Three correlates of classroom effectiveness will be described:

(*1*) The proportion of time spent in task behavior by class members
(*2*) The predictability of the teacher's behavior
(*3*) The amount of achievement produced by the class

Although all three of these variables are related to classroom effectiveness, none is perfectly related to it. We shall consider each, in turn, along with a scale that quantifies it.

A. *Time Spent in Task Behavior*

In one study of classroom behavior, Cabot and D. E. P. Smith[8] identified 19 categories that included some 60 behaviors occurring in a classroom (see table of classroom behaviors). They recorded the incidence of occurrence of each behavior category during a specified period each day for some 30 days. Six children were observed. Six experienced teachers each observed one child through a

[8] Unpublished study.

Classroom Behaviors

1. WITHDRAWAL: PSYCHIC
   Sleep; immobility; staring in space; daydreaming (including doodling without attention, i.e., aimless drawing). **Comment**: At the extreme, "paralyzed with fear"; less extreme, escape from reality when physical escape cannot be managed.

2. WITHDRAWAL: PHYSICAL
   Leaving room; hiding from teacher or peers (not to include moving to a booth to work). **Comment**: Interpreted as **situation fear**, fear that can be reduced by moving out of the situation. It is possible that some bizarre behavior ("dangerous games") is akin to this and to categories 4, 5, and 6.

3. NARCISSISM
   Grooming; thumbsucking; masturbation; nose picking; chewing clothes; hair; finger-nails; using materials as toys (but breakage is category 11); singing (plus concomitant motions); chewing gum; eating; belching; laughing to self; random task behavior.

4. VISUAL PURSUIT: TEACHER
   Looking at or toward teacher or teacher's zone of operation; looking at student with whom teacher is working.

5. VISUAL PURSUIT: PEER
   Looking at or toward peer or peer's zone of operation (except when with teacher); copying (competition falls in category 14, Attacks Peer; Visual Pursuit is to be differentiated also from category 13, Responds to Peer; there is no apparent attack in the case of 5).

6. RULE TESTING
   Violation of "no-talking" rule or of "one person out at a time" rule; defined by enforcement by the teacher.

7. TASK I
   Work; without neurotic movements.

8. TASK II
   Work: small movements (hand, foot, head).

9. TASK III
   Work: large body movements (trunk, leg, arm).

10. SELF-ATTACK
    Pushing objects into self; pulling hair, skin, eyes; nail biting; biting lips, inside of cheeks (differentiation from category 3 by vigor).

11. OBJECT ATTACK
    Punching holes in books; breaking pencil; hitting desk, wall; scribbling; doodling (with care).

12. MANIPULATES PEER
    Initiates conversation; encourages ("Do it!" "Don't do it!"); smiles; enlists support; seduction.

13. RESPONDS TO PEER
    Reacts to any peer behavior (other than by observing).

14. ATTACKS PEER
    Swings at or kicks at, with or without contact; threatening gestures; throws things at (recorded as attack even though it may appear friendly).

15. **MANIPULATES TEACHER**
    Smiles at; asks for help; exhibits work.
16. **RESPONDS TO TEACHER**
    Blushing; stammering when in contact with teacher.
17. **ATTACKS TEACHER**
    Throws object; verbal abuse; gestures; facial expressions; any physical contact with teacher.
18. **ACTING-OUT ROOM**
    If acting-out is sufficient to hurt child or peer or to contage or if child would lose face by acting out in classroom, he is removed. Time out of room is recorded as category 18.
19. **HABITUATION**
    "Getting ready to act," perhaps decision making, essentially no activity momentarily before acting. Includes random page turning.

---

one-way window and tallied the current behavior every third second (20 tallies per minute) for 50 minutes each day.

Read through the list of behaviors in the table to answer the following questions:

> 1. Which categories include **work behavior**?
>
> _____, _____, _____.

> 2. Which category refers to "getting ready to work"?
>
> _____

> 3. How does the list describe "asking the teacher for help"?
>
> _____ _____.
>
> (All tasks in this room were self-instructional. Children did not need help at any time in order to complete tasks.)

Cabot and Smith determined the relationship between the incidence of each behavior and achievement in the target task (learning to read).

Only three categories were related to gains in reading—you can probably guess which three. Yes, the ones you noted in question 1.

Cabot and Smith concluded that achievement is related to the proportion of time spent working. This does not mean that children who work all the time necessarily succeed. But it does mean that **no work** tends to be accompanied by **no achievement**. In fact, in the programmed curriculum that the children were following, achievement in reading was dependent upon completing the curriculum. So the relationship worked both ways: (*1*) the less the work, the less the achievement; and (*2*) the more the work, the more the achievement.[9]

THE *P* RATIO GRID

The *P* Ratio Grid (p. 93) is an observation schedule. It will allow you to make a quick assessment of time spent in task behavior. Total observation time is less than 10 minutes.

Look at the form. Look at it now.

Now imagine yourself observing in a classroom. Select 10 children. Observe each one in turn for trial 1 and write in *P, N,* or *T*. When all 10 have been observed, do it again (trial 2). Continue for 10 trials. Work out the average *P* ratio for each child and for the total group. (See the example on page 101.)

Carry out the procedure for each of three classrooms. Enter group results for each classroom on the criterion test. A "Group Total %" average of 80% is a highly productive classroom. An average of 50% or below indicates a classroom in trouble. (If possible, use an independent work period.)

B. The Predictable Teacher

The teacher may be thought of as a catalyst of change. A catalytic agent facilitates change without itself being changed. The teacher manages the classroom enterprise in such a way that her behavior remains a constant in a sea of change.

Carl Semmelroth has provided the theoretical foundation for viewing the **predictable teacher**, that is, one who does not change from moment to moment or day to day, as the most effective classroom manager. Read the following section to find out:

(*1*) What are "leftover" behaviors?

(*2*) What are "stylized behaviors" of a teacher?

---

[9] After these findings, the research team set about determining how to increase working time and were able to increase it to 93% of total class time.

P RATIO GRID[10]

School_____ Date_____

Observer_____ Time_____

Trials	Names / Suzy Jones									Group Total %
1	P									
2	P									
3	N									
4	T									
5	P									
6	P									
7	P									
8	T									
9	N									
10	P									
Individual % Total	60%									Average

Key: *P* = Participating (actively involved in learning)
  N = Not participating (talking, dawdling)
  T = Transient (getting new materials, answer keys, etc.)
  P ratio is *P*/10

Directions: Take 10 samples of behavior from the same 10 students at fairly close intervals. Compute *P* ratio from these samples. In the course of a week cover all students. In the example, notice that Suzy was participating 6 out of 10 times. Dividing 6 her *P* ratio is 60%.
  10

[10] This noncopyrighted page was provided by the staff of the Reading Center, Omaha, Nebraska, Board of Education. After Cohen (1971).

Name two categories of classroom behavior.

1. _____

2. _____

What does it mean to say that one has a **teaching style**?

_____

_____

_____

_____

HOW TO TELL A WELL-MANAGED CLASSROOM
WHEN YOU SEE ONE[11]

Our topic is the well-managed classroom; specifically, how do you tell such a classroom if you happen to see one? There are two kinds of descriptions that might satisfy this purpose. First, we can describe the outcomes which might characterize a well-managed classroom. For example, what you might see in this type of classroom is orderly, relatively quiet, successful students.

For someone who might not happen to observe a well-managed classroom, this kind of description is not very helpful. Similarly, a description of a home run hitter as a person who hits a fair ball out of the park is not helpful to most ballplayers. We'd all agree, to begin with, that it's better to be rich and healthy than sick and poor, and it's better to have a happy, serious, knowledgeable class than it is to have an ignorant, noisy, unhappy class.

A second way of describing a well-managed classroom is to attempt to describe some behavior which is not itself the outcome of the classroom, but which appears to be intrinsic to it. That is, what would we invariably see happening in a well-managed classroom besides the outcomes referred to above? This is the problem I am addressing in this paper.

I am also assuming a rather "utopian-minded" approach to the problem. That is, I shall be attempting to describe an ideal combination of factors from the point of view of an assumed ideal outcome. This ideal outcome is, to put it bluntly, to have the teacher in charge of the classroom. What do I mean by "in charge"? What I mean is that the total effect of his influence on the behaviors of members of the class is more than the total influence of the class members on

[11] Reprinted, with permission, from the article of the same title by Carl Semmelroth in *The Reading Specialist*, 1969, 7, 21–23.

each other's behavior. Notice, I did **not** say that the teacher controls a majority of the child's behavior; rather, the teacher has more control of a child than the control exerted on that child by other students. The distinction here is an important one. It takes into account the obvious, but often overlooked, fact that a child's behavior is regulated by things such as tasks, books, and pictures on the walls as well as by other people present. If you are bothered by the notion of the child's behavior being regulated by "things" such as books and self-instructional programs, then you can think of these behaviors as being "self-control" behaviors without disturbing the distinction drawn here.

Why have I partitioned the behaviors of a child into those which are controlled by things and those which are controlled by people? The reason is that the interactions between a person and a thing (whether the thing is a book or a sophisticated piece of programmed instruction) are comparatively simple and tend toward stability, whereas person–person interactions tend to be relatively unstable and complex.

Before examining why this should be and what it has to do with classroom management, I will outline the assumption I am making about what constitutes control. This assumption is simply Thorndike's **law of effect**; that is, behavior is regulated by its consequences. It follows, then, that whoever controls the consequences controls the behavior. If consequences are presented by a book or a puzzle, then the book or puzzle control (perhaps a better word is "regulate") behavior. If consequences are presented by another person, then that person controls or regulates the behavior.

An example of behavior regulation by an object is that of an adult doing an arithmetic problem: every time he performs an operation in long division, there is a consequent arrangement of stimuli which is familiar and which guides his next behavior. Unfortunately, a long division problem does not serve to regulate a child's behavior unless the child knows how to do long division. There are, however, ways to construct materials so that they will guide a child's behavior through a series of "double" steps and he ends up doing long division. These are so-called "programmed" or self-instructional materials.

An example of behavior regulation by another person is that of a teacher smiling at a student after or during a recitation by the student. This consequence will often result in the student's waving his hand to recite and watching the teacher's face while he is reciting. Another example of person–person behavior regulation is that of the student who waves his hand at the teacher when the teacher has previously called on him and smiled. This will often result in the teacher's ignoring the student's waving hand. The point of these two examples is that, when people are seen as administering consequences to one another which serve to regulate each other's behavior, we have a complex and often unstable situation. In this case, the student raised his hand, the teacher called on him, the student recited, the teacher smiled, the student raised his hand, the teacher ignored him, the student waved his hand, etc. Behavior can become unstable because behaviors are at once shaped by and shaping other behaviors. In short, given the behaviors in a classroom which are not successfully regulated by tasks, programmed books or such "things," these leftover behaviors are what need to be "managed," in so far as the situation is seen as being a "classroom."

We have, then, one answer to how we tell a well-managed classroom when we see one: namely, a classroom in which there is no "class," only a room full of task-regulated behaviors. That is, when all the behavior is regulated by tasks, there is no interaction among students or between student and teacher. Therefore, there are no left-over behaviors for the group or the teacher to regulate. However, we ordinarily want to have classes in which there is interaction, if for no other reason than that we don't have enough tasks, nor are they "good" enough to effectively regulate student behavior for the lengths of time which the educational enterprise is required to deal with students. So, we return to the original question stated in a slightly different way: Given the behaviors in a classroom which are not regulated by academic tasks, how do we tell if the teacher has more influence on those behaviors than the influence generated by the interregulation among the class members? Or put in terms of consequences, how do we tell whether the teacher has more control of the consequences of behavior in the classroom than do the students?

When the question of management is framed in terms of having "majority control" of non-task behavioral consequences, two stubborn aspects of reality come to the fore. First, the arithmetic of class size is definitely not on the teacher's side. If we assume that each child in a class has an opportunity to administer a behavioral consequence to every other child in the class and count up these opportuniites, we might have a rough measure of the amount of behavioral control the classroom administers to itself. For example, consider a classroom with three students, Jack, Henry, and Sally: Jack can administer consequences to Henry and Sally's behaviors (that's two); Henry can administer consequences to Jack and Sally (that's four); and Sally can administer consequences to Henry and Jack (that's six). On the other hand, the teacher of this class can administer behavioral consequences to three people. So in terms of the raw arithmetic of the balance of power, the teacher is a two-to-one underdog with a class size of three.

Consider what happens to this arithmetic if we increase class size. For a class size of 5, the score is 20 to 5, or 4 to 1; for a class size of 10, it's 90 to 10, or 9 to 1, and so on. In terms of the number of two-person interactions possible as class size increases, we have 90 in a class of 10 students, 380 in a class of 20 students, 600 in a class of 25 students, and 1560 in a class of 40 students. According to this arithmetic, if we were to pay a teacher $10,000 a year to manage a class of 10 students, then we ought to pay her $173,300 a year to manage a class of 40 students, since there are 1733 times more to manage in a class of 40 than in a class of 10.

Aside from the arithmetic of class size, a second stubborn aspect of reality comes to the fore when we pose the problem of classroom management in terms of whether or not the teacher has more influence on non-task behaviors than do the students. This has to do with the fact that students administer consequences to the teacher as well as the other way around. Now, in order for the teacher to have any kind of chance at managing the classroom, she cannot be entirely "managed" by these consequences. If her behavior is managed by the class in the sense that it changes according to the consequences it produces, then the class will inevitably be more in control than she is. What this means is that, if the classroom is well-managed and if we watch her behavior over a period of time, she will exhibit a style which is independent of the particular outcomes of her behaviors in class. Notice I did not say she would exhibit some particular style of behaviors, but that she would exhibit **some** style. This means, especially, that when she is "punished" for a behavior, she continues to exhibit it. For example, asking John to sit down and then having to go and sit him down because he would not do what she asked him to do is a punishing experience. If the teacher were being managed by the consequences administered to her by John, then she would gradually (or not so gradually) cease to ask John to do anything which she didn't feel he would do.

I am expressly leaving the door open here on what set of behaviors, i.e., what style, may be better than some other. In fact, I think it is possible that it is relatively unimportant whether a teacher runs a classroom by punishing, cuddling, buddying or rule-mongering. What is extremely important, if she does not want the class to manage itself (and her with it), is that she be relatively impervious to the short-term consequences of her behavior; this means that she will look pretty much the same day to day. Put another way, she has a style.

We have, then, a second way of telling when we see a well-managed classroom, that is, a classroom in which the teacher is in charge. We watch the teacher. If the teacher responds the same way to events day by day, then the class is well-managed.

In summary then, I am suggesting that the essence of a well-managed classroom consists of two things. First, that the proportion of task-regulated behaviors to people-regulated behaviors be large enough to give the teacher a fighting chance at behavior regulation. Second, the essence of a well-managed class is that the teacher controls more of the consequences to student behavior than the students do. The only way that a teacher can exert more influence than the students is to have her behavior be unaffected by its consequences. A sign that this is the case is that her behavior is characteristic, i.e., essentially unadaptive in the day to day context of the classroom.

Semmelroth does not tell us **what** teacher behaviors we should look for to assess predictability. But as his long-time colleague, I would guess that one of those behaviors is **rule-related behavior.**

Substantial data gathered by D. E. P. Smith and T. Walter (1972) lead to the following conclusions:

(*1*) The most common teacher behaviors are those used to maintain classroom control. One of these is rule enforcement.

(*2*) Rules exist to be tested (and enforced).

(*3*) If a rule is enforced less than 80% of the times it is tested, it tends to continue to be tested at a high rate. If enforced 80% or more, rule testing decreases. (That is, if a rule is tested 10 times during a period, enforcement on eight or more occasions tends to result in less rule testing.)

(*4*) If a teacher must enforce more than three rules, he will be unable to reach the 80% criterion.

Note that, according to Semmelroth, the more behaviors under task control, the fewer leftover behaviors must be managed. **Productive classrooms demonstrate little rule testing and dependable enforcement.**

Rule	Enforcement
No talking.	"Joe, the rule is 'No talking.' "
No throwing papers.	"Joe, the rule is 'no throwing papers.' "
One person at a time.	"Joe, the rule is 'one person at a time.' "

It follows, then, that one way to estimate classroom productivity is to count **the rule tests** and **the rule enforcements**. Then express them as a ratio:

$$\text{Rule enforcement ratio} = \frac{\text{enforcements}}{\text{rule tests}}$$

Example: In one short work period, there were 20 rule tests and 2 enforcements:

$$\frac{2}{20} = \frac{1}{10} = 10\%$$

Try this:

Joe observed a 20-minute independent work period. He counted 10 rule tests and 9 enforcements. The rule enforcement ratio (RER) was _____%.

To observe and record, take the following steps:

Step 1 Arrange to observe for 10 to 20 minutes in each of three classrooms. Try to arrange to be there during an independent work period.

Step 2 Ask the teacher what the class rules are, if any.
  (a) If there are rules, select no more than three for observation.
  (b) If there are no **stated** rules, figure out the unstated ones by observing the teacher's control techniques.

Step 3 Tally:
  (a) Rule tests
  (b) Enforcements

Step 4 Write your results in the appropriate place on the criterion test at the end of this module.

C. Productivity

We have considered and measured student participation and teacher predictability in order to assess classroom effectiveness. Each of these is related to the progress of learners. But each leaves something to be desired. Other than final criterion tests, the best measure of productivity is the daily work output of the class.

Charting work output requires that some number value be assigned to completed tasks. In some cases, that is easy to do:

	Points
• Mastery of 10 spelling words	10
• Completion of three workbook pages with 15 tasks per page	45
• Reading a story:	
Grade 3: 16 paragraphs = 16 4 questions = 4	20
Grade 6: 8 pages = 8 10 questions = 10	18

Other tasks require more arbitrary values:

• Passing a criterion test	10
• Writing a paragraph of four correct sentences:	

Sentences   = 4
     Relationship (coherence)   = 3
     Beginning and ending punctuation = 4
	11

• Oral response in class	5

In general:

(1) Assign **one point** for a **task response** of one or a few words.

(2) Assign **two points per minute** on tasks that utterly defy measurement. For example:

- Reading a book: 2 hours   = 120 X 2
- Library research: 1 hour   = 60 X 2
- Building a bird house: $3\frac{1}{2}$ hours = 210 X 2

To assess the **Class Productivity Index** (CPI), arrange to observe a class during a work period.

Step 1   Select five children at random. (To randomize, number each desk and select every fifth desk in a 25-child room, every sixth desk in a 30-child room.)

Step 2   Make up a point chart. Note the length of the activity period.

CLASS 1

Begin:	9:10 ⎫	20
End:	9:30 ⎭	minutes

	Points
Joe	6
Judy	10
Sam	3
John	14
Suzy	7
Total	40

Step 3   Use the point procedure just described to count the productivity of each child. Add up the points.

Step 4   Determine the **average production** of the group by dividing the total by 5 (number of children).

$$\frac{40}{5} = 8 \text{ points/child}$$

Step 5   Determine the CPI, the average production **per minute**.

$$CPI = \frac{\text{average production}}{\text{minutes of work}}$$

$$CPI = \frac{8 \text{ points}}{20 \text{ minutes}}$$

CPI = .40 points/minute ($\frac{4}{10}$ points/minute or 1 point every $2\frac{1}{2}$ minutes)

Step 6 Carry out steps 1–5 with two more classes. Values across classes will range from .10 to about 3.00 (a point in 10 minutes to 3 points/minute).

Step 7 Enter the CPI for each class in the appropriate places on the criterion test.

EXAMPLE

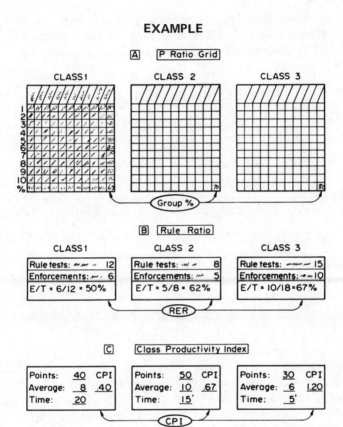

You may have noticed that all data can be collected in 3 half-hours of observation.

	Time	Days	Classes	Activity
A. *P* Ratio Grid	10 minutes	1	3	Work time

B. Rule Ratio	10–20 minutes	1	3	Work time

C. Class Productivity Index	10–20 minutes	1	3	Work time

These can be collapsed into 30 minutes of observation in each class, 10 minutes of *P* ratio observations and 20 minutes of rule enforcement. The 20 minutes (or all 30 minutes) can be used for the point production time.

Criterion Test

	A *P* Ratio Grid (Group Total % Average)	B Rule Ratio	C Class Productivity Index
1. Class 1	_____	_____	_____
Class 2	_____	_____	_____
Class 3	_____	_____	_____

2. Which of the three classes was most effective—1, 2, or 3? Why do you think so? _____
_____
_____
_____
_____
_____
_____

3. Set up a point procedure for these activities:
   a. Three pages of workbook tasks, 10 tasks per page   _____
   b. A visual search task requiring finding all the letters of the alphabet **once, in order**.   _____
   c. Reading an SRA story of four paragraphs and answering six questions   _____
   c. Preparing and giving a 3-minute talk on any topic   _____

Domains
of Language

Listening
Speaking
Reading
Writing

LISTENING

FRANK'S STORY

It was a sunny Monday morning in mid September. Millie had arrived early, as usual, to arrange the day's activities for her first grade scholars. The chairs were still upended on the desks after the weekend cleaning.

Frank had also arrived early and was standing, his back to the wall, staring vacantly at the disordered desks. Millie wondered about this quiet boy who never seemed to do anything. He either merely observed the other children—or appeared withdrawn: frightened? retarded? catatonic? Or, possibly, just over-whelmed? Well, let's find out:

"Frank?" A small response, a slight, ear-raising twist of the head.

"Frank?" An eyebrow-raising look in Millie's general direction.

"Frank?" Discovery! *That's teacher saying my name.* A bobbing of the head meaning "What?"

"Frank, will you take that chair off the desk and put it on the floor, please?" Forehead creasing, Frank leaned forward, his total being locked on Millie's face.

"Frank?" Head nod. "Will you take that chair off the desk and put it on the floor?" Frank looked at the chair. Then he looked back to Millie.

"Frank, will you take that chair . . . [he looked at the chair] off the table . . . and put it on the floor?" Frank looked at the floor, then at the chair, then at the

105

floor, then back to Millie. Then a sudden smile broke over his face. He leapt forward and lifted the chair off the desk.

But wait! Something was wrong. The chair had its back to the desk and Frank was momentarily confused. Three seconds passed. Suddenly, Frank picked up the chair, turned it around, and placed it under the desk.

He looked up at Millie with a small smile of satisfaction. "Thank you, Frank. That's very helpful."

*   *   *   *   *

Frank has normal hearing and normal intelligence. He must not be classified as retarded. Millie, with the wisdom and skill of a first grade teacher, found out what she wanted to know. Frank was overwhelmed by stimuli, unable to "process information" rapidly in this room. Simply take him, step by step, through the requirements of the first grade culture and help him become a normal second grader.

*   *   *   *   *

About a month later, Frank could be seen immersed in picture books during independent work period. Day after day, he searched out illustrated books and studied the pictures. And, suddenly, he began to draw.

His Thanksgiving drawing was judged "Best Picture" among first graders.

In a rough way, listening is to speaking as reading is to writing. Listening and reading are **receptive** of information; speaking and writing are **expressive**. But both listening and reading are active rather than passive receptive processes. Listening as **attending** (e.g., "Listen to this!") is merely the first step in receiving information. Listening as **hearing something** or, more precisely, as responding to what someone is saying is what constitutes a communication event. In a similar way, reading as **attending to print** has long been excluded from definitions of reading. Reading is generally viewed as **responding** to print or, better, as responding to one's own voice when one is looking at print.

The gap between attending and responding when children listen is the problem facing the teacher. The gap can be filled by appropriate training. And the strategy to be followed is somehow to get the child to make appropriate responses to language units—to utterances, to words within utterances, and to sounds within words. Before specifying the training further, let us place listening in the total language act.

I. What Is Known

The relationships among reading, writing, listening, and speaking are far from being unraveled. Despite long and intensive study by psychologists and linguists, only a few hard findings are available and those are virtually unrelated to instruction.

For example, it is known that the babbling of infants includes most sounds comprising the phonemes[1] of most languages; that the infant early distinguishes speech sounds from other sounds in his environment; that the sounds he makes that have a consequence tend to be continued, whereas others are lost; that those that are continued tend to drop out and to reappear later (thus giving rise to terms such as *stage of development*); and that there tends to be an orderly development of response to (and use of) syntactic signals such as noun and verb endings, with most of the basic regularities of the language in use by school entry.

Concerning language instruction, linguistic scientists tend to be pessimistic about the usefulness of imitation and other methods of direct instruction. Wardhaugh (1971) quoted McNeill (1966) in this context:

> One child, in the phase of producing double negatives while developing the negative transformation, had the following exchange with his mother:
>
> Child: Nobody don't like me.
> Mother: No, say "Nobody likes me."
> Child: Nobody don't like me.
>
> (eight repetitions of this dialogue)
>
> Mother:, No, now listen carefully; Say **"Nobody likes me."**
> Child: Oh! Nobody don't likes me.
>
> The exchange . . . demonstrated the relative impenetrability of the child's grammar to adult models, even under the instruction (given by the mother's "no") to change [McNeill, 1966, p. 69].

We must agree that the mother's instruction is inefficient, although she has produced one of the two changes desired. But I think we need not be as pessimistic as McNeill. Both imitation—the use of models—and direct instruction can be effective when properly engineered. There are paradigms of second language instruction that have proved effective (Bereiter & Englemann, 1966; see Dale, 1972, pp. 280 ff.) and others that are both effective and **painless** (Knudsvig, 1975). The way to more efficient language learning appears to be through intensive listening training. We shall return to this point in a discussion of dialect (Chapter 5).

[1] Sounds of a language that differentiate words from one another. /Bit/ and /bet/ have different phonemes in the middle position.

II. Assumptions

There is relatively little evidence on the relationships among language skills. To get on with instruction, we shall make certain guesses or assumptions about the what and why of listening. These assumptions derive from theory and from practice and do not, at present, run counter to laboratory evidence.

The infant and child attend to an undifferentiated array of auditory stimuli. When attention to some part of the array (like mother's voice) tends to be followed by a positive consequence, that part begins to stand out, to be discriminated, to become a discriminative stimulus or **target stimulus**. Certain important sounds and utterances become target stimuli. With sufficient experience, the infant and child come first to recognize the sound (indicated by anticipatory responses like sucking) and then to reproduce it. Reproducing the sound sometimes has the effect of controlling the consequence. The reproduction of the sound is called **speaking**.

Assumption 1. (See Vol. 1, pp. 33–34.) Speaking, the reproduction of sounds and utterances, tends to bring out characteristics of the stimulus not previously noticed (and not needed for recognition). For example, /hops-ital/ and /hot-sittal/; /bus-ghetti'/; /bwek-mas/, /bek-fit/, /bref-kit/, /bres-kit/, /bref-skit/, /brek-sit/, and /brek-fit/. These approximations to words are transformed into acceptable pronunciations by making it possible for the child to note the contrast between his product and that of an adult. To say it another way, these stimulus characteristics (correct sounds) serve as stimuli for further recognitions and reproductions. Therefore, expressive or reproduction learnings (speaking and writing) are facilitated by the training of receptive responses (listening and reading) and vice versa.

Assumption 2. (See Vol. 1, p. 23.) Language responses are hierarchical, with new discriminative responses "distinguishing the (hitherto unnoticed) features of a rich input [Gibson, 1966, p. 320]." First responses are to tonal patterns, later ones to the lexical content of utterances (the meaning), to single words, and to parts of words, in that order.

Neither of these assumptions implies that learning occurs in a straight line, from listening to speaking to reading to writing, or from tonal patterns to parts of words. Rather the course of learning appears to be **alternating and cyclical**: Children become much involved with auditory input, then visual, then auditory. They move back and forth from stories to sounds to word play, and so on. This leads us to Assumption 3.

Assumption 3. Instructional materials are best organized and patterned from simple to complex but children must have free access to tasks at various levels of complexity. In other words, freedom of choice (self-selection) must be possible with those materials.

Assumption 4. Concerning the nature of tasks: Although we will try to have children respond to utterances, words, and parts of words, we do not assume that every response **must** be learned simply because it **can** be learned. Rather, we will train children to **attend** to language stimuli—by providing language stimuli to which children can respond. And we will not provide sounds of trains, buses, birds, and bees. Though such sounds are interesting, they have little or nothing to do with language. What then should we provide, specifically?

III. What to Teach

No matter what method of teaching reading is used, a number of listening competencies are required. For example, children must learn that the utterances /littleboy/ and /fatboy/ are not simply different words and that, in fact, the sound they have in common is seen in print as [boy]. They must learn that /my country tizaltee/ and /of thee high C/ are only rough approximations to the lines of the patriotic song, that /thisaft/ will appear in book writing as [this afternoon], and that /lieberry/ is spelled [library]. And, in order to read, in order to sound out words, they must discriminate sound differences far more subtle than these.

The number of auditory discriminations required to achieve independent reading is difficult to estimate but easily runs into the thousands. For example, at one of several levels of word discrimination, **words from similar words**, some 600 tasks using minimal contrastive pairs of words[2] are required to bring first grade children to mastery. It is not surprising, then, that so few auditory training programs have useful results. Most of them contain nonlanguage stimuli (target stimuli unrelated to reading), language stimuli improperly graded, and, finally, not enough language stimuli to make a difference.

Not all these thousands of discriminations must be purposefully taught to all children, of course. It is possible to teach **attentional strategies** having some generalizability; for example, children can be trained to focus on the beginning, ending, or middle of words at will. But, whether or not we teach all responses, it is useful to know which ones are necessary, and to know when they have been achieved. One cannot know when to stop training without goal measures.

Listening skills may be classified by language units, that is, as **utterances** (spoken sentences), as **parts** (segments) **of utterances** (such as single words), and

---

[2] Minimal contrast: two words differing in only one phoneme, as /pit/ and /pet/.

as **groups of utterances**. Or, they may be classified by the visual representations of language, words and sentences (and, later, paragraphs and discourse).

Although the second method of classification is only roughly equivalent to natural spoken language, it does simplify instruction in reading because reading begins with print. When children sound out or decode words, they look at words first, then isolate letters and groups of letters and try to match them to sounds. Letters have slightly different sounds in different words, so the matching process is difficult. In fact, the sound–symbol equivalents used in sounding (or phonics) are not at all self-evident.

For example, Judy was out of school with rheumatic fever when the other children learned to read. She learned to read, of course, but without phonics instruction. On her return to school, she was asked during a lesson to identify the middle sound in /lake/. (There is no middle sound in /lake/.) She responded /lake/, to the great amusement of the other children—who **knew** the answer was /a/. (Put the word on audiotape and cut out the middle portion. Then splice the cut ends and run the tape. You will hear /lake/. You cannot remove the vowel sound since it "colors" beginning and ending consonants.) Judy was right: The middle sound in /lake/ is /lake/. The children were, unknowingly, using a phonics convention: "Let us assume that we can isolate the middle sound. What would it be? Yes, the long *a*." A phonics convention is a letter–sound pairing in which **the most likely sound** for that letter is tried.

Although conventions introduce distortion in the coded words, they are still useful rough-and-ready techniques. Another such technique is the addition of junctures (speech interruptions) where none would occur in normal speech: /little . . . boy/ for /littleboy/; /sit . . . down/ for /siddown/.

Despite difficulties with matching letters to sound, we shall use the categories of words and sentences to facilitate instruction. Since the child looks at the visual representation of a word (i.e., the printed word) before sounding it, we must have a classification system for language as it appears in print. Such a system appears in the following chart:

FEATURES OF SPEECH

Suprasegmental	Segmented
Tonal Pattern	*Utterances*
Pitch	
Stress	*Visual Equivalents*
Juncture	Words
	Sentences
	(and punctuation)

The categories of concern include tonal patterns and the items derived from utterances. As it stands, the **training domain** of speech categories has limited usefulness. It does not tell us what sounds to teach, it provides no ideas on how they may be taught, and it says nothing about how we may know whether or not they have been learned.

To determine which sounds should be learned, we shall look to linguistic science to find relevant distinctions:

(*1*) A **communication event** may be described as the reception of information (meaning) transmitted by a speaker.

(*2*) Within any communication event, there may be units of information at several levels of analysis—the **phonological**, the **grammatical**, and the **referential**.[3]

(*3*) It is possible to detect differences in sound (phones), some of which make a difference in meaning (phonemes).

Phonological level. A **phone** is a detectable unit of sound that may or may not make a difference in meaning:

/bottle/   /boddle/   /bo?el/

(wherein ? indicates a glottal stop). The middle sound or phone is different in these three enunciations of *bottle*, but the word remains recognizable; the meaning remains the same. On the other hand, /bad/ and /bed/ have a detectable sound difference that makes a difference in meaning: *bad* and *bed* are different words. The smallest detectable sound difference that also signals a meaning difference is called a **phoneme**. Therefore, (*1*) **we must discriminate phonemic differences**.

Differing patterns of stress within utterances also may be used to signal differences in meaning:

/those are **my** books/   (not yours)
/**those** are my books/   (not these)
/those are my **books**/   (not old newspapers)

Therefore, (*2*) **we must discriminate stress differences**.

Pitch differences are used in our language for many purposes—for example, to signal a question:

/that's a hat/   (the name of that is *hat*)
/that's a hat/   (the name of that is *monstrosity*)

Therefore, (*3*) **we must discriminate pitch differences**.

---

[3] Some writers refer to the grammatical and referential levels by the roughly analogous terms, *syntactic* and *semantic*.

Combinations of stress, pitch, and juncture make up **tonal patterns**. For example, the dinner signal at my house,

$$\overset{\rightarrow}{\text{/It's}}\ \overset{\searrow}{\text{al}}\ \overset{\nearrow}{\text{read}}\ \overset{\rightarrow}{\text{y/}}$$

constitutes a musical pattern with emphasis (stress) on /read/. When dinner time approached, our very young children, 1–2 years old, were heard to give a similar signal without words. The tonal pattern, then, can signal meaning. But linguists have found such signals to be variable in meaning depending on the larger language transaction and social context. Thus we should probably not attempt to teach particular responses to tonal pattern, except those differentiating questions, statements, and commands.

Grammatical level. Many common words sound enough alike that most children are unaware that they are different. They respond to such words differently because the words are embedded in differing contexts. Our language is sufficiently redundant that we seldom depend on a single sound to interpret a message. When reading, however, we are often dependent on a single cue for decoding a word. The word /pin/, for example, will often be found in a sewing context. The word /pen/, on the other hand, is usually in a writing context. The statement /give me the pin/ will cause confusion unless other cues are present. In a story, other helpful cues may or may not be present. Other confusable words:

> *he hit me, he bit me*
> *tree, three*
> *six, sick*
> *crown, clown*
> *next, nests*
> *scream, stream*
> *scrap, strap*
> *fine, vine, pine*

The distinctions here are obvious to a good **reader**, considerably less obvious to a beginning **listener**. Therefore, (*4*) **we must discriminate similar-sounding words**.

A morpheme may be a whole word (**unbound** morpheme). But many morphemes are parts of words and have meanings of their own (**bound** morphemes). For example, the *pre* in *prefix* and *prelude* means "before," therefore is classified as a morpheme. A morpheme is the smallest indivisible unit of language: If divided further, it loses or changes its meaning. Therefore, *ed* in *waited* is a morpheme (its meaning is its indication of past tense); furthermore, the *s* in *waits* and *s* in *waiters* are both morphemes, but different ones (*s* signifies the third person, present tense in the first case and the plural in the second). Many parts of words, then, carry meaning. Therefore, (*5*) **we must discriminate sounds within words**.

Nor is this all. I have already mentioned discriminating words within utterances (/littleboy/ and /fatboy/) and phonemes within words. There are also initial blends, digraphs, phonograms, and syllables.

The foregoing explication was not designed to overwhelm you with trivia—even though, like Frank, you may have felt overwhelmed. I have tried to make a case for the "great silent area" of instruction, the auditory training component of literacy. Auditory training tends to be given too little and too late in virtually all the commercially prepared materials used in American schools (see Spache & Spache, 1973, pp. 125–126). If the method of teaching reading used does not include a substantial auditory program, the teacher must supplement it to bring all children to a critical level of competency. The **what** of training is summarized in Table 4.1. The **how** is summarized in Table 4.2 and discussed in a subsequent section of this chapter.

In Table 4.1, note that the levels of task are numbered (arbitrarily) from one to six. A brief description of the contents or domain of each is given and followed by a test number from the *Standard Achievement Recording System (STARS)*, Word Level: Auditory Skills. Finally, sample test items are given.

Questions about Table 4.1

What skills are involved at the sentence level?
Mainly **sentence memory**, distinguishing statements from questions, and so on. Although there is, in fact, some training required in tonal pattern, it is best handled in the training program for speaking.
Isn't there a lot of overlap in the domain subheads for words (Level 2)?
Yes.
In Level 3, why do you say "consonants: final, then initial position"?
A good question. Most programs begin with listening for initial consonants, partly because they contain most of the information required when sounding out words. However, endings are more easily discriminated, on the whole, than are initial sounds. The initial sound is masked by following sounds; the final sound is not masked. Therefore, I suggest that you teach final sounds first.
Some of the directions are missing under "Sample Test Item." Why?
There wasn't enough space. See Volume 2 for complete tests.
Why do you sometimes use triads (cap . . . cat . . . cap) for minimal pair training?
We give children a picture (of a cap) and the word *no*. If the words are the same, they circle the picture; if not the same, they circle *no*. Young children confuse the task. They respond as if to a naming task. (Is it a hat?) The third choice, repeating the first, gives them a chance to recover and respond to the contrast task by using the second and third words.

Table 4.1

Components of Auditory Training (What to Teach)

Level	Class	Domain	Test[a]	Sample Test Item
1	Utterances: word or sentence	Sentences of increasing length and/or complexity	1	· Say the sentence just the way I say it: *Where could he work?*
		Statements, questions, commands (directions)	2	· Say the letters I say: *m . . . o . . . t* *bi . . . ck . . . o*
2	Words from similar words	Minimal pairs representing all phonemes	5	Single words: · I will say some words. If they are the same, circle the word. If they are not the same, circle *no.*
		Sight words from readers	6	*cat . . . cap . . . cat*
		Spelling words	7	*fat . . . fan . . . fat*
		Common nouns, verbs modifiers, function words	8	*soap . . . soup . . . soap*
		Words in idiomatic phrases and frequently occurring word groups	9	Words within sentences: · Listen for *from:* *Here is a letter for you.*

114

#				
3	Sounds in words: (a) Phonemes[b]	Consonants: final, then initial, position c-v and v-c combinations	4 10 11	• I will say words that start the same. You tell me another. *bean, bird, bunch* • Listen for *ish . . . fin* • Listen for *ca . . . cat* • Say the underlined sound then cross out one that does not have that sound: *fun . . . phone . . . laugh . . . ghost*
			⎡Letter— ⎣sound 11 12	
4	(b) Morphemes (bound)	Endings on nouns, verbs Prefixes, suffixes, roots	12 13 14	• Circle the number that tells how many words I said: *My mother is not home.* 1 2 3 4 5 6 7 8
5	(c) Blends and phonograms	*sh, wh, th, ch* *bl, br, pl, gr, sp, st,* *tr, thr, cr, etc.* Families	3 15 16	• I will say words that rhyme. You tell me another word. *mat, fat, sat* • I will say words. If they start the same, circle *yes*. *shop, shock, shot*
6	(d) Syllables	All common polysyllabic words	17 18	• I will say a word . . . count the syllables. *world misunderstanding*

[a] All tests are from *STARS*, Word Level, Auditory Skills with the exception of the bracketed entries.
[b] Lists of common sounds are available (see, e.g., Spache & Spache, 1973, p. 470).

115

IV. How to Teach

Table 4.2 presents a good deal of information about how training materials should be constructed. Notice first that the six levels of Table 4.1 appear also in Table 4.2. Notice next the three major columns, Listening 1 (Match), Listening 2 (Identify), and Listening 3 (Equate). Each of these recognition tasks is followed by a production task (not surprisingly, called Speaking): miming or mimicking, completing, or generating words or utterances. Matching units, identifying units within larger units, and equating (equivalence of sound or meaning) are three stages in learning:

(1) Matching tasks consist mainly of triads (three words or sounds). The middle item is different from the first and last items on half of the tasks; the middle item is the same as the first and last items on the other half.

(2) Identifying tasks are more difficult than matching tasks. Learners are required to hold a unit "in mind," then to try matching it to parts of a larger unit.

(3) Equating is more complex than it appears to be. The equivalence is based on meaning (which words mean the same) and on sounds that must have "unit value." For example, the child must compare *harm* and *alarm*, identify the *arm* sound, then match it to either *ring* or *farm*. In effect, the phonogram becomes a tool for sounding out unknown words.

Reference to the norms for *STARS* (Volume 2) will show a training period starting in kindergarten and ending at second grade for these skills. In fact, intensive work will enable virtually all children to pass the last tests by the end of the first grade.

Summary

Frank seems to have had a problem of information overload. He processed auditory information (and visual, too) very slowly.

An examination of what is known about language learning unearthed very little of relevance to training problems. On the other hand, examination of distinctions from linguistics suggested that children must discriminate (1) utterances from other utterances, (2) words within utterances, (3) words from similar words, and (4) a number of sounds within words: phonemes, morphemes, blends, phonograms, and syllables. The domain of each of these classes was specified, tests were identified, and teaching paradigms were illustrated.

Now let us do a similar kind of survey of speaking.

Table 4.2
Paradigm for Teaching Auditory Discrimination (How to Teach)[a]

Level	Listening 1 Match		Listening 2 Identify		Listening 3 Equate (sound or meaning)	
1	Sentences: • Same or different? /He is my dad/ /He is our dad/	SPEAKING: → Mime	• Listen for *this is our little baby*: That is mom. That is Dad. That is a baby Yes No	SPEAKING: → Complete (reproduce, with aid)	• Which one tells who lost something? /The baby lost her shoe/ /Where can it be?/	SPEAKING: → Generate (produce)
2	Words: • Same or different? /can . . . can . . . can/ /cap . . . cat . . cap/		• Listen for *this*: /This is Jack Yes No /He is a boy/ Yes No		• Which one means about the same? /dog: puppy Kitty/ /horse: cow pony/	
3	Phonemes: • Same or different? /ca . . . ca . . . ca/ /ba . . . da . . . ba/		• Listen for *s-s-s*: /horse/ Yes No /kiss/ Yes No /good/ Yes No		• Which one ends the same as *was*? /bus . . . does/	
4	Morphemes (bound): • Same or different? /boy . . . boys . . . boy/ /girl . . . girl . . . girl/	Mime	• Listen for *z-z-z*: /boys/ Yes No /girl/ Yes No		• Which means more than one? /boy/ /boys/	
5	Blends and phonograms • Same or different? /ite . . . ite . . . ite/ /arm . . . aim . . . arm/		• Listen for *arm*: /farm/ Yes No • Listen for *arm*: /same/ Yes No	Complete	• One rhymes with *harm, alarm*. Circle/ring/ or /farm/	Generate
6	Syllables: • Same or different? /mar . . . ma . . . mar/ /row . . . ra . . . row/	Mime	• How many syllables? /throw/ 1 or 2? /tomorrow/ 2 or 3?		• Complete the rhyme: /And when out walking We're always _____./	
	• Say what I say: /He is my dad/ /can . . . cap . . . cat/ /ca . . . at . . . ca/		• Complete this sentence: Jack is a _____/ • Which one? (sn) /ake/		Generate words and sentences within certain constraints. See Fluency Program (Chapter 5).	

[a]General paradigm is found in Volume 1, Appendix B.

SPEAKING

THE FLUENCY LESSON

Visualize a first grade classroom. As you walk in the door, the teacher is standing at the chalkboard and pointing to a child. The child shouts at another child: "Carrot!" The next child shouts "Turnip!" The next hesitates and then, in the same tone of voice, shouts "Blue!" Next, "Red!" Next, "Green!" At each word, the teacher puts a tally on the board and points to the next child.

The posture, the tone of voice, the angry look on the face of each child as he shouts all suggest that these words are epithets, bad names. These children are attacking each other with color names. Indeed, as the shouting continues, you suddenly hear "Pig!" "Poop!" "Ass!" (nervous giggling follows). You look at the teacher. She goes on serenely, pointing to children and drawing tallies.

Suddenly she announces, "Time!" The children count the tallies and the total number of words is entered on a graph on the chalkboard (see p. 120 for graph). The curve shot up today. The children cheer.

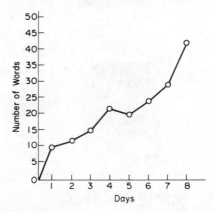

When one listens to the babbling of young preschool children, it comes as a surprise to discover language deficits in a substantial proportion of first grade children. The deficit is discovered when they are asked to generate words for sentence slots. For example,

> Direction: Finish this sentence:
> *When my best fried moved away, I was* _____.

A few children will be able to produce more than one word that fits; *sad, unhappy, lonely*. But most children are unable to produce more than one word.

This deficit looms as a major problem when children are sounding out words. **They must generate alternatives for the unknown word, the word to be "unlocked."**

The production of words under a time constraint is called **word fluency**. The *Stanford-Binet Intelligence Scale* uses such a constraint: "Say as many words as you can in one minute. Any words will do." Other intelligence tests use a sound constraint. "Say as many words as you can that start with *s-s-s*."

If word fluency is a skill necessary for success in reading, perhaps it can be taught. With this assumption, we tried increasing the word fluency scores of first grade children, with the surprising results you have just witnessed. We first worked with the total class. In these sessions, children tended to be careful. They chose very common, socially acceptable words. The number of words produced was graphed on the chalkboard. In later sessions, uncommon words began to appear as pressure increased to "make the line go up." At the next stage, taboo words began to appear.

Then, the air became blue with "bad words." The teacher simply recorded the words without comment. After some three sessions of such experimental activity, there was a spurt in fluency by the total group. At the same time, great anger seemed to be unleashed—harmlessly.

As the group output continued to increase steadily, we added individual sessions. Children were paired and tallied words for each other. Other group and individual fluency activities were added thereafter. Some are illustrated later in this chapter.

The result of this training was apparent within a few weeks. Substantial growth in verbal skill occurred in all class members. Children were now better able to generate alternative words when sounding out unknown words.

Most schoolchildren spend more time with their teachers than they spend with their parents. Therefore, the teacher is in a unique position to influence the child's speech—by **modeling** and by **shaping** good speech behavior. Clarity, both of speech and of thinking, may be modeled; fluency may be taught by the careful use of reinforcers.

Problems in speaking are largely of two kinds:

(*1*) Deficits in form and/or content, such as
  · sparse vocabulary
  · inappropriate sentence patterns
  · incorrect usage
(*2*) Deficits in delivery, such as
  · refusal to speak
  · low volume
  · single-word responses
  · inadequate articulation
  · stuttering

Both classes of problems are amenable to training. Deficits in form respond to appropriate instructional material. Those of delivery respond to behavior modification techniques.

Problems attributable to differing dialect and differing first language (if these two are, indeed, different) will be treated separately.

I. Problems in Delivery

Children learn their language in a particular language community, consisting of parents, siblings, and near neighbors. In addition, they learn a style of delivery, a manner of speaking: slow, laconic, rapid, redundant or cliché ridden, unique, unpredictable. These differences in style of delivery are largely modeled after adults in the language community and members of the peer group.

But problems in delivery are more likely due to the **consequences** of speaking.

The child who responds predictably with "I dunno" is making a safe response, one for which he has probably not been punished or for which the punishment has been predictably small. More extreme behaviors are those of children who do not respond at all, the shy child and the angry child.

Both these children, in effect, punish the teacher for calling on them, the shy one by embarrassing others who identify with him, the angry one by looking hostile, by acting as though he has been challenged. After a few encounters, teachers tend not to call on such children, indeed, to forget that they are there. By the end of first grade, such children have learned to "disappear into the woodwork," the end result of a teacher–child conspiracy to overlook each other.

Inadequate volume and single-word responses are variants of nonresponse. Each tends to fulfill the requirements, "the letter of the law," but at a minimum level, thus failing to fulfill "the intent of the law." Once more, these problems appear to be ways of avoiding punishment and are, most probably, learned behaviors.

Some articulation disorders clear up rapidly in the first grade, particuarly those caused by inadequate auditory discrimination training or the operation of low standards outside of school. If baby talk or other forms of poor enunciation have been rewarded, i.e., have been effective for getting needs satisfied, the child will continue to use such forms of speech.

More extreme kinds of speech problems are stammering and stuttering. These have been found to be amenable to behavioral training, usually by speech clinicians using techniques that can be applied in the classroom.

In short, most delivery problems in speech have been shaped in children—that is, they are present in strength because of their consequence history. As learned behaviors, they can be either eliminated completely or reduced significantly by appropriate teacher behaviors.

II. Shaping Acceptable Speech

The concept of shaping is, on the face of it, simple. Behold Theresa, nick-named "Mouse." Theresa responds to teacher questions in a very quiet voice. Each day, during word fluency training, the teacher gives the same directions except for one or more constraints. For example, "When I point to you, say a word. Any word will do. Say it loud enough." Or, "When I point to you, say a word that begins with s-s-s. Any word will do. Say it loud enough." Or, "When I point to you, say a word that ends with *ful*. Any word will do. Say it loud enough." The children know that, if unable to generate a word, they may repeat the word given by the last child.

To shape Theresa's volume, the teacher applies three standards to any response the child gives:

Standard 1 Does the response fit the constraint? (For example, does it being with *s-s-s*?)

Standard 2 Is it loud enough?

Standard 3 Is it louder than last time?

If the answer to standard 1 is *no*, the teacher must say, "No, *zebra* [Theresa's word] starts with *zee*. Say a word that starts with *s-s-s*."

If the answer to standard 1 is *yes,* the teacher applies standard 2: Is it loud enough? If not, the teacher must say, "Say it louder." and again apply standard 2.

If the answer to standard 2 is *yes*, the teacher applies standard 3: Is it louder than last time Theresa recited? If *no*, the teacher points to another child and the exercise continues.

If the answer to standard 3 is *yes*, it is louder than last time, the teacher says "Good!" and points to another child. (The only other case in which the teacher says "Good!" during this exercise is when a unique or unusual correct answer is given.)

Shaping is a procedure whereby a desirable behavior is strengthened by being reinforced or an undesirable behavior is weakened by being punished or ignored. To reinforce is to apply a consequence that increases the likelihood of occurrence of the desirable behavior. The teacher's saying "Good!" will have the effect of reinforcing louder speech (in most children) if used carefully, i.e., if used in the manner just described. In effect, the teacher's "Good!" says to Theresa, "You really did say it louder and that's a good thing." In short, the teacher's comment provides information to Theresa on her progress. (Moving on to another child, even without saying "Good!" also provides information. It says to Theresa, "You said a word beginning with *s-s-s* and you said it loud enough." The teacher does not move on until an acceptable response occurs.)

Oral work of the kind described here is one of the best classroom opportunities for using on-the-spot systematic behavior-shaping with a social reinforcer. With 30 children, it is difficult for a teacher to remember every child's last response in several subject matters.

Two other examples will, however, illustrate the value of a teacher's *nonresponse* for reducing or extinguishing undesirable behaviors.

John had a history of being a crier. Throughout kindergarten, John managed to cry three or four times a day for one reason or another. Of course, the children were very sympathetic. Now, John had arrived in the first grade and was still crying.

The children had opened to page 17 for their 10-minute listening training. The tape had begun and all the children were responding. When the direction was given to turn the page, John turned to page 16 (instead of 18). The pictures did not fit what the voice was saying. In a panic, he whispered desperately to the teacher, "I lost my place . . . I lost my place."

Being a bright, responsible, and warm person, the teacher understood what had happened and was about to move toward John when I signaled to her not to respond. She stopped. When no help was forthcoming, John began to cry. He cried through pages 18 to 24. And the lesson was over.

Next day, he lost his place again. Again he whispered desperately—and cried when given no help. But this time, he looked at the books of nearby children and found his place before two pages of words elapsed—and he completed the lesson. The third day passed without incident. On the fourth day, he lost his place, cried, and found his place. **For the remainder of the first grade, he did not cry in class.** (If the reader's response to this example is to damn the writer as calloused, cold, and cruel, I must respond: One of the things schools do best is to train children to be dependent. It is very difficult to contain one's sympathy and do what is best for the **child**.)

A second example of the effectiveness of nonresponse by the teacher also concerns independent behavior. Joe and Michael were responding to the listening tape; rather, Michael responded to the tape and Joe responded to Michael. When the voice said "ball . . . ball . . . ball," Michael circled a picture of a ball. Joe observed Michael's response and circled his own picture of a ball. When the voice said "hat . . . hit . . . hat," Michael circled *no* across from the picture of a hat. Joe followed suit.

Michael tried to cover up his work. Joe managed to see it. Michael looked beseechingly at the teacher. No response. Then: Michael tried "saving up" his responses: He circled nothing on the page until the last item was given, then quickly answered all six items and turned the page. Joe appeared upset. He tried to predict Michael's responses. The only way to predict them was to listen to the words. He found that, by listening to the words, he could circle what Michael circled. After a page of this, he paid Michael no further attention. He simply listened to the tape and responded in his book.

This is an example of "shaping out" an undesirable behavior, in this case, Joe's copying behavior. Michael's variability in signals and the tape's consistency in signals were necessary ingredients, as was the teacher's nonresponse. Note that Michael also solved his problem without help.

Shaping can be used with stuttering children also. It would be well to discuss a program with a speech therapist. But the training should occur **in the classroom** if it is to transfer to normal speech situations with other children. If no speech therapist is available, include these minimum conditions:

(*1*) Direct the child to take a deep breath before speaking and to speak before the inspiration is complete.

(*2*) Ask for brief answers (*yes, no*) to begin with; then gradually increase constraints so that phrases and sentences are required.

(*3*) Say "Good!" when the child takes a deep breath. When this habit begins to regularize, withhold "Good!" Then say it whenever a response is completed without a stutter. Finally, use it only when a longer answer is given without stuttering.[1]

III. Teaching Language Behavior

Most of the spoken language skills required of children in Grades K to 3 are shown in Tables 5.1 and 5.2. The column of sample items consists of single tasks at each level taken from the *STARS* test indicated. The sample is an example of the kinds of responses listed in each domain.

More than that, the sample demonstrates the form of training tasks that are effective. What is required is a systematic program, requiring only a few minutes each day, but designed to be cumulative.

Figure 5.1 presents a sample page from such a program. Each day one fluency entry (such as Word Fluency or Pattern Fluency) is carried out during a 5–10-minute period. Exercises remain similar but increase in complexity, week by week, as various constraints are added. The cumulative effect over a full year can be impressive.

STRATEGIES

A learning paradigm for listening was given in Chapter 4. Each of the recognition stages was followed by a production stage. The production stages constitute a paradigm for speaking.

	Discriminate	Produce
Listening 1	*Match* (same–different)	
Speaking 1		*Mime*
Listening 2	*Identify* (present–absent)	
Speaking 2		*Complete*
Listening 3	*Recognize* (equate)	
Speaking 3		*Generate*

Miming

- "I will say a word. When I point to you, repeat the word I say." (Use words from preprimers.)

---

[1] For other techniques used successfully with stuttering, see Goldiamond (1965).

Table 5.1
Components of Training in Speaking (Fluency: Word, Phrase, Clause)

Level	Class	Domain	Test	Sample item (and training task)
1	Grammatical closure	Verb, verb phrase; noun, noun phrase; adverb, adverb phrase; adjective, adjective phrases; clauses	*STARS* (Word) Vocabulary: Fluency 1	• Tell me a word to finish the sentence—as fast as you can. *In the morning I like to _____.* Time: 10 sec Standard: verb, verb phrase
2	Names	Names	2	• Tell me the names of as many things as you can. Time: 30 sec Standard: 10 names
3	Actions	Verbs (transitive)	3	• Tell me the names of all the things you can do. Time: 30 sec Standard: 10 actions
4	Subject Modifier Preposition	Common nouns Noun modifiers Prepositions	4	• Tell me different words that could go in the blank. *The _____ is on the floor.* Time: 30 sec Standard: 3 items
5	Initial sounds	All single consonants: initial position	5	• Tell me as many words as you can that start with *s*. Time: 30 sec Standard: 10 items
6	Final sounds	Phonograms	6	• Tell me as many words as you can that end with the sound *ow*. Time: 30 sec Standard: 5 items
7	Initial blends	All consonant blends	7	• Tell me as many words as you can that start with *tr*. Time: 30 sec Standard: 5 items

Table 5.2
Speaking (Sentence)

Level	Class	Domain	Test	Sample Item
1	Phonology	Junctures Emphasis (statement, question, exclamation, quotation)	Sentence: oral reading 1–3 Paragraph: oral reading	· Read aloud: *Can you come out to* *play?* *"Jim!" Tom gasped.* *"Throw me a rope and* *yell for help!"*
2	Memory	Length (3–8 words) Complexity (independent clause)	Words: Auditory Test 1 Sentence: Memory Tests 1,2	· Repeat after me: *How did you get* *here?* *Jane found the* *treasure under the* *table.*
3	Transforms	Number Tense Negation Pronouns Auxiliary verbs Passive voice Links Order	Sentence: Transforms 1–16	· Restate, making it singular: *We are going home.* · Restate, making it negative: *They have seen this* *before.*
4	Directions	Cross out Underline Draw line, circle Through, under, over, from–to.	Sentence: Directions 1,2	· Cross out the word above *red*. · Draw a line from the *Y* to the *M*.
5	Questions	Who What Where When Why How	Sentence: Questions 1–6	· Make up a *who* question answered by this sentence: *This book belongs to me.* · Make up a *how* question answered by this sentence: *He soaked his feet* *to get them clean.*
6	Equivalent statements	Constraints (internal, external, paragraph, idioms, metaphor)	Sentence: Meaning 1–3; Figurative Language 1–4	· Which sentence goes with the picture? · Does this make sense? *The bush smiled at me.* · Which means the same? *I came off with flying* *colors.* *( ) I did it well.* *( ) I did it fast.*

WORD FLUENCY

I will say a word. When I point to you, repeat the word I say. * (Say words at random, as before. Include words from any Pre-Readers which the learners have read.)

When I point to you, say a word. Any word will do. Say it loud enough. *

When I point to you, tell me something that is in this room.

When I point to you, tell me something that is in your own house.

PATTERN FLUENCY

(Ask students to place a book on their desks for this exercise. As you say the sentences, point to the learner's book in an appropriate way.)

I will say a sentence. When I point to you, say the sentence in the same way.

1.	This is a <u>book</u>.	4.	This is not my <u>pencil</u>.
2.	This is <u>my</u> book.	5.	This <u>is</u> my book.
3.	This is <u>not</u> your book.		

CONCEPT FLUENCY

Pretend that you saw a girl this morning.

I will ask you questions about this "pretend girl."

1.	What was her name:	4.	Tell me one thing she was wearing.
2.	Where was she?	5.	What was she doing?
3.	How big was she?		

SENTENCE FLUENCY

I will say some sentences that have the words <u>I am</u>. Listen for <u>I am</u>.
I am Jack.
 I am a teacher.
  I am very tired.
   I wonder where I am.
    I am here.
When I point to you, tell me a sentence with <u>I am</u>. *

PERFORMANCE FLUENCY

When I say "go," say as many words as you can in one minute.
Any words will do. Try not to repeat. I will tell you when to stop.
...Now go.

Name: _____ _____ _____ _____ _____

Word Tally: _____ _____ _____ _____ _____

Figure 5.1. Sample page. (Reprinted, with permission, from *Speaking: Fluency Program Script Book, Michigan Language Program*, by D. E. P. Smith & J. M. Smith. New York: Random House, 1975. © 1970 Donald E. P. Smith.)

- "I will say a sentence. When I point to you, say the sentence in the same way."

    (*1*) *This is a* **book**.

    (*2*) *This is* **my** *book*.

    (*3*) *This is* **not** *your book*.

    (*4*) *This is not my* **pencil**.

    (*5*) *This* **is** *my book*.

The miming stage is critical. You use it whenever you repeat a name after being introduced to a stranger (thus substantially increasing the likelihood of remembering the name); whenever you repeat a technical word in a course (e.g., *dĭs·crĭm'·ĭ·nāte', ar·tĭc'·ū·la'·tion, mĭm'·ing*); whenever you read over your notes preparatory to giving a talk.

We discovered that 10–15% of first grade children were unable to handle the matching tasks in listening until they were given miming practice. This finding suggests that production (miming) should come before recognition (discrimination), rather than the reverse. I have taken the position that back-and-forth processes, of which we are unaware, probably occur. If a child cannot do matching tasks, he should receive miming training.

Note that single words and longer utterances, sentences, should be practiced so that the information provided by tonal pattern is recognized.

Completing (internal constraints). First, for sentences:

- "I will say part of a sentence. You finish it in any way that makes sense: *In the morning, I like to* _____." (Leave out nouns, verbs, auxiliaries, modifiers. Leave them out, one at a time.)

Completion of any utterance requires the child to respond to two kinds of internal constraints, syntactic (*I like to* ____ requires a verb) and semantic (the verb must be some act of which a person is capable).

Practice of this kind pays off in what reading specialists call **sensitivity-to-context clues**. When the child meets an unrecognized word during reading, he must be able to generate possible words for that slot. Then he uses analytic skills to choose among the alternatives.

Our original interest in teaching word fluency was our discovery of deficits in children with reading problems. It was not uncommon to find that a child possessed good word-analysis skills but failed to use them. One reason was that he tended to generate only one possibility for a slot. If that one were incorrect, he appeared to be stymied, unable to generate another possibility.

Next, for words:

- "I will say some words that start with *s*. As I say them, listen for *s-s-s*: *seat, sack, sun, sink, six*. When I point to you, tell me a word that starts with *s*."

At this stage, children are generating words on the basis of some clue internal to the words—initial or final sound, presence of a given prefix or suffix, and so on.

The task is similar to that of sentences except that the constraints emphasize letters and sounds in words. These are the foundation skills for word analysis.

Generating (external constraints)

- "When I point to you, tell me the name of something smaller than you."
- "When I point to you, tell me the name of a letter of the alphabet."
- "Pretend you saw some food.
  (*1*) What kind of food was it?
  (*2*) What color was it?
  (*3*) How did it taste?
  (*4*) Where was the food?
  (*5*) What could you do with it?"
- "When I point to you tell me a sentence using *very fast*."

The constraints used in these tasks are probably self-evident:

- Given an item, cite its relative size.
- Given a class name, cite a member.
- Given an item, give its class membership, identifying characteristics, and function.[2]
- Given a part, generate an appropriate whole.

Sample tasks shown here are all taken from the *Michigan Language Program* booklet *Speaking: Fluency Program Script Book* (D. E. P. Smith & J. M. Smith, 1975). After a careful reading of this little book (28 pages), the reader will be able to construct his own lesson plans for a total speaking program.

IV. Dialects

The contribution of differing dialects to the problem of learning to read has received careful scrutiny. In particular, psychologists and linguists have focused on **black dialect** or as used hereafter, **black English vernacular** (BEV). Professor Glenn Knudsvig, a psycholinguist, has described developments occurring between 1960 and 1975. He has analyzed differing dialects and developed and evaluated a promising instructional procedure to be used by teachers. Excerpts from his report follow.

---

[2] Taken from an ideal definition: A hammer (item) is a hand tool (class membership) consisting of a heavy head attached to a handle (physical structure or characteristic) and used for pounding (function).

LANGUAGE DIFFERENCE VERSUS LANGUAGE DEFICIT[3]

A major dispute among educators, psychologists, and linguists is the nature of the language abilities of certain black children, namely those whose speech reveals phonological and syntactic features and patterns different from those of the linguistic code generally labeled as standard American English (SAE) (Williams, 1970; Labov, 1972). Attempts to resolve educational problems relating to language development and reading may be facilitated both by resolution of the dispute and by increased awareness of the linguistic issues (Baratz & Shuy, 1969; Figurel, 1970; Rutherford, 1970). The points of view in the controversy may be labeled the language deficit position and the language difference position.

The Language Deficit Position

The language deficit position, sometimes referred to as the "verbal deprivation theory," became formalized in the 1960s through a wide range of studies and reports by investigators who based their conclusions on casual observations as well as on objective test data. These researchers, primarily educators and psychologists, did not consider the code used by speakers of black English vernacular (BEV)[4] to be functionally adequate or structurally systematic (Bernstein, 1961; Hess & Shipman, 1965; Bereiter & Englemann, 1966; Deutsch *et al.,* 1967; Blank & Solomon, 1968; Houston, 1970). It was also proposed that the underdeveloped code, even if it were somewhat systematic, might lead to cognitive deficits (Jensen, 1969).

With regard to educational policies, the deficit position suggested that there be early, pre-school intervention for speakers of BEV to reduce cognitive damage and to minimize the gap between the child's skill and the school's demands. Language is considered to be the core of all differences and must, therefore, receive the greatest attention in the hopes of preventing further cultural and, eventually, economic disadvantages (Bereiter & Englemann, 1966).[5]

---

[3] Reprinted, with permission, from *Cross-Dialect Learning*, by G. Knudsvig (1975).

[4] Labov has described black English vernacular as "the relatively uniform dialect spoken by the majority of black youth in most parts of the United States today [1972, p. xiii]."

[5] Bereiter and Englemann were among the very few deficit theorists who actually designed an instructional system (1966). Others were Blank and Solomon, who designed a language-based tutorial program (1968).

The Language Difference Position

At the same time as the deficit position was evolving, there emerged the work
of a number of researchers, primarily linguists, who proposed that dialects such
as BEV should be studied as systems in themselves. Their position was that
variations in systems reflect distinctions among well developed, but different,
linguistic systems (Cazden, 1966; Lenneberg, 1967; Labov & Cohen, 1967;
Baratz & Povich, 1968; Baratz, 1969; Wolfram, 1973).

> All linguists who work with BEV recognize that it is a separate system, closely
> related to standard English but set apart from the surrounding white dialects
> by a number of persistent and systematic differences [Labov, 1970a, p. 184].

Thus, BEV has its own rule-governed, equivalent ways of expressing the same
logical content and of preserving the distinctions found in other dialects. For
example, the embedded yes—no question in BEV does not utilize the com-
plementizers *if* and *whether* but preserves the meaning through a word order
rule. Thus, the SAE sentence *I asked him if he wanted to go* is expressed in BEV
as *I asked him did he want to go*.

Persons supporting the difference position suggested that what is observed in
school problem situations is very often a display of differences, not of deficits.
Many problems are the result of discrepancies between the primary linguistic
code of the student and that of the school. Accordingly, solutions to the
problems lie, in part, in acknowledging that the child has a well established
linguistic code which should be taken into account and utilized in any instructional program.

As regards the manner in which the BEV dialect should be utilized, there have
been a variety of suggestions and programs. The most far-reaching utilization of
BEV as an instructional base is in the use of dialect readers (Stewart, 1969;
Baratz, 1970). These materials or books, designed to be used especially for initial
reading instruction, are written so as to present the child's system of expression,
particularly the grammatical system. Characteristic phonological and semantic
differences may also be incorporated into the reading material.

> The advantages of such a program would be three-fold; first, success in
> teaching the ghetto child to read; second, the powerful ego supports of giving
> credence to the child's language system and therefore to himself, and giving
> him the opportunity to experience success in school; and third, with the use of
> transitional readers the child would have the opportunity of being taught
> standard English so that he could learn where his language system and that of
> standard English were similar and where they were different. Such an op-
> portunity might well lead to generalized learning and the ability to use
> standard English more proficiently in other school work [Baratz, 1970, pp.
> 21–22].

Another manner in which the vernacular code of the child can be taken into account is to allow the child to read standard materials using his own vernacular patterns (Goodman, 1969). This, of course, requires the teacher to be very knowledgeable of BEV so that a distinction can be made between dialect-based differences of expression and actual skill deficits or errors.

Utilization of the vernacular is also central to the techniques borrowed from the field referred to as English for Speakers of Other Languages (Wolfram, 1969; Zintz, 1970). Developing greater aural—oral control of SAE is the primary goal of these techniques. This training precedes formal training in reading so that the child will have aural—oral control of the material he is expected to read. This model has been most widely applied to situations where the dominant language of the children is Spanish.

Current Status of the Dialect Problem

Inasmuch as the deficit position, whether under this name or another, seems to have exerted the greater influence in educational settings, many language centered problems continue to exist. Writing in a joint publication of the National Council of Teachers of English and the Center for Applied Linguistics (1970), William Labov describes American education as being concerned about "nonstandard English," but primarily in a negative way. "It has been an object to overcome rather than something to be studied and understood in its own right." He goes on to say that "current textbooks and the approach of most educational research show that the underlying negative assumptions about nonstandard English remain unchanged."

Thomas Horn, writing in the introduction to *Reading for the Disadvantaged: Problems of Linguistically Different Learners*, a project of the International Reading Association, states, "When this book was in the planning stages, it became apparent that the role of linguistic differences as a major contributing factor to reading disability was being generally misunderstood or overlooked entirely by both educators and laymen." He continues to say that: "Since it is a truism that language constitutes the main vehicle for instruction in our schools, a new focus on oral language and reading, particularly for disadvantaged populations, is long overdue [1970, p. 3]."

As one example of a frequent conflict regarding dialects, Labov describes the "pluralistic ignorance which prevails in the classroom; the teacher does not know that the students' dialect is different from his own and the students do not know just how the teacher's system differs from theirs [1970b, p. 43]." Thus, he sees as the chief difficulty not the dialect differences, but the ignorance of those differences.

In a publication of the International Reading Association (1970a), Roger Shuy discusses the "incredible situation" in which teachers are not trained to hear, distinguish, and analyze the language to which most of a child's reading will relate. He also describes how teacher training programs have preserved and passed on many of the unfounded language stereotypes regarding the so-called non-verbal, deficient, disadvantaged child.

The combination of lack of training and lack of understanding of language systems has prevented the type of progress which is needed, particularly in the urban schools.

In an effort to remedy language problems, many teachers, unskilled in analyzing the differences in the codes, have relied on instruction consisting primarily of modeling. Labov describes this as "all of the teaching method and philosophy that has been required in school [1970b, p. 4]." Because the teacher and the book both use SAE, the student is expected to pick it up and should be corrected when he is in error. Obviously, the degree to which this works has varied according to home, school, peers, environment, and other variables.

Another example of a situation which has arisen from the lack of understanding of language differences is found in the field of speech therapy (Shuy, 1970b). First of all, many speakers of BEV are referred to speech therapists because their language development is considered abnormal while it is, in fact, quite normal, but for a different system. Secondly, unless speech therapists have had specific training, it is very difficult for them to distinguish a pathological problem from a code difference.

The lack of awareness of systematic differences also has a great impact on student and teacher performance through the attitudes which are generated. A teacher with the deficit viewpoint observes students from that bias and is therefore reminded of the child's deficiencies every time a BEV pattern is used. Gradually this view of the student comes to be used by the teacher as justification for the student's lack of progress. The blame is placed upon the culture and environment rather than upon the instructional program.

Efforts to compensate for deficits and to reform students also create negative attitudes on the part of the students and their families when it appears that efforts are being made to take away their primary culture as represented by their language.

In light of the continuing educational problems apparent where the schools' expectations and programs with respect to language and the actual language behavior of students differ, there is considerable need for research and new approaches related to solving some of the language centered problems. A group of foremost educators and linguists has stated that among the issues concerning oral language development for linguistically different speakers are these which are "desperately in need of more intensive research."

> To what extent should the curriculum be modified to ... provide for oral
> fluency in standard American English?

What is the optimum point for beginning instruction in a second language or second dialect?

Is listening alone enough to overcome language deficiencies? Are informal learning experiences in school adequate for learners with non-standard language, or must structured oral language instruction be provided, initially and/or subsequently?

What are the most promising techniques for developing fluency in standard oral American English? Is it necessary to provide different exercises for speakers of the various languages and dialects common to American school populations that have been found to interfere with learning through the language of instruction? [Horn, 1970, p. 5]

The instructional program and study described herein is a partial response to the issues regarding oral language training and is meant to provide a model for the design and development of other instructional materials for cross-dialect learning.

A Proposed Instructional Program in Cross-Dialect Learning

The difficulties encountered by the speaker of BEV when attempting to use SAE represent a language intrusion of one code (the dominant system) upon the structure of the second code (Baratz, 1969). This difficulty in code-switching may occur when the second code (SAE) is not as well learned as the first (BEV) or when neither code is well-learned.

Learning the second code can be accomplished through associative learning of equivalences of the two codes. This learning requires that those responses to be learned are systematic in both codes as determined by a linguistic analysis.

The assumption of this study is that the learning of equivalences can be accomplished through auditory discrimination training. Inasmuch as there doesn't appear to be research which has had either this same objective or has used this approach, this study may provide a model for further research into dialect problems relating to phonology and syntax.

The Instructional Domain

Designing instruction for language learning requires a description of the kinds of discriminative responses to be learned, the language functions being learned, and the kinds of tasks leading to mastery, as well as a description of the stimuli to which the learner will respond [D. E. P. Smith, 1976].

The products of instruction may be thought of in terms of the kinds of responses learned, i.e., recognition, reproduction, and substitution. Recognition requires a particular response to a particular stimulus. When a child has made such a discriminative response it can be said that he can recognize the item. One such discriminative response occurs when the child discovers that two sentences which had seemed to be the same are different in form although their meanings are the same. The child who fails to pronounce a word accurately, even when corrected repeatedly, or the child who repeats the teacher's well-formed sentence in his own pattern of expression may well have failed to discover that there are differences between the model and his own utterance. In these cases, the child has not yet made certain discriminations which are prerequisite to the next kind of response, i.e., reproducing the stimulus. Instruction must therefore be provided at this learning level.

After the learner is able to recognize the stimulus, he is ready to learn to reproduce the stimulus, and then to make substitutions. The target of instruction in the auditory modality is that the learner be able to reproduce, through speaking, the auditory stimulus.

Any kind of paired associate task, such as the learning of equivalents in two language codes, requires that substitution responses be learned. This learning is of two kinds:

1. Stimulus substitution in which a response to one stimulus comes to be elicited by a second stimulus.
2. Response substitution in which a stimulus which elicits one response comes to elicit a second response.

Thus in order for substitution to be possible, all three kinds of responses are necessary. Both elements of the equivalence must be learned, thereby requiring the ability both to recognize all stimuli and to reproduce them.

The target language functions for this study are the auditory functions of hearing and saying. In the learning process, recognition can be considered the output for the hearing function and reproduction and substitution the outputs for the saying function.

The stimuli to which the learners will respond in any piece of instruction are those units, e.g., letters or words, which are appropriate to the instructional goals. Stimuli for auditory functions include such units as phonemes, words and words in sentences, and sentences and sentences in connected speech.

Smith [1976], in discussing the sequencing of these units for instruction, has suggested that the process of learning these units is "reminiscent of Gesell's principle of the **reciprocal, interweaving spiral** of growth." Thus, the steps in language development might be described as being on an alternating, interlocking pathway wherein any new skill surfaces in a primitive form, then disappears or regresses while another skill appears, and then reappears in a more complex form. The critical point in the interlocking hierarchy is that primitive wholes, such as ideas or utterances expressing ideas, must exist before the parts constituting the whole are mastered. Such an order or progression is one of the conditions for retrieval of responses as well as for the apprehension of meaning. That is, an entity such as a sentence, or utterance, must be perceived before the words within it elicit contextual meaning. The reason for this is that part of the meaning of the word derives from the word's relationship to the whole sentence or utterance. In regard to this word–sentence relationship, Goodman (1970) speaks of the inadequacy of word recognition alone since one also obtains information from the syntactic use of the word and the semantic meaning that it conjures up.

Phoneme contrasts are most easily learned when common minimal pairs are contrasted. Therefore, assuming a primitive command of the language, the initial training will take place at word level. The training will terminate at the associative level of sentence since the grammatical structures being learned occur at the sentence level.

PROGRAM DEVELOPMENT[6]

Pedagogic Analysis—Evaluation Instruments

It was determined that mastery should be demonstrated through two types of tasks. One is the **repetition task** in which the student is directed to repeat the sentence that he hears. In this case, the student who has displayed BEV speech patterns is asked to repeat a sentence expressed in SAE.

Labov (1970b) has called this the most useful means of getting at the grammatical competence of children since it is very difficult to remember and repeat back sentences unless they follow the same grammatical rules as those of the speaker.

The well known bi-dialectal study of Baratz (1969) obtained its data from the administration of a repetition task involving "standard and non-standard" sentences. The subjects were from an inner city school and a lower middle class suburban school. The results indicated that the black children performed significantly better than the white children on the sentences characterized by BEV patterns and, on the SAE sentences, the converse was true.

---

[6] Reprinted, with permission, from *Cross-Dialect Learning* by G. Knudsvig (1975).

The second task is an **equivalence task** which requires the student to produce the SAE sentence which is the equivalent of the BEV sentence provided as the stimulus. In this task the student thus demonstrates an even greater control over the second or new code since it requires that one know what category of intent is being dealt with and what grammatical requirements exist for expressing the thought in the second dialect.

Evaluation Instrument Tryout

The next stage of development consisted of administering both types of tasks to a racially mixed sample of 35 kindergarten and first and second grade students in the school where the validation study later took place.

The tasks contained sentences which also focused on grammatical constructions other than the two which were to be used in the instructional materials. They are all constructions which involve differences between the SAE and the BEV manner of expression. They include the following: third person subject–verb agreement, negation, past tense markers, possessive markers, and plural markers. [Table 5.3 provides examples of each of these constructions as they appear in SAE and in BEV. Knudsvig then proceeded to develop instructional programs to teach the BEV–SAE equivalents for the first three examples under BEV in the table. They were tested on individuals and small groups, then revised.]

Table 5.3
Sample Test Items[a]

BEV Sentences—Equivalence Test

Zero copula	*He in the car.*
Zero auxiliary *be*	*She buying the new book.*
Zero *if* + verb + subject in embedded question	*Ask can you go with us.*
Zero third person marker	*He want to go to the store.*
Double negation	*She can't play no more.*
Zero past tense marker	*They listen to the record yesterday.*
Zero possessive marker	*He has Donna books.*
Zero plural marker	*I see four book on the desk.*

SAE Sentences—Repetition Test

Presence of copula	*She is in the kitchen.*
Presence of auxiliary *be*	*He is coloring the picture.*
If + subject + verb in embedded question	*Ask if she can play with us.*
Third person agreement	*She lives in Detroit.*
Negation	*They don't have any money.*
Past tense marker	*I colored that picture yesterday.*
Possessive marker	*I see Mary's books.*
Plural marker	*He has many toys in his room.*

[a]From Knudsvig (1975).

The two revised programs were then administered to the small groups. The primary purpose of this tryout was to determine whether the program provided enough practice in each of the lessons to reach mastery level. Results from the tryout indicated that several of the lessons in the indirect question program did need more practice so these were added to the final program.

Description of the Instructional Programs

Each of the two programs used in this study, i.e., one on the copula and auxiliary *be* and the other on the indirect yes/no question, consists of two parts. Part I of each provides training in BEV patterns only. Part II provides training in the SAE equivalent sentences. The lessons in each part of the two programs follow the same sequence, which begins at word discrimination level and progresses through to identification of equivalent BEV—SAE sentences.

The BEV patterns are presented first and separately since it cannot be assumed that a particular code, although dominant, is under the active, conscious control of the speaker. Thus, if the listener—speaker is to hear contrasts and ultimately be able to produce equivalences, the system of the first code must be as well learned and under the same control as that of the second code. Indeed, one of the difficulties encountered in trying to switch codes is in identifying when there is a contrast and what the actual point of contrast is.

Lesson 1 of each part of both programs operates at the perceptual level and requires the auditory discrimination of words. The use of common minimal pairs provides for the learning of phoneme contrasts. The words used in these frames are primarily those that occur in the sentences used in the programs. Some of the foils do not occur in the sentences but are chosen for the purpose of providing a minimal pair contrast or because they are frequently confused with the target word.

The following lessons are samples only. The samples provided are all from Part I of the copula program.

TAPE SCRIPT

Lesson 1, page 1
Directions: I am going to say some words. If they are the same, circle the word. If they are not the same, circle the NO. (Provide examples) 1. you   he   you 2. she   you   she

3. he   he   he
4. in   on   in
5. happy   happy   happy
6. we   she   we
7. reading   running   reading
8. car   can   car

STUDENT RESPONSE PAGE

PAGE 1

1. you   NO
2. she   NO
3. he   NO
4. in   NO
5. happy   NO
6. we   NO
7. reading NO
8. car   NO

Lesson 2 of all parts also operates at the perceptual level, but with sentence stimuli rather than word stimuli. In the BEV part of a program the sentences are all expressed according to the rules of that system, as in the sample below.

TAPE SCRIPT

Lesson 2, page 1

Directions: I am going to say some sentences. If they are the same, circle the sentence. If they are not the same, circle the NO. (Provide examples)

1. She my new teacher.   She my new teacher.
2. He happy.   He happy.
3. He in the car.   They in the car.
4. You happy.   You happy.
5. The boy tired from running.   They tired from running.
6. They on television tonight.   They on television tonight.

STUDENT RESPONSE PAGE

PAGE 1

1. She my new teacher.   NO
2. He happy.   NO
3. He in the car.   NO
4. You happy.   NO
5. The boy tired from running.   NO
6. They on television tonight.   NO

TAPE SCRIPT

Lesson 2, page 15

1. He watching television. He watching television.
2. You not reading. You not running.
3. He buying a record. He buying a car.
4. They reading now. They reading now.
5. He running fast. He reading fast.
6. She playing the record. She playing the record.

TAPE SCRIPT

Lesson 2, page 18

1. They not reading. He not reading.
2. He my teacher. He has a teacher.
3. You the leader. You see the leader.
4. You playing the new record. You playing the new game.
5. You the leader. You the reader.
6. His name Joe. His name Joe.

Lesson 3 operates at the conceptual level wherein the learner identifies a word as it occurs in the context of a complete sentence. The learner identifies words occurring in all parts of the sentence and thereby receives training in attending to the entire sentence. This attention to the total sentence is essential if the learner is to have the awareness and active control over language which is necessary in identifying contrasts between his own dominant language patterns and other patterns.

TAPE SCRIPT

Lesson 3, page 4

Directions: I will say a word. Then I will say a sentence. If you hear the
word in the sentence, circle the word. If you do not hear the
word in the sentence, circle NO. (Provide examples)

	word	sentence
1.	watching	He watching television
2.	records	You not reading.
3.	they	He buying a record.
4.	reading	They reading now.
5.	reading	He running fast.
6.	buying	She playing the record.
7.	she	She reading the book.
8.	watching	He buying the record.
9.	playing	The boy watching television.
10.	record	The girl buying a record.

STUDENT RESPONSE PAGE

PAGE 4

1.	watching	NO
2.	records	NO
3.	they	NO
4.	reading	NO
5.	reading	NO
6.	buying	NO
7.	she	NO
8.	watching	NO
9.	playing	NO
10.	record	NO

In lesson 4 the learner begins associating the spoken utterance with a simple
picture. It is necessary to learn the name and the intent of each picture so that it
can be used as a token in Part II of the program where the student learns an
equivalent name, i.e., SAE sentence.

TAPE SCRIPT

Lesson 4, page 2

Directions: I will say a sentence. Circle the picture that the sentence is about.
1. He the leader.
2. They on television.
3. She watching television.
4. He in the house.
5. You happy.

STUDENT RESPONSE PAGE

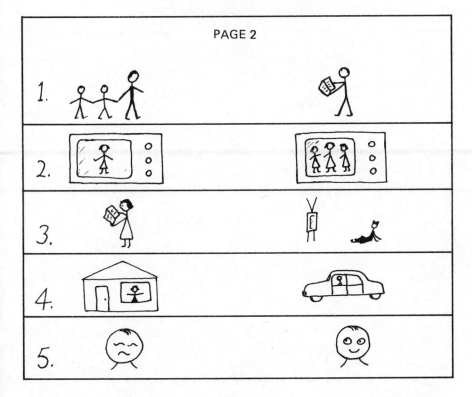

PAGE 2

Lesson 5 requires the learner to recognize whether a sentence (auditory stimulus) is appropriate to a picture on the response page. Thus, the learner proceeds from visual to auditory, while in lesson 4 the learner was directed to proceed from auditory to visual.

TAPE SCRIPT

Lesson 5, page 2

Directions: Look at the picture by number 1. I will say a sentence. If the sentence is about the picture circle the picture. If it is not about the picture, circle NO.
1. She my new teacher.
2. He the leader for the game.
3. He buying a car.
4. He running.
5. He in the car.

STUDENT RESPONSE PAGE

Part II of the program, in which the SAE patterns are learned, follows the same sequence of lessons as Part I. The sentences which are used in the practices are the SAE equivalent of the sentences used in Part I. Even though many of the words will have been practiced extensively in Part I, word discrimination is again the first lesson since the students must now begin to use these words in a new linguistic environment and must be able to perceive these as parts of a new whole, i.e., a new sentence pattern.

In the copula program, Lesson 1, word discrimination, and Lesson 3, identifying words in sentences, put a special emphasis on the finite forms *is* and *are* since the expression or non-expression of these is the observable point of difference in the two dialects. A special emphasis is also put on contrasting the target forms of the copula with other verbs, e.g., *is/has* or *is/does*, and on contrasting it with other tenses of the copula, e.g., *is/was* or *are/were.* Making these discriminations will help keep the learner from situations commonly observed when speakers try to use patterns new to them or to their linguistic code. That is, the speaker realizes that a certain kind of word should occur in a certain slot, but he has not learned appropriate possibilities.

Just as the finite forms of *be* receive special emphasis in the SAE part of the copula program, the second program, that on the indirect question, places particular emphasis on the complementizer *if* in the SAE part of the program. Establishing *if* as a discriminative, functional element is perhaps more difficult than treating the copula since, while the copula is familiar in varying degrees to most learners, the word *if*, and certainly its syntactic function, are much more unfamiliar to the speakers of BEV.

Part II of both programs includes a sixth lesson which provides practice in associating the equivalent BEV and SAE sentences. The token of the association is the picture which has been named by a sentence in both the BEV part and the SAE part of the program.

TAPE SCRIPT

Lesson 6, page 3

Directions: I will say two sentences. If both of them are about the picture and mean the same thing, circle the picture. If they are not about the same picture, circle NO. (Provide examples)

1. She is a teacher.   She has a teacher.
2. He happy now.   He is happy now.
3. He has a teacher.   He is a teacher.
4. She is in the car.   She in the car.
5. They running fast.   They are running fast.

STUDENT RESPONSE PAGE

PAGE 3		
1.		NO
2.		NO
3.		NO
4.		NO
5.		NO

To summarize, 21 children received training in the two most troublesome constructions:

(*1*) The copula and auxiliary *be:*

BEV	SAE
You tired.	*You are tired.*
He a teacher.	*He is a teacher.*
You lazy.	*You are lazy.*
They in the pool.	*They are in the pool.*
She running fast.	*She is running fast.*

(*2*) The embedded yes/no question:

BEV	SAE
I asked him did he want to play.	*I asked him if he wanted to play.*
I wonder do he like to play ball.	*I wonder if he likes to play ball.*
I asked her do she like to read books.	*I asked her if she likes to read books.*

The trainees consisted of 12 boys and 9 girls, ranging in age from 7 to 10 years, all having completed first or second grade. Median reading achievement (*Wide Range Achievement Test*) was Grade 1.4 (range 1.0–1.7). There were 30 meetings, each of 25 minutes, during a 6-week summer program.

Two kinds of tests were used:

(*1*) Equivalence: Given a sentence in BEV, produce the SAE equivalent correctly.

(*2*) Repetition: Given a sentence in SAE, repeat it correctly.

One set of tests was designated **mastery** and included sentences used in

Table 5.4
Results of Training in the Copula and Auxiliary *Be* Construction as Shown by Percentage Scores on Mastery Equivalence and Repetition Tests[a]

| | Equivalence test[b] | | | | Repetition test[b] | | | |
| | Pretest | | Posttest | | Pretest | | Posttest | |
Student	Points	Percentage	Points	Percentage	Points	Percentage	Points	Percentage
A	5	42	12	100	7	58	12	100
B	0	0	12	100	5	42	12	100
C	3	25	12	100	6	50	12	100
D	4	33	12	100	5	42	11	92
E	4	33	12	100	6	50	12	100
F	3	25	12	100	5	42	12	100
G	2	17	12	100	6	50	12	100
H	2	17	9	75	6	50	12	100
I	5	42	12	100	6	50	12	100
J[c]	3	25	12	100				
K	0	0	12	100	2	17	12	100
L	3	25	9	75	5	42	12	100
M	3	25	12	100	2	17	12	100
N	2	17	12	100	9	75	12	100
O	2	17	10	83	4	33	10	83
P	3	25	12	100	5	42	11	92
Q	4	33	11	92	6	50	11	92
R	2	17	11	92	4	33	12	100
S	2	17	11	92	3	25	12	100
T	4	33	12	100	9	75	12	100
U	2	17	9	75	7	58	12	100
Mean %		23.9		93.5		45.1		97.9

[a]From Knudsvig (1975).
[b]Points possible: 12.
[c]Unavailable for testing on repetition test.

training. A second set of tests, designated **independent**, contained new sentences in order to determine whether training would generalize.

Results were very similar for both mastery and independent tests. All gains were substantial. For example, on the mastery test for repetition of the copula sentences, the pretest score was 23.9%; the posttest score was 93.5%. Table 5.4 (preceding page) demonstrates the consistency of results.

Summary

Although shaping and modeling good speech are necessary and effective procedures, the most powerful procedure of all is probably training in auditory discrimination. Certainly, as shown by Knudsvig, second language or second dialect learning is greatly facilitated by such training. When a fluency training program is added, there should be no difficulties in reading and writing attributable to deficits in listening and speaking.

* * * * *

For a sound linguistic basis for handling dialect differences in BEV, read Module 3, Black English Vernacular.

MODULE 3
Black English Vernacular[7]

Purpose

This module is designed to teach you to recognize and reproduce various forms of Black English Vernacular (BEV) pronunciation and grammar.

Objective

Upon completion of this module, you will be able to discriminate at least four black nonstandard (BEV) variations in pronunciation and approximately eight

---

[7] By Mary Lee Bronzo, Ann Congeni, and Marija Kaunelis. Reprinted by arrangement with the authors.

grammatical variations from their standard English (SE) equivalents and produce both forms.

Directions

(*1*) Work through Mini-module 1, answering the questions appropriately as you go and checking your answers with those given in the key (p. 159).
(*2*) Complete the criterion test, making sure your answers correspond with those given in the key (p. 160).
(*3*) If 100% is achieved on the criterion test, proceed to Mini-module 2 and continue as before until the entire module is completed and 100% is achieved throughout.

Introduction

Although it may not be the precise way we as individuals speak, dictionaries, spelling books, and grammatical authorities dictate the proper way to express ourselves. We recognize and accept this "doctrine of correctness." Most dialects, especially middle class, deviate only slightly from these examples and thus the speakers suffer little stigmatization or learning difficulties. Black nonstandard English speakers are not so fortunate.

A child's linguistic competence influences his comprehension and performance of school tasks. If the child's competence and that of the teacher are dialectally similar, communication problems between the two are generally minimal. However, differing dialects can cause serious communication problems and this can interfere with learning. Performance and task can be misunderstood and the child's potential may be incorrectly evaluated. This often happens when a standard-speaking teacher confronts a student with nonstandard speech.

An understanding of nonstandard speech is the first step in understanding the nonstandard-speaking student and helping him achieve his basic goals. We attempt here to present some of the more common elements of black nonstandard English with hopes that this briefing may help you to teach more efficiently and effectively. We also want to remind you that the following examples are not used exclusively among blacks nor is this to say that all blacks necessarily use these forms. Also, the use of any one of these characteristic linguistic features does not indicate use of any of the others.

Pretest

Test your knowledge of Black English Vernacular on the pretest that follows. Check your answers against the answer key (p. 158). If you cannot easily and successfully answer these questions, continue to read through this material and you will be asked some of these same questions in the criterion test at the conclusion of each mini-module.

A. The following words are approximations of BEV pronunciation. The standard spelling is shown in parentheses. Suggest what characteristics of the child's dialect might contribute to the variation:
   1. *bet (bed)*
   2. *bin (bend)*
   3. *dak (dark)*
   4. *woof (wolf)*
   5. *skreet (street)*

B. Give the BEV equivalents of the following sentences:
   1. *Mary likes hot dogs.*
   2. *She'll walk again.*
   3. *I asked him when he was coming.*
   4. *Who's going to go tomorrow?*
   5. *The teacher gave two tests.*
   6. *There's a nice place to eat just down the block.*
   7. *There isn't anything I can do that will help him any.*
   8. *We go to see him every day at five.*
   9. *He is a big boy now.*

MINI-MODULE 1

Pronunciation of Black English Vernacular[8]

Overview of Word, Sound, and Contrast Variability

There are three kinds of pronunciation differences:

(*1*) Word variability—alternative pronunciations of individual words which vary from speaker to speaker.
(*2*) Sound variability—predictable variations of particular sounds within a dialect.
(*3*) Contrast variability—loss of contrast between two words that are usually pronounced differently.

[8] The answer key is on p. 159.

Part I

Pronunciation can vary in three different ways. The first of these is **word variability**.

Word variability is the most basic kind of pronunciation variability since it is simply the **use of alternate pronunciations for individual words**. This alternation varies from speaker to speaker and may even occur within the same region or family. No generalization about the speaker's dialect can be drawn from such variability.

Examples would include

- *adult* pronounced *a'-dult* or *a-dult'*
- *economic* pronounced *ĕ-co-nom-ic* or *ē-co-nom-ic*
- *syrup* pronounced with the first syllable as *sere* or *sir*

Circle the letter of the example that shows word variability.

1. a. *creek* pronounced *crick* or *creek*
   b. *schedule* pronounced *timetable* or *bulletin*

2. a. *stream* pronounced *creek* or *brook*
   b. *ration* pronounced *ră-tion* or *rā-tion*

3. Write down three examples of word variability:
   a.
   b.
   c.

As members of a socially distinct group, **black speakers have pronunciations for a few random words that show word variability.** Common examples include

- *street* pronounced *skreet*
- *threw* pronounced *thew*
- *pattern* pronounced *pattren*
- *supposed to* pronounced *posed to*

Using what you have just learned, circle the letter of the comparison item showing possible other common word variability by speakers of Black English Vernacular (hereafter, BEV):

4. a. *business—bidness*
   b. *circus—carnival*

5. a. *ask—ax*
    b. *street—road*
6. a. *Detroit—De'-troit*
    b. *pair—pare*

Because word variability is universal, random, and unsystematic, it is less stigmatized than other pronunciation differences and causes fewer learning difficulties. We all simply learn to associate our pronunciation with the conventional spelling.

Word Variability Check

7. T F   In conversation it is likely that you would not notice examples of word variability.

8. T F   Word variability causes many learning problems.

9. T F   If a person says *root* for *route*, she is also likely to say *crick* for *creek*.

Part II

A second, more complicated type of variability is **sound variability**. It can be defined as a variance of a **particular sound in predictable situations**. Hence, every word that contains that particular sound differs in pronunciation from the same words in another dialect. **It is a consistent and predictable variance.** So, many, many words may be involved in a single variance of pronunciation.

A common standard English (now abbreviated to SE) example would be the Philadelphian pronunciation of the *ou* or *ow* diphthong in each word of the sentence *How now brown cow?* While SE speakers from the upper Midwest or far West would use the same sound found in the pronunciation of *house*, a person from Philadelphia or farther south might use the sound like the vowel in *bat* or *cap*.

Usually associated with Brooklyn is the pronunciation of such words as *girl*, *world*, and *first* with the same vowel sounds as words like *toy* or *boy*. Unlike word variability, predictability is evident in these types of pronunciation differences—if a person says *girl* as *goil*, chances are good that he will also say *woild* and *foist*.

Also unlike word variability, sound variability is clearly noticed in another's dialect. One can hardly speak a complete sentence without displaying some characteristic sound, but word variability is random so a word showing such contrast may never appear even in extended conversations. Generally it is the vowel that shows this contrast since consonant pronunciation in English is fairly stable.

Circle the letter of the word pair that demonstrates sound variability:

10. a. *learn—learning*
    b. *turn—toin*
11. a. *sad—bad*
    b. *round—răwnd*

Many vowel sounds in BEV are pronounced with a characteristically Southern drawl. One such example of this would be the sound variability shown in the group of words using the long *i* like *time, my*, and *find*. Speakers of BEV and most white Southern speech have a tendency to open the mouth wider on the pronunciation of the vowels in these words and to lengthen the sound. Try to say these words in such a manner. It is much easier to hear the sound, whether in your own speech or that of another, than to merely read a description on paper.

In words such as *head, led*, and *met*, the vowel sound is diphthongized, or made to **sound like two vowels** in addition to being lengthened. Try to say these words. A phonetic approximation of head would be *ha-aid*.

Another group of words, such as *good, should,* and *would,* are said with less puckering of the lips, the tongue raised, and the vowel diphtongized. Say these aloud in such a manner.

Circle the letters of the series of words that might show sound variability in BEV:

12. a. *red, dead*
    b. *darn, barn, charm, farm*
13. a. *can, pan, sand, man*
    b. *hook, foot, look, book*
14. a. *I, ride, side, lied*
    b. *me, he, see, tree*

Sound Variability Check

---

15. T F Sound variability is not a predictable occurrence in a person's speech.
16. T F Sound variability is clearly noticed in another's dialect.
17. T F Sound variability usually occurs in vowels.
18. T F When telling a story in dialect you are unconsciously using your knowledge of that dialect's sound variability.

Part III

The third type of pronunciation variability, and the most complicated, is **contrast variability**. This is also the most important type, since it causes so many misunderstandings between student and teacher.

Consider the word *contrast* in its usual meaning. Generally we would say that if two items, words, or sounds contrast, they are different. So it seems clear to SE speakers that the words *write* and *wrote* contrast, and *right* and *write* do not.

Circle the letter of the word that contrasts with the first word:

19. *rode*:   a. *road*   b. *ride*

20. *bear*:   a. *bare*   b. *bore*

Many SE speakers make contrasts in their language that other SE speakers do not make. Consider the following pairs of words:

> *witch—which*
> *wear—where*
> *marry—merry*
> *fairy—ferry*
> *poor—pour*

Many speakers hear and say these pairs as **homophones** (pronounced identically), while some distinguish their sounds. The *wh* in *which* and *where* is pronounced with a puff of air and the *w* of *witch* and *wear* is pronounced with none for the latter group of people. The last three pairs of words show contrast (or lack of contrast) between vowels. As with sound variability, contrast variability occurs infrequently among consonants.

Say the word pairs just listed. Do you have contrast between the words of each pair? Whether you contrast the words or not, you can easily find others nearby who would disagree with you on the pronunciation of one or more of the pairs. It is important to point out that all people call some words homophones that others contrast. It is also typically human to think that the only valid and truly important contrasts are the ones we make ourselves.

Like sound variability, contrast variability shows a systematic relationship and more than one word is involved, but unlike sound variability, there is little predictability from one dialect to the next. Understandably, when dialects differ in which contrasts they make, spelling of the specific words will be approached differently. For example, if a child makes a contrast between *w* and *wh*, his reasons for spelling the words in such a manner will be different from one who does not contrast them, because the child who lacks the contrast will just have to memorize the correct spelling. Of course we all have homophones (words that sound the same) but some people have more than others and in some ways, the more homophones you have, the more spelling difficulties you will encounter.

BEV speakers usually have more homophones than SE speakers. BEV speakers may lose contrasts that SE speakers, as a whole, maintain. One common occasion is the loss of vowel contrast before a nasal consonant (*n* or *m*). In such a case, the following words would be homophones in BEV.

pin—pen
bin—Ben
Jim—gem
think—thank

---

21. Circle the letter in front of a nasal consonant:

   a. *p*   c. *n*
   b. *c*   d. *f*

---

22. Which word contains a nasal consonant? Circle it.

   terrace   blue   cried   surprise   new   direct

Circle the letter of the pair of words that might be considered homophones in some dialect of BEV:

23. a. *lid—led*
    b. *sit—set*
    c. *tin—ten*

24. a. *bill—bell*
    b. *gin—Jen*
    c. *missed—messed*

If contrast has been lost before a nasal consonant, which words would rhyme with the first word? Circle the correct letters:

25. *den*   a. *bin*   b. *dead*   c. *glen*
26. *Penny*   a. *Ginny*   b. *Lenny*   c. *Jerry*
27. *drink*   a. *sank*   b. *thank*   c. *sick*

Contrast Variability Caused by Loss of Consonants

Final consonants are the most often affected when loss of contrast occurs in BEV. The most significant variability appears there. The consonants most often "lost" or altered are *r, l, t,* and *d*.

r

This consonant is generally dropped after a vowel, such as in the words *car, fear, Martha, fort.*

Circle the letter of the words that would be homophones:

28. a.   *fort—fought*
    b.   *lark—dark*
    c.   *sack—back*

29. a.   *fool—full*
    b.   *God—guard*
    c.   *bring—bing*

30. a.   *pin—pen*
    b.   *four—door*
    c.   *poor—poe*

Occasionally an *r* may be omitted between two vowels as in *Paris* or *interesting.*

Circle the letter of the homophone pair if this applies:

31. a.   *car—card*
    b.   *terrace—Tess*
    c.   *Jim—gem*

---

l

Much the same thing happens with *l* as happened with *r*. In some cases the *l* is weakened but in others the *l* is lost completely after a vowel, making the words *help* and *hep* homophones, for example. BEV speakers will make this complete reduction more often than SE speakers. The *l* can be lost when followed by a consonant, or when it comes at the end of a word as in *toll,* which may then be pronounced just like *toe.*

Circle the letter of the word that could not be considered a homophone of the first word:

32. *tool*   a. *too* b. *two* c. *tale*

33. *bolt*   a. *bait* b. *boat* c. *bote*

$$\boxed{t \text{ and } d}$$

The letters *t* and *d* are like *r* and *l* in that they are most often lost when followed by a consonant and also primarily in final consonant blends. The word *last* would be simplified to *lass*, for example.

Circle the letter of the word pair that shows this reduction:

34. a. *tow—toe*
    b. *first—firs*
    c. *first—last*

35. a. *mend—men*
    b. *send—sends*
    c. *bolt—boat*

As you see from your answers, a consonant often precedes the *t* or *d* reduction and this is ordinarily the rule.

Another interesting change often occurs in BEV. The final *d* may be pronounced as a *t*. So a student may say, *I got a goot grate.*

---

36. If *t* is pronounced as *d*, then which of the following pairs would be homophones? Circle the correct response.
    a. *treat—tee*
    b. *meet—met*
    c. *bed—bet*

Contrast Variability Check

---

37. T F   Contrast variability causes many misunderstandings between teacher and student.

38. T F   Loss of contrast between two words produces homophones.

39. T F   Loss of contrast does not produce spelling problems for the student.

40. T F   The consonants *r, l, t*, and *d* are most likely to be "lost" in BEV.

To practice your understanding of these concepts, complete the variability map that follows.[9]

(*1*) Select a word pair from the list.

(*2*) Decide which type of variability it demonstrates.

[9] The answer key is on p. 160.

(*3*) Write it in the correct column.

(*4*) Look back to pages 150–157 for other examples.

Word Variability	Sound Variability	Contrast Variability

<table>
<tr><td>crick—creek</td><td>cheer—chair</td><td>roof—roof</td></tr>
<tr><td>mirror—mirrah</td><td>pen—pin</td><td>been—been</td></tr>
<tr><td>third—thoid</td><td>price—prod</td><td>which—witch</td></tr>
<tr><td>route—rout</td><td>Mary—merry</td><td>can't—cahn't</td></tr>
<tr><td>ask—ax</td><td>for—four</td><td>skreet—street</td></tr>
<tr><td>girl—goil</td><td>sender—cinder</td><td>world—woild</td></tr>
</table>

Criterion Test for Mini-module 1

A. Assuming standard pronunciation for the following words, write in the blank a possible BEV pronunciation:

1. *toll* _____

2. *penny* _____

3. *fooled* _____

4. *lark* _____

5. *send* _____

B. Suggest what characteristics of the child's dialect might create the first pronunciation. The standard spelling is shown in parentheses.

1. *bet (bed)* _____

2. *bin (bend)* _____

3. *dak (dark)* _____

4. *woof (wolf)* _____

5. *skreet (street)* _____

Check your answers with the answer key on p. 160.

Answer Key for Pretest

A. 1. Pronunciation of *d* as *t*

   2. Loss of contrast between vowels before nasal and loss of final *d*

   3. Loss of *r* after a vowel

4. Loss of *l* before a consonant (or after a vowel)
5. Word variability
B. 1. *Mary like hot dogs.*
   2. *She walk again.*
   3. *I asked him was he coming.*
   4. *Who gonna go tomorrow?*
   5. *The teacher gave two tesses.*
   6. *It's a nice place to eat just down the block.*
   7. *Ain't nothing I can't do that won't help him none.*
   8. *We be going to see him every day at five.*
   9. *He a big boy now.*

Answer Key for Mini-module 1

1. a
2. b
3. Possible targets:
  ahnt—aunt
  advertise'ment—adver'tisement
  marine—mahrine
  drawer—draw
  schedule—shedule (British)
  often—ofen

4. a	23. c
5. a	24. b
6. a	25. a, c
7. T	26. a, b
8. F	27. a, b
9. F	28. a
10. b	29. b
11. b	30. c
12. b	31. b
13. a	32. c
14. a	33. a
15. F	34. b
16. T	35. a
17. T	36. c
18. T	37. T
19. ride	38. T
20. bare	39. F
21. c	40. T
22. new	

Speaking

Map Key

Word Variability	Sound Variability	Contrast Variability
crick–creek	third–thoid	cheer–chair
mirror–mirrah	girl–goil	pen–pin
route–rout	world–woild	Mary–merry
ask–ax	turn–toin	for–four
r̄oof–r̆oof	round–răwnd	sender–cinder
bēen–bĕen	red–kept–deck	which–witch
skreet–street	hook–foot	fairy–ferry
business–bidness	ride–side	poor–pour
Detroit'–De'troit		wear–where
		tin–ten
		fort–faught
		God–guard
		toe–told

Criterion Test Key for Mini-module 1

A. 1. *toe*
   2. *pinny*
   3. *foo or food*
   4. *lak*
   5. *sin or sind*

B. 1. *D* pronounced as *t*
   2. Loss of contrast between vowels before nasal and loss of final *d*
   3. Loss of *r* after a vowel
   4. Loss of *l* before a consonant (or after a vowel)
   5. Word variability

MINI-MODULE 2
Black English Vernacular Grammar, Part 1[10]

Introduction to Mini-modules 2 and 3

From a linguistic point of view one dialect is as good as another, and both BEV and SE are seen as logical linguistic systems, with slightly divergent grammar and pronunciation rules.

However, BEV dialects that contain grammatical deviations from SE are highly stigmatized. Attitudes of dialect correctness are formed at an early age and they are supported by strong emotional commitments to family and peers. Considering human nature, these feelings are understandable, but they are, in part, responsible for many prejudiced attitudes toward both dialects.

The grammatical elements of BEV programmed in Mini-modules 2 and 3 were chosen because they occur with high frequency and are therefore highly stigmatized and often the cause of communication and learning problems.

Verb Tense

Third Person Singular

In SE the third person singular is marked with *s* or *es* or an irregular form.

---

1. Check the SE form:
   a. _____ *He play hard.*
   b. _____ *He plays hard.*

In most BEV dialects the *s* or *es* is dropped:

He, She, or *It*	*walk good.*
	sing good.
	do good.
	have good sense.

---

[10] The answer key is on p. 171.

Check the correct BEV form:

2. a. _____ *She sings a song.*
   b. _____ *She sing a song.*

3. a. _____ *He like candy.*
   b. _____ *He likes candy.*

4. a. _____ *It show through.*
   b. _____ *It shows through.*

5. a. _____ *She has troubles.*
   b. _____ *She have troubles.*

6. Fill in the BEV form:

   a. *He _____ like a butterfly.*
   b. *He _____ like a bee.*
   c. *She_____ too much.*

7. Write two sentences. Use the third person singular BEV form of *smile* in (a) and *look* in (b):

   a.
   b.

8. Write the same sentences using the SE form of *smile* in (a) and *look* in (b):

   a.
   b.

Past

The past tense of **regular** verbs in SE is often marked with *ed*:

> *I walked to school yesterday.*
> *She passed away.*

The past tense of **irregular** verbs is the same in SE and BEV

> *The corn grew tall last year.*
> *He drove to Chicago.*

However, the past tense of **regular** verbs is often dropped in BEV, because of the frequent loss of consonants in the final position. (See page 155 in Mini-module 1.)

Before *t* or *d*. The final consonant is often dropped when the next word begins with *t* or *d*.

> *I walk to school last week.*
> *I want doughnuts yesterday.*

Before vowels. The final consonant is often dropped when the next word begins with a vowel:

> *I look in last week.*
> *You yell at me yesterday.*

Why is the past tense marker *ed* dropped in these sentences? (Choose *a* or *b*.)

a. The next word begins with *t* or *d*.
b. The next word begins with a vowel.

9. _____ *I look at him.*
10. _____ *I want to go.*
11. _____ *I walk down the hill.*
12. _____ *He jump over it.*

Check the common BEV form of the past tense;

13. a. _____ *I smell that fire they had.*
    b. _____ *I smelled that fire they had.*
14. a. _____ *Tom played dodge ball and won.*
    b. _____ *Tom play dodge ball and won.*
15. a. _____ *I smile at you this morning.*
    b. _____ *I smiled at you this morning.*
16. a. _____ *He kissed me last time.*
    b. _____ *He kiss me last time.*
17. a. _____ *She swam in that meet.*
    b. _____ *She swim in that meet.*

18. Fill in the correct BEV forms of *play, run, walk*:
    a. *Sally _____ at my party.*
    b. *I _____ all the way home.*
    c. *I _____ to work last week.*

19. Write a sentence using the BEV form of *wink*:

20. Write a sentence using the SE form of *wink*:

Labov's Test for Standard Dialect Past Tense Rule. A teacher of BEV-speaking students should consider whether or not these students use the SE *ed* marker for the past tense. William Labov has suggested the use of this test sentence:

When I passed by I read the sign.

If the student says the past form of the verb *read*—then he applies the SE rule for past formation. Most important, if the student uses the present tense of *read*, then he will need some special help to learn the SE rule for past tense.

21. Choose an alternate test sentence to use in place of Labov's sentence:
    a. *When I went to work I read the sign.*
    b. *When I smiled at her she laughed.*
    c. *When I walked by I read the sign.*

Future Tense

Will. Both SE and BEV use *will* to form the future tense, in both full and contracted form:

SE: *I will go—I'll go*
BEV: *I will go—I'll go*

However, in BEV if *will* is used in a contracted form it is often reduced (dropped):

I'll go tomorrow—I go tomorrow
You'll be happy then—You be happy then

The reduction of contracted forms is common in BEV (see Copula section of this module). So there are three alternatives:

(*1*) Full form: *I will go.*
(*2*) Contracted form: *I'll go.*
(*3*) Reduced form: *I go.*

---

22. Check the sentences that contain a reduced BEV future tense:

    a. _____ *She'll walk again.*
    b. _____ *She walk again.*
    c. _____ *You never make it better.*
    d. _____ *You'll never make it better.*
    e. _____ *I never do it again.*

---

23. Write your own BEV sentence forms of a contracted and reduced form of the future tense using:

    a. *will eat*
    b. *will fly*
    c. *will get*

Gonna. Another frequent future tense form in BEV and SE is formed with *gonna. Gonna* is reduced from the words *going to* and it can exist in both dialects in various degrees of reduction.

> Example: *I'm gonna go.*
> *I am going to go.*
> *I gon' go.*
> *I'ngna go.*

In SE the rule is to use the verb *to be* + *gonna*:

> *You are gonna go.*
> *I am gonna go.*

In BEV the rule for the use of *gonna* is to delete the *to be* form.

> *You gonna go.*
> *I gonna go.*

---

24. Check the BEV use of *gonna* below:

    a. *I gonna be mad at you.*
    b. *I am gonna be mad at you.*
    c. *I gonna go real fast.*
    d. *You gonna get in trouble.*
    e. *Sam is gonna get in trouble.*

25. Using the verbs *play, think,* and *live,* construct BEV sentences containing *gonna*:

Verb Tense Check

26. Which of these statements are true?
    a.   *He look real strong* is a correct BEV sentence.
    b.   *The girl wore red* is a correct BEV sentence.
    c.   Lack of an *ed* past rule is impossible to detect.
    d.   A BEV speaker can form the future tense a variety of ways.
    e.   *I gon' go* is a common BEV future tense form.

Question Patterns

Questions.   In SE and BEV the most common question pattern is formed by reversing the order of the subject and the verb or auxiliary:

I can go.	*Can I go?*
He is smart	*Is he smart?*

These are called **yes—no questions** because they require a yes or no answer.

Wh **Questions.**   The question pattern that contains *wh* question words is treated differently by each dialect. In SE pattern, the speaker **must reverse** the subject and verb or auxiliary order:

Where is he going?
What can I do?

The BEV pattern can be the same as the SE pattern, but there is also an **alternative** pattern, in which the subject and verb order is not reversed. Both patterns are acceptable:

Where is he going?	or	*Where he is going?*
What can I do?	or	*What I can do?*

---

27. Which sentences are BEV patterns?
    a.   _____ *Are you going downtown?*
    b.   _____ *Where you are going?*
    c.   _____ *What you can do about that?*

28. Write two BEV patterns of a *when* question:

   a.

   b.

Note: Each dialect has different rules that control the order of the subject and verb according to the type of sentence pattern.

Embedded *Wh* Questions. An embedded sentence or question is found within a longer sentence. When the *wh* question is embedded in a sentence, the SE pattern **does not** contain a reverse of the subject—verb order:

> *I know where he was going.*
> *You asked him how he is doing.*

The BEV pattern can be like the SE pattern, but there is also an alternative pattern in which the subject and verb order **is reversed** in the embedded sentence:

> *I know where was he going.*
> *You asked him how is he doing.*

29. Which sentences are possible BEV patterns?

   a. _____ *I know how you did it.*

   b. _____ *I asked when was she coming.*

   c. _____ *You know how he is doing.*

   d. _____ *She asked what was the big idea.*

30. Write two BEV patterns of a *wh* embedded question:

   a.

   b.

Yes—No Embedded Questions. This type of embedded question is treated differently by each dialect. In SE this type of question is marked by *if* or *whether*, which signals the kind of sentence to follow:

> *I thought about whether I should go.*
> *I asked him if he liked me.*

In BEV there is no use of *if* or *whether* to form this type of question. The speaker **must reverse** the order of the subject and verb or auxiliary:

> *I thought about should I go.*
> *I asked him did he like me.*

Note the insertion of *did* when the verb lacked an auxiliary part to reverse.

---

31. Which sentences are BEV forms of *yes–no* embedded questions?

    a.   _____ *I wondered can I do it.*

    b.   _____ *I wondered if I can do it.*

    c.   _____ *I asked him whether he wanted one.*

    d.   _____ *I asked him did he want one.*

---

32. Write two BEV forms of *yes–no* embedded sentences:

    a.

    b.

Hypercorrection

Hypercorrection is a linguistic term. Hypercorrection is a misapplied linguistic rule. It is done unconsciously and it occurs often in the speech of a BEV speaker who is assimilating SE forms into his own dialect. Common patterns of hypercorrection follow:

(*1*) Third person singular *s*:

SE form:	*I go to school.*
	He goes to school.
BEV form:	*I go to school.*
	He go to school.
Hypercorrect BEV form:	*I goes to school.*
	He goes to school.

The idea of *s* marking third person singular is misapplied to first person singular.

---

33. a. *I* _____ *a tune.*

    b. *You* _____ *pretty.*

    c. *I* _____ *my dog.*

(*2*) Pluralization of words ending a consonant cluster.

SE:	*desk, desks*
BEV:	*des'(k), desses*
Hypercorrect BEV:	*desk, deskes*

Hypercorrect plurals are formed when the final cluster is not reduced, and the dialect pluralization is used:

desk

deskes

---

34. Write the hypercorrect plurals for these words:

    a.   *test* _____

    b.   *ghost* _____

    c.   *risk* _____

    d.   *post* _____

(*3*) Hypercorrect possessive. In SE dialect possessive is marked by adding *'s*:

the boy's hat

John Johnson's hat

In BEV dialect possessive is marked by word order:

the boy hat

the girl dress

Hypercorrect possessives are common in a possessive form of first name and surname. They are formed by a hypercorrection application of the *'s* to the first name:

John's Johnson's car

---

35. Write BEV forms of the following possessives:

    a.   *the dog's tail* _____

    b.   *the baby's bottle* _____

    c.   *John's car* _____

---

36. Write a hypercorrect BEV form of a surname possessive:

    a.   *Sally Flynn's cat* _____

    b.   *Bob Smith's house* _____

    c.   *Florence Brown's car* _____

37. Check the hypercorrect BEV forms:
    a. _____ *The girl doll is cute.*
    b. _____ *Bob's Simon's dog is big.*
    c. _____ *That girl's hair is curly.*
    d. _____ *Andy's Brown's nose is big.*
    e. _____ *The boy book is muddy.*
    f. _____ *He has the girl's dime.*
    g. _____ *Marcia's Stone's house is far away.*

Question Pattern and Hypercorrect Form Check

38. Check which statements are true:
    a. _____ *You asked him if he was going.* This sentence has an embedded sentence in it.
    b. _____ In BEV question patterns the subject and verb order is often reversed.
    c. _____ The BEV speaker has more alternative question patterns available to him than the SE speaker.
    d. _____ The word *hypercorrect* means overcorrect.

Criterion Test for Mini-module 2

Write the BEV equivalents of the following sentences:

1. *I asked him when he was coming.*
2. *I wonder if I can do it.*
3. *I'll show him which way to go.*
4. *I walked to school yesterday.*
5. *I smiled at him.*
6. *Who's going to go tomorrow?*
7. *She'll walk again.*
8. *Jerry is going to get it.*
9. *Mary likes hot dogs.*
10. *He sings a song.*
11. *The teacher gave two tests.* (Give hypercorrection.)
12. *Sally Brown's car is dirty.* (Give hypercorrection.)
13. *I go to the movies.* (Give hypercorrection.)
14. Would this sentence be a good test for the existence of an *ed* past rule? Circle *yes* or *no*.
    When I smiled she read the joke.

Check your answers against the answer key on p. 172.

Answer Key for Mini-module 2

1. b
2. b
3. a
4. a
5. b
6. a. *fly*   b. *sting* or *others*   c. *talk* or *others*
7. a. *He smile at everyone.*
   b. *She look good.*
8. a. *He smiles at everyone.*
   b. *She looks good.*
9. b
10. a
11. a
12. b
13. a
14. b
15. a
16. b
17. a
18. a. *play*   b. *ran*   c. *walk*
19. *He wink at me yesterday.*
20. *He winked at me yesterday.*
21. a, c
22. b, c, e
23. a.   *You eat better tomorrow.*
    b.   *She fly to Chicago for Easter.*
    c.   *I get over there soon.*
24. a, c, d
25. a.   *You gonna play with me?*
    b.   *I gonna think on it.*
    c.   *I gonna live till I die.*
26. a, b, d
27. a, b, c
28. a.   *When are you coming?*
    b.   *When you are coming?*
29. a, b, c, d
30. a.   *I knew where was he playing.*
    b.   *I asked when you are coming.*
31. a, d
32. a.   *You wondered did I like it.*
    b.   *I asked can he go.*

33. a. *whistles*   b. *looks*   c. *loves*
34. a. *testes*   b. *ghoses*   c. *riskes*   d. *postes*
35. a. *dog tail*   b. *baby bottle*   c. *John car*
36. a. *Sally's Flynn's cat*
    b. *Bob's Smith's house*
    c. *Florence's Brown's car*
37. b, d, g
38. a, b, c, d

Criterion Test Key for Mini-module 2

1. *I asked him when was he coming.* (or left the same)
2. *I wonder can I do it.*
3. *I show him which way to go.*
4. *I walk to school yesterday.*
5. *I smile at him.*
6. *Who gonna go tomorrow?*
7. *She walk again.*
8. *Jerry gonna get it.*
9. *Mary like hot dogs.*
10. *He sing a song.*
11. *The teacher gave two tesses. (testes)*
12. *Sally's Brown's car is dirty.*
13. *I goes to the movies.*
14. *Yes*

MINI-MODULE 3
Black English Vernacular Grammar, Part 2[11]

Dummy *It*

The phrase *there's* is not used by many BEV speakers. Instead *it's* is used. Thus, in BEV *It's a dog in the house* could mean *There's a dog in the house.* So in BEV:

> *There's* is replaced by *it's.*

[11] The answer key is on p. 185.

Circle the letter next to each sentence in which *there's* has been replaced by *it's*:

1. a. *It's a nice resturant down the block.*
   b. *It's a nice restaurant with a good decor.*

2. a. *It's a good stereo and it costs a lot.*
   b. *It's a stereo at the store which I want to buy.*

3. a. *It's a good movie for kids to see.*
   b. *It's a good movie down at the theatre tonight.*

4. a. *It's a policeman on every corner.*
   b. *It's the policeman with the long hair.*

5. a. *It's a lot of fun to be with nice people.*
   b. *It's a lot of fun to be had with nice people.*

6. a. *It's a topic that has been discussed by many people.*
   b. *It's a lot to be said on that subject.*

7. a. *It's very little to doing okay in school.*
   b. *It's not hard to do okay in school.*

8. a. *It isn't much I can do.*
   b. *It isn't too much to ask for.*

9. a. *It's no way to get out of it.*
   b. *It's a situation in which no escape is possible.*

10. a. *It's a case of not being able to back out.*
    b. *It isn't anybody who can stop me now.*

---

11. Now write a SE sentence beginning with *there's* and change the *there's* to *it's* to form the BEV version. For example, SE: *There's a fly in my soup.* BEV: *It's a fly in my soup.*

    a. (SE) _____
    b. BEV _____

---

12. Write the BEV version of the following sentence: *There's no way I can get up that early.*

Negation

Overview

The two basic rules for negation in SE are

(*1*) Place the negative in the first possible location in the sentence.
(*2*) Move the negative from the first possible location one place to the right to the second possible location for the negative.

BEV accepts those rules of negation but then goes even further in what is possible. Thus, the basic rule for negation in BEV, in addition to the foregoing, is

(*3*) Copy the negative into all later indefinites.

The four optional rules for negation in BEV are

(*1*) Copy the negative from the preceding indefinite into the auxiliary.
(*2*) Copy the negative into embedded sentences.
(*3*) Invert the positive of the preverbal indefinite and the auxiliary.
(*4*) In those negative sentences that begin with *it is*, delete the *it*.

Most SE sentences are negated by placing the word *not* **after the auxiliary verb.** SE speakers learn this rule when they are children and continue to use it intuitively throughout their lives. They negate sentences like *He goes to school* by placing the auxiliary *do* before *goes* where it is automatically changed to the third person singular *does* and then placing *not* after it. The result is *He does not go to school.* Thus, the most common rule of negation in SE is

Place the word *not* after the auxiliary.

Circle the letter next to each sentence that is correctly negated according to this rule:

13. a. *He does not read the book.*
    b. *He not does read the book.*

14. a. *I do like not ice cream.*
    b. *I do not like ice cream.*

15. a. *The TV does sit on not the table.*
    b. *The TV does not sit on the table.*

16. a. *The dog does not run often.*
    b. *The not dog does run often.*

17. a. *You will not go today.*
    b. *You will go not today.*

If there is an indefinite, for example *some* or *somebody*, at the beginning of the sentence, SE speakers must place the negation with the indefinite instead of after the auxiliary. Thus, in the sentence *Somebody left the door open,* **somebody** would become **nobody**. The negative would then be *Nobody left the door open*. So the second rule of negation in SE is

If there is an indefinite before the verb, the negation must be placed with the indefinite.

Circle the letter next to each sentence that is correctly negated according to this rule:

18. a. *Somebody not did know that.*
    b. *Nobody knew that.*
19. a. *Nothing can happen.*
    b. *Something cannot happen.*
20. a. *No one will go.*
    b. *Everyone will not go.*
21. a. *Anybody knows nothing.*
    b. *Nobody knows anything.*
22. a. *Nothing is taken care of.*
    b. *Something is not taken care of.*

Now we understand that the most common rule of negation in SE is to place the word *not* after the auxiliary verb. This applies in all cases **except** when an indefinite appears before the verb, in which case the indefinite must be negated. Both these rules can be combined into one simple rule, which states

Place negation in the first possible location in the sentence.

Circle the letter next to each sentence that is correctly negated according to this rule:

23. a. *John and Maggie did not go to town.*
    b. *John and Maggie did go not to town.*
24. a. *Someone did not go to town.*
    b. *No one went to town.*
25. a. *The plane is not ready to take off.*
    b. *The plane not is ready to take off.*
26. a. *We did not have much fun.*
    b. *We had no fun.*

27. a. *No one will know what we did.*
    b. *Someone will not know what we did.*
28. a. *I will have none.*
    b. *I will not have any.*
29. a. *She did not visit her grandmother.*
    b. *She not did visit her grandmother.*
30. a. *I will wear no blue clothes.*
    b. *I will not wear any blue clothes.*
31. a. *The plant grew well not.*
    b. *The plant did not grow well.*
32. a. *No oil was found.*
    b. *Some oil was not found.*

There is one more rule of negation in SE that is used in formal contexts. It is most often found in formal writing and is rarely used in speech but it should be mentioned here because of the many times students are asked to write formal papers. This rule allows the user to move the negation from the auxiliary **one** place to the **right,** to the next available location for a negative. Thus, in the sentence *I will not go anywhere* the negative can be moved down one place to the right so that the sentence reads *I will go nowhere.* Note that this rule does not apply in sentences in which the negative is already attatched to the first indefinite. So the final rule of negation in SE is

Move the negative **one** place to the **right.**

Circle the letter next to each sentence that is correctly negated according to this rule:

33. a. *I do not have any.*
    b. *I have none.*
34. a. *We did not strike any oil anywhere.*
    b. *We struck no oil anywhere.*
35. a. *Diane cannot have any candy.*
    b. *Diane can have no candy.*
36. a. *The cat will not go anywhere.*
    b. *The cat will go nowhere.*
37. a. *I know nothing.*
    b. *I do not know anything.*

In SE one and only one negation is allowed in a negative sentence. This is not true of BEV. In BEV the most common rule of negation is to copy the negative, which has been placed in the first available location, into **all** later indefinites. Thus, the SE sentence *I don't have any* becomes *I don't have none*. So the **first** rule of negation in BEV which builds on the previously mentioned SE negation rules is

Copy the negative into all later indefinites.

Circle the letter next to each sentence that is correctly negated according to this rule:

38. a. *We struck no oil nowhere.*
    b. *We didn't strike no oil nowhere.*
39. a. *I don't want to go nowhere.*
    b. *I don't want to go anywhere.*
40. a. *Nobody has nothing.*
    b. *Nobody has anything.*
41. a. *You don't see anybody.*
    b. *You don't see nobody.*
42. a. *The dog isn't barking at nothing.*
    b. *The dog isn't barking at anything.*

The preceding rule is used almost all the time in BEV but there are four additional rules that can be applied if the BEV speaker wishes to do so. The first of these is to copy the negation from the preceding indefinite into the auxiliary. This means that if the negation has been placed in the first possible location, which happens to be an indefinite in a preverbal position, then the negation is copied into the auxiliary and the sentence becomes *Nothing can't happen*. So the **first optional rule** of negation in BEV is

Copy the negative from the preceding indefinite into the auxiliary.

Circle the letter next to each sentence that is correctly negated according to this rule:

43. a. *Nobody has nothing.*
    b. *Nobody hasn't got nothing.*
44. a. *Nobody knew that.*
    b. *Nobody didn't know that.*
45. a. *Nothing doesn't seem right about this.*
    b. *Nothing seems right about this.*
46. a. *Nobody saw nothing.*
    b. *Nobody didn't see nothing.*

47. a. *Nobody isn't going nowhere.*
    b. *Nobody is going nowhere.*

The **second optional rule** is to copy the negative into embedded sentences. Thus, the sentence *Nobody didn't know he did* becomes *Nobody didn't know he didn't*. So the second optional rule of BEV is

> Copy the negative into the embedded sentence.

Circle the letter next to each sentence that is correctly negated according to this rule:

48. a. *I don't believe it's not no God.*
    b. *I don't believe it's not any God.*
49. a. *There wasn't no trick that could shun her.*
    b. *There wasn't no trick that couldn't shun her.*
50. a. *Nothing can't happen when you pay some attention.*
    b. *Nothing can't happen when you don't pay no attention.*
51. a. *I didn't know that couldn't happen.*
    b. *I didn't know that could happen.*
52. a. *There isn't no cat can't get in any coop.*
    b. *There isn't no cat can't get in no coop.*

The third optional rule of negation in BEV is applicable only when there is an indefinite in a preverbal position. This indefinite and the auxiliary can switch positions so that the auxiliary now precedes the indefinite. Thus, the sentence *Nobody don't break up a fight* becomes *Don't nobody break up a fight*. The **third optional rule** of negation in BEV, then, is

> Invert the position of the preverbal indefinite and the auxiliary.

Circle the letter next to each sentence that is correctly negated according to this rule:

53. a. *Didn't nobody see nothing.*
    b. *Nobody didn't see nothing.*
54. a. *Didn't nobody know that.*
    b. *Didn't know nobody that.*
55. a. *Nobody ain't going nowhere.*
    b. *Ain't nobody going nowhere.*

56. a. *Can't nothing happen.*
    b. *Nothing can't happen.*

57. a. *Nothing ain't gonna stop me.*
    b. *Ain't nothing gonna stop me.*

The final optional rule of negation in BEV has to do with sentences beginning with the phrase *it is*. In these sentences it is possible to drop the *it* completely. For example, *It ain't nothing you could do* becomes *Ain't nothing you could do*. So the **fourth optional rule** of negation in BEV is:

In those sentences that begin with *it is*, delete the *it*.

Circle the letter next to each sentence that is correctly negated according to this rule:

58. a. *It ain't no cowboy who could beat him.*
    b. *Ain't no cowboy who could beat him.*

59. a. *It ain't no dog wouldn't want no bone like that.*
    b. *Ain't no dog would want a bone like that.*

60. a. *Ain't no man in the whole house.*
    b. *It ain't no man in the whole house.*

61. a. *It ain't no cop around to see us.*
    b. *Ain't no cop around to see us.*

62. a. *It ain't no pie like pumpkin pie.*
    b. *Ain't no pie like pumpkin pie.*

Thus, multiple negation in BEV consists of copying negation into all indefinites in a sentence. The BEV speaker can also choose to copy the negation into the auxiliary. He or she can further choose to copy the negative into embedded sentences. A negative sentence that begins with an indefinite can be inverted so that the auxiliary precedes the indefinite. Finally, in negative sentences that begin with *it is* the *it* can be deleted.

Circle the letter next to each sentence that is correctly negated according to all the rules of BEV:

63. a. *Don't nobody care about anything.*
    b. *Don't nobody care about nothing.*

64. a. *Can't nobody stop me now.*
    b. *Can't stop nobody me now.*

65. a. *We didn't find no man nowhere.*
    b. *We didn't find no man anywhere.*

66. a. *I didn't see anybody that nobody knew.*
    b. *I didn't see nobody that nobody knew.*

67. a. *That man don't like nothing.*
    b. *Don't that man like nothing.*

---

68. Correctly negate the following sentence, first in SE, and then in BEV:
    Somebody can always see him.
    a. (SE) _____
    b. (BEV) _____

---

69. Correctly negate the following sentence in BEV: *There is something I would like to do more.*

    _____

Invariant *Be*

In BEV *be* is commonly used to denote a habitual or repetitive state or action. The sentence *I be hungry*, for example, would mean *I am often hungry*. It is important to understand this because misunderstandings may result if a SE speaker does not comprehend the use of the word. A student might say, for instance, *My head be hurting* and mean *My head hurts often*. A teacher, however, might think that the student simply meant *My head hurts right now*. So the rule for using *be* in BEV is

   Be refers to a habitual or repetitive state or action.

Circle the letter next to each sentence that uses *be* correctly according to BEV:

70. a. *I be hungry right now.*
    b. *I be hungry every day.*

71. a. *I be running to catch the bus.*
    b. *I be running to catch the bus in a minute.*

72. a. *I be late for work.*
    b. *I be late for work today.*

73. a. *I'll be seeing you.*
    b. *I be seeing you.*

74. a. *I have to be there by nine.*
    b. *I be there by nine.*

---

75. Now imagine that the restaurant you frequent has hired a cook who continually makes very bad coffee. Describe the cook in one sentence first in SE and then in BEV using *be*.

    a. (SE) _____

    b. (BNE) _____

---

76. Write the BEV version of the following sentence: *My dog always barks at night.*

    _____

Note: BEV-speaking students, when trying to correct their English, often change the *be* in, for example, *He be busy*, to *bees* so that the sentence reads *He bees busy*. When they realize that this also is not right, they change it into *will be*. So BEV speakers are apt to misread the SE *He is busy* as showing immediacy and *He will be busy* as indicating repetition or long duration as well as futurity.

Copula

The copula refers to the verb *to be* and its various forms. The most common forms are *is, are,* and *am.* In all except formal SE the copula is contracted so that *You are leaving tomorrow* usually becomes *You're leaving tomorrow.*

Circle the letter next to each sentence that shows the correct informal version of the copula in SE:

77. a. *He is a fast runner.*
    b. *He's a fast runner.*

78. a. *We going to church on Sunday.*
    b. *We're going to church on Sunday.*

79. a. *The dog's asleep in the shade.*
    b. *The dog be asleep in the shade.*

80. a. *You are just too critical.*
    b. *You're just too critical.*
81. a. *She's very pretty.*
    b. *She very pretty.*

BEV speakers carry this one step further and completely delete the copula so that the sentence would be *You leaving tomorrow* in BEV. This rule applies, however, only in those situations in which it is possible to contract the copula in SE. Thus, in the sentence *He isn't too tall, is he?* it would not be possible to say *He isn't too tall, he's?* in SE so it would also not be possible to say *He isn't too tall, he?* in BEV. Therefore, in BEV:

It is possible to delete the copula except in those cases in which it cannot be contracted in SE.

Circle the letter next to each sentence that uses the copula correctly according to BEV:

82. a. *I going to school tomorrow.*
    b. *I'm going to school tomorrow.*
83. a. *We are late for the show.*
    b. *We late for the show.*
84. a. *Tell what it's.*
    b. *Tell me what it is.*
85. a. *He a bad boy.*
    b. *He is a bad boy.*
86. a. *Here I am.*
    b. *Here I is.*

87. Now write the following sentence, first in the contracted form of SE, and then in the deleted form of BEV: *He is at home now.*

    a. (SE) _____
    b. (BEV) _____

88. Write the BEV form of the following sentence. *We are one big, happy family.*

    _____

Note: BEV-speaking children use the deleted form of the copula most frequently. They use the full form less frequently and the contracted form hardly ever. Teachers should keep this in mind when teaching contractions or when giving students primers to read that contain many contractions.

Summary

In this part of the module four grammatical rules for BEV have been presented. The **first** rule is that *there's* is replaced by *it's*. For example, *There's no time like the present* becomes *It's no time like the present*. The **second** rule is negation and this is how it works:

Positive Sentence: *I like anyone who likes any of my friends.*

Negative:

(*1*) Place negation in the first possible location in the sentence:
I don't like anyone who likes any of my friends.
(*2*) Move negative and place to the right:
I like no one who likes any of my friends.
(*3*) Copy negative into later indefinites:
I don't like no one who likes any of my friends.

The following rules are optional:

(*1*) Copy the negative from the preceding indefinite into the auxiliary:
Positive: *Someone likes me.*
Negative: *Nobody don't like me.*
(*2*) Copy the negative into embedded sentences:
Positive: *I like anyone who likes any of my friends.*
Negative: *I don't like nobody who don't like none of my friends.*
(*3*) Invert the position of the preverbal indefinite and the auxiliary.
Positive: *Someone likes me.*
Negative: *Don't nobody like me.*
(*4*) In those negative sentences that begin with *it is*, delete the *it*.
Positive: *It's a real victory for everyone.*
Negative: *Ain't a real victory for nobody.*

The **third** rule is that *be* refers to a habitual or repetitive state or action. Thus, the sentence *The cops come by all the time* can be rephrased as *The cops be comin' by*.

The final, or **fourth** rule, refers to the copula. In BEV the copula can be deleted in all cases except when the full form could not be contracted in SE. For example, *I'm going to be famous* becomes *I going to be famous*, but *I can't tell you how happy I am* remains the same.

Criterion Test for Mini-module 3

Give the BEV equivalents of the following sentences:

1. *There's a nice place to eat just down the block.*

2. *There's going to be a great party tomorrow.*

3. *He can't bring any books anywhere.*

4. *There isn't anything I can do that will help him any.*

5. *We go to see him every day at five.*

6. *He does that puzzle over and over again.*

7. *He is a big boy now.*

8. *I am going to be late for work at this rate.*

Check your answers against the answer key on p. 186.

If you desire further information on this topic, we recommend the following references:

Baratz, Joan C., & Shuy, Roger W. (Eds.). *Teaching black children to read*. Washington, D.C.: Center for Applied Linguistics, 1969.

Burling, Robbins. *English in black and white*. New York: Holt, Rinehart and Winston, 1973.

Kochman, Thomas (Ed.). *Rappin' and stylin' out: Communication in urban black America*. Urbana: University of Illinois Press, 1972.

Labov, William. *The language of the inner city*. Philadelphia: University of Pennsylvania Press, 1973.

Labov, William. *The study of nonstandard English*. Champaign, Ill.: National Council of Teachers of English, 1970.

Williams, Frederick (Ed.). *Language and poverty*. Institute for Research on Poverty Monograph Series. Chicago: Markham, 1970.

Wolfram, Walter A., & Clarke, Nona H. (Eds.). *Black—white speech relationships*. Washington, D.C.: Center for Applied Linguistics, 1971.

Answer Key for Mini-module 3

1. a
2. b
3. b
4. a
5. b
6. b
7. a
8. a
9. a
10. b
11. a
    b
12. *It's no* way *I can get up that early.*
    Ain't no way I can't get up that early.

13. a	38. b
14. b	39. a
15. b	40. a
16. a	41. b
17. a	42. a
18. b	43. b
19. a	44. b
20. a	45. a
21. b	46. b
22. a	47. a
23. a	48. a
24. b	49. b
25. a	50. b
26. a	51. a
27. a	52. b
28. b	53. a
29. a	54. a
30. b	55. b
31. b	56. a
32. a	57. b
33. b	58. b
34. b	59. b
35. b	60. a
36. b	61. b
37. a	62. b

63. b
64. a
65. a
66. b
67. a
68. a. *Nobody can always see him.*
    b. *Nobody can't never see him.*
69. *Ain't nothing I wouldn't like to do more.*
70. b
71. a
72. a
73. b
74. b
75. a. *The cook makes bad coffee all the time.*
    b. *The cook be making bad coffee.*
76. *My dog be barking at night.*
77. b
78. b
79. a
80. b
81. a
82. a
83. b
84. b
85. a
86. a
87. a. *He's at home now.*
    b. *He at home now.*
88. *We one big, happy family.*

Criterion Test Key for Mini-module 3

1. *It's a nice place to eat just down the block.*
2. *It's going to be a great party tomorrow.*
3. *He can't bring no books nowhere.*
4. *Ain't nothing I can't do that won't help him none.*
5. *We be going to see him every day at five.*
6. *He be doing that puzzle (over and over again).*
7. *He a big boy now.*
8. *I going to be late for work at this rate.*

READING

GEORGE'S STORY

George's kindergarten teacher recommended special-room placement for him at the end of the year. She was not sure of her recommendation. His language development seemed average, but he could not **do** anything. He was clumsy, dropped everything, could not write his name, could not draw at all, was unable to respond to pictures, could not follow directions—in short, he acted retarded. Except for his language!

Nevertheless, he was placed in the special room. During his third year there, he was referred for testing. His teacher said, "He can't read or write at all, but I don't think he's retarded."

The school psychologist found a language IQ of 115 (bright normal) and a performance IQ of 46 (severely retarded). His diagnosis: perceptually disturbed.

* * * * *

George was referred to the reading center of a nearby university for training. He had one meeting with the staff and did not return.

* * * * *

George reappeared at the center 5 years later. He was now 15 years old and in his eighth year in the special room. His mother reported that they had not returned to the center earlier on the advice of the school psychologist. "He said that our own school would be providing perceptual training soon." And that was 5 years ago.

A reading test given him at age 15 showed George to be reading at Grade 1.3. He could not write his name legibly. He dragged his feet as he walked the halls. He was unable to focus on any training task for more than 4 minutes. He described himself as stupid—and very unhappy.

* * * * *

At this writing, George has had 15 hours of training. The results:

	Initial	Current
Basic sight words	7	63
Oral reading		
(Talking Dictionary)	32 words/2 min	71 words/3 min
Auditory skills (*STARS*)		
(18 tests to mastery)	3 tests	9 tests
Auditory training: Accuracy		
(MLP: Listening 1)	87%	98%
Sentence comprehension:		
(Cloze procedure)	18 tasks/5 min	45 tasks/5 min
	56%	76%

These progress data give an incomplete picture of the gradual metamorphosis George is undergoing. However, they do show the increments in accuracy, speed, absolute numbers of words recognized, and **staying** power. By the fifteenth hour, George worked virtually the whole hour.

* * * * *

The training program was designed to develop these skills:

- **Visual discrimination:** letter matching; word matching; cursive writing
- **Auditory discrimination:** word matching; initial, final, and medial sounds; auditory memory
- **Reading tasks:** letter names; letter—sound equivalents; sight words; sentence comprehension
- **Writing tasks:** Cursive writing; story writing; spelling
- **Independent work:** read and follow directions; operate tape player; operate timer; select tasks for day's work; graph results.

George is not out of the academic woods yet. But the odds on achieving literacy are now in his favor. At his present rate, he should approximate the goal of independent reading and writing by the fiftieth hour.

In its simplest form, reading consists of saying the name of something while looking at it. Some authors insist that the infant is reading when he looks at a person or a toy and indicates recognition. According to the foregoing definition, the infant's action would not qualify as reading. He must name the item recognized.

Representations of experience. The most primitive form of reading seen in schools is illustrated by the series of pictures shown in Figure 6.1. The words are chosen to represent the pictures exactly—or vice versa: Pictures and words are designed to be equivalent.

Experience (A) is represented by pictures (B), and pictures are represented by print (C). If $A = B = C$, then $A = C$. Whether or not it is possible to construct exact equivalents, the child must understand very early that speech is represented by printed words and sentences. This is a serious problem for children having a dialect only roughly related to book language, as discussed earlier.

Subroutines. Another serious problem arises whenever either side of an equivalence statement is ill defined. For example, Ray (Grade 7, Reading Grade 1.2) insisted that d and b are the same letter. "They both got a circle and a stick. They're the same. It's the same letter." If the difference between two confusable letters (or sounds, or faces, or names, and so on) **cannot** be distinguished, as in Ray's case, each remains ill defined. Then the equivalence of [b] = /b/ cannot be established because sometimes [b] = /d/.

Faces are defined by being identified (and recognized) in varying contexts.[1] We have all had the experience of embarrassment at failure to recognize an acquaintance "out of context" (the milkman at church, the store clerk at a wedding, another teacher at the theatre). Letters, like faces, **look different** in differing contexts. Their unique characteristics stand out when they have been identified and recognized or named in several contexts. Then, like a unique personality, you would "recognize it anywhere" (To the child the two d's in [dad] look quite different, just as the two c's in /circus/ sound quite different.) The defining and recognizing of sounds has been treated at length in prior

---

[1] J. J. Gibson puts it this way: ". . . the important question emerges of how animals and children detect those distinctive features of things that are invariant under changes in perspective [1966, p. 320]."

A cat

A cat in a tree

A man

A man sees a cat in a tree

A dog

A man and a cat in a tree

Figure 6.1. The most primitive form of reading: exactly equivalent pictures and words. (Reprinted, with permission, from *Pre-reader A, Michigan Language Program*, by D. E. P. Smith & J. M. Smith. New York: Random House, 1975. © 1970 Donald E. P. Smith.)

chapters. These essential responses are sometimes called **subroutines**. A subroutine is an automatic, basic, low-level sequence of responses, upon which is built more sophisticated responses. If subroutines are ill defined, higher level skills requiring more of the organism's resources must be used to compensate for them.[2]

Subroutines include attending to letters and sounds and recognizing them, attending to sight words and to common utterances (like teacher directions) and recognizing them, drawing legible letters and saying recognizable words, responding reliably to the phonology and syntax of utterances and to the visual representations of them (function words, punctuation, transition words, and so on). If these are present in the behavioral repertoire of entering schoolchildren, they will learn to read with routine instruction. **If such subroutines are missing, or if the method of teaching does not establish them, the most brilliant method used by the most brilliant teacher will probably fail.**

I. Domain of Skills

The problem of what to teach has plagued reading teachers for generations. The domain of skills shown in Table 4.2 is one way of resolving that problem. The skills shown there were identified by following an engineering strategy. The method is described in Volume 1. In brief, we specified a level of skill using a criterion test. (A criterion test differs in several ways from a standardized test, as described in Volume 2. Mainly, it specifies all the responses the child must make.) The criterion test represented certain reading and writing skills, which together constitute literacy. Children were given the test, and the responses of those failing to pass were isolated to determine deficiencies. Instruction was designed to handle minor deficiencies, then the final test was readministered. Those still failing to pass were analyzed further, revealing even lower level missing skills. As a result, a domain, graded in difficulty, was identified. As in the case of listening and speaking, the ordered nature of this domain does not imply that skills should be **taught** in this order.

On the other hand, there is a strong tendency for some critical portion of lower level skills to be **completed** prior to mastery of higher level skills depending upon them. The resulting sequence of learnings tends to be cyclical: lower → higher → lower, and so on, as shown:

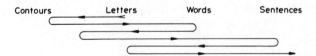

| Contours | Letters | Words | Sentences |

---

[2] After a brilliant rundown and tackle by a defensive back following a pass reception, the coach was asked, "Wasn't that a brilliant defensive play?" The coach replied, "If he'd been playing his position, he wouldn't have had to do it." If a football player handles fundamentals well (like being in the right place on defense), he can use his energy wisely.

Table 6.1
Components of Training in Reading

Level	Class	Domain	Test
1	Contour		
2	Letter	a–z A–Z *a - ʒ* *a - ʒ* Italics Boldface	*STARS*: Letter Shapes Names Manuscript Cursive Letter-sound Functions

3	Word	Boundaries (spaces between words)
		Basic words (Dolch and others)
		All words in preprimer
		Common nouns, verbs
		Common phonemically regular, then irregular
		  words (Coleman list)
			STARS: Word
			Shapes
			Recognition
			Vocabulary
			  range and
			  power

4	Sentence	Boundaries (initial capital and end punctuation) Punctuation Transformations Directions Questions Meaning	*STARS*: Sentence Punctuation Transforms Directions Questions Meaning

5	Paragraph	Format
		  Form conventions
		  Grammatical patterns
		  Phonological patterns
		  Universe of discourse
		Content:
		  Topic
		  Plot
		  Links
		  Information
		Equivalents:
		  Summarization
		  Induction (inference)
		  Deduction
		Impact:
		  Focus
		  Point of view
		  Mood
			STARS: Paragraph
			
			same

6	Discourse	Fiction Nonfiction Textbooks Reference works Periodicals Letters	*STARS*: Book same

The cyclical nature of learning is better shown in Volume 1 (Figure 3.13).

One important conclusion to be drawn from this description is that children should be free to take progress tests **at any level** of the hierarchy **in any sequence**. To provide for that condition, one needs a graded series of tests at each level (see Table 6.1). There are book-level skills appropriate for kindergarten children and word–letter skills appropriate for sixth grade children.

II. The Process of Learning to Read

The learning-to-read process has been described in a picture sequence in Volume 1.[3] That material is reproduced here.

A. *Naming and Drawing Pictures*

When the 2-year-old interacts with pictures, he takes several steps:

(1) He looks at the picture, hears its name, and says the name.
(2) He confuses the picture with other similar-appearing pictures and the name with other similar-sounding names. He has a discrimination deficit.
(3) When he corrects his errors, lines of the picture and sounds of the words become better defined, and he names the picture correctly more often.
(4) He tries to draw the picture, first by tracing or copying it, and later by drawing it from memory.

These four steps, *(1)* attending, *(2)* confusing and discriminating, *(3)* recognizing, and *(4)* reproducing are illustrated next, as a 2-year-old might follow them in the process of naming and drawing pictures.

ATTENDING

1

The child looks at a picture,
hears its name, and says the name.

[3] Reproduced, with permission, from *Learning to Read and Write: A Task Analysis*, by D. E. P. Smith (New York: Academic Press, 1976).

He looks at a picture,   hears its name,   and says the name.

But, like you and me, 2-year-olds have problems.

Problem

To resolve these problems, he must discover some differences:

(*1*) how the pictured object differs from similar-appearing objects;
(2) how the object's name differs from similar-sounding names.

DISCRIMINATING

2

Objects differ from similar objects. Names differ from similar names.

RECOGNIZING

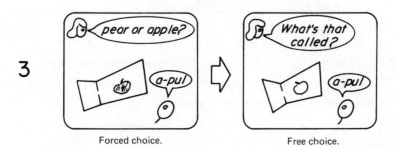

3

Forced choice.   Free choice.

By now, he can name the picture—first, with prompting (given two choices only: **forced choice**); then, without prompting (given unlimited possibilities: **free choice**).

REPRODUCING

4

Drawing by tracing,   by copying,   and from memory.

Finally, he may try drawing the picture, first by tracing or copying, later by drawing from memory.

The four steps taken to learn pictures and names are basically the same steps taken to learn reading and writing, and just about everything else that involves language:

Step 1 Looking at a picture, hearing its name, and repeating the name—we have called **attending** (or **attention**).

Step 2 Discovering ways pictures and the sounds of names differ from similar pictures and names—we have called **discriminating** (or **discrimination**).

Step 3 Naming the picture in a free choice situation—we have called **recognizing** (or **recognition**).

Step 4 Drawing a picture, from memory—we have called **reproducing** (or **reproduction**).

These steps are called by many different names:

Attending—listening to, looking at, observing, noticing, viewing, echoing, miming, surveying, imitating.

Discriminating—identifying, searching, matching, matching to sample.

Recognizing—knowing, naming, identifying, understanding, "reading."

Reproducing—drawing, writing, speaking, spelling,

B. Reading and Writing Words

When a child learns to read and to write a word, he carries out the same steps—and in this order.

1. HE ATTENDS TO THE WORD

Auditory		Visual	
He listens to the sound.	He mimics the sound.	He looks at the word.	He traces the word.

2. HE DISCRIMINATES THE WORD
Auditory

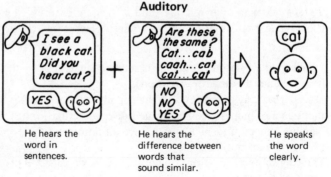

He hears the word in sentences.

He hears the difference between words that sound similar.

He speaks the word clearly.

Visual

| He finds the word in sentences. | He sees the differences between words that look similar. | He copies the word. |

To take step 3, the child must have taken steps 1 and 2 with these words: *cat, dog, I am a cat, I am a dog, I, am, a.* In step 3, hearing is viewed as auditory input, saying as auditory output.

3. HE RECOGNIZES THE WORD

Auditory in, Visual out   **Visual in, Auditory out**

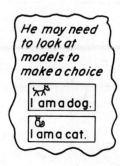

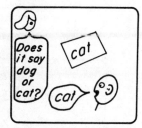

He sees and recognizes the word (as a picture) when he hears its name (forced choice).

He hears and recognizes the name of the word when he sees its picture (forced choice).

Visual and Auditory Matching

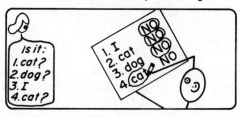

Reading

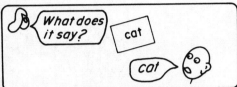

Free choice: silent reading test   Free choice: oral reading test

The reading shown here is the simplest form, the recognition of **sight words,** that is, words that do not require sounding out.

4. HE REPRODUCES THE WORD

He says the names of the letters in the word and draws them.

He reads the word to check his spelling.

Notice that in order to write (or spell) a word, it is helpful for the child to say letter names. He must be able to read and write (or draw) letters. But simply to read the word, he does not need to know his letters.

C. Decoding

Some may argue that knowing sight words is word calling rather than reading, and that the child may not really understand what he is reading. But recognizing sight words and responding to sentences consisting of sight words is actually a major step in learning to read. Most children need to master between 50 and 100 sight words in order to take the next major step, reading sentences containing unfamiliar words, words needing **decoding**.

Sight words are needed for at least three reasons:

(*1*) Such words as *of, the, was, which, after,* and *then*—a group of about 200 words that **connect** nouns and verbs and phrases and clauses—make up about 70% of the text of primary readers. These **function words** must be recognized quickly during reading in order to provide a context for the 3000 or more unknown words (Dolch, 1945).

(*2*) Many function words resist sounding out because they are phonemically irregular—they do not follow the rules of phonics. They are more easily learned as sight words.

(*3*) **Phonic chunks**, consonant–vowel combinations that have about the same sound in many different words, are used in sounding out words. The *ca* and the *at* in *cat* are chunks. These chunks or sound–symbol regularities are most easily used as tools when they are located **within** known words. So sight words can be used to teach the chunks of phonics. (Teachers call these chunks **phonograms** or **spelling patterns**.)

D. Decoding: Sounding Out and Context Guessing

Children learn many sight words by themselves, but sight words are not enough. Their acquisition by the learner is too slow to handle the 200,000 or more words in our language. The child is capable of using problem-solving strategies to unlock or decode printed words he does not recognize.

1. HE USES THE CONTEXT TO GENERATE POSSIBILITIES

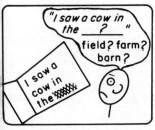  

He uses the context to generate possible words.

He identifies a phonogram (chunk) and tries to match its sound with the sounds within the possibles.

He distorts the sound of the phonogram and finally achieves a match.

The context provides syntactic clues (*I saw a cow in the___* requires a noun) and semantic clues (*a cow in the___* requires the name of a place where one would expect to find a cow). Using the clues, the child generates possible words.

Next, he identifies a part of the unrecognized word, usually the initial phonogram. He tries matching the sound of the initial phonogram with the initial sounds of his generated words. A match allows him to continue reading.

Sometimes the context provides so little information for generating possibilities that the child will use the initial phonogram for generating.

2. HE USES A PHONOGRAM TO GENERATE POSSIBILITIES

| He meets an unre-
cognized word and finds
no context clues. | He identifies the first
phonogram (*hor*)
and generates words. | He identifies the last
apparent phonogram
(*ed*), and the sentence
makes no sense. | He identifies the last
phonogram (*fied*) and
produces a distortion,
recognizable as an
appropriate word. |

Decoding the unrecognized word proves too much for many children. To carry out this step, the child must be able to do the following:

(1) Use an average speaking vocabulary and recognize synonyms.

(2) Discriminate letters and letter names.

(3) Generate words as follows:

    (a) Given a syntactic signal requiring a noun or a verb or an adjective or an adverb, produce several words of the specified kind. For example, *He drove the car* (adverb).

    (b) Given a semantic signal requiring particular classes of words, produce several words that make sense.

    (c) Given a visual symbol (letter, letter group), produce a corresponding sound. Given a sound within a word, produce several words containing that sound in the same position (initial, medial, final).

    (d) Given a word, search it for the following parts: *(i)* known whole words (e.g., *play*ground); *(ii)* known beginnings or endings (e.g., *un*forgive*able*); *(iii)* known phonograms (e.g., h*arvest*).

(4) Recognize common words on hearing distorted versions of them, such as occur when sounding out. For example, *horfied.*

(5) Use all these skills alone or in combination, as required, when faced with an unknown word.

This is a formidable list of skills. Most phonics systems used in schools devote most of their attention to item *3, c,* and somewhat less to item *3, d.* However, to be successful in reading, the child needs **all** these skills.

E. Reading and Writing Letters

PROBLEMS

The basic building blocks of reading and writing are obviously the letters of the alphabet. Problems that arise in mastering them are numerous.

Lack of meaning. Most children can learn to name five to seven letters by rote. After that, the information load is too great. The letters become confused with one another. Confusion can be reduced by adding meaning. For example, if a letter is part of a word, the letter can be more easily identified (*TV, Kay*). Techniques that add meaning to letters facilitate learning by reducing confusion.

Size of the domain. We think of the alphabet as having 26 letters. In fact, it has at least 104 letters:

(1)	Manuscript, small	26
(2)	Manuscript, capital	26
(3)	Cursive, small	26
(4)	Cursive, capital	26
		104

In addition, there are variations in size of type and type style (e.g., italics). And, finally, there are many symbols, other than letters, that are similar enough to be confused with them:

$$0 \quad 1 \quad 2 \quad 3 \quad 4 \quad 7 \quad \$ \quad \cent \quad \# \quad * \quad ! \quad \& \quad \flat$$

Subtlety of differences. Look at the following letters and note the discriminanda (points of difference):

$$\boxed{a\ d}\quad\boxed{h\ n}\quad\boxed{c\ e}\quad\boxed{v\ y}\quad\boxed{d\ b}\quad\boxed{p\ q}\quad\boxed{u\ n}$$

These, then, are the kinds of problems facing the child—the sheer number of letters to be identified and named, the number of variations and of similar symbols with which they may be confused, the subtlety of the visual differences, and their lack of meaning.

WHAT MUST BE LEARNED?

Children must handle tasks like these:

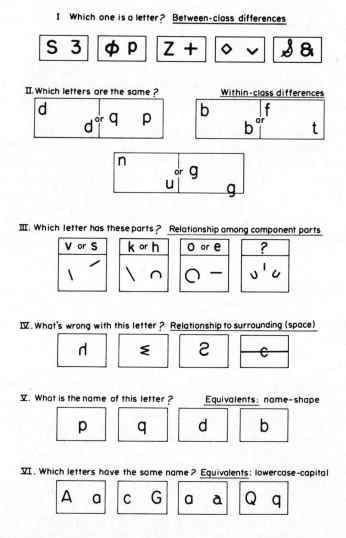

The learnings tested by these tasks are often called **perceptual learnings** and the child who has difficulty with them is often called **perceptually handicapped**. In fact, most of the items are visual discrimination tasks. If a child has difficulty with them, it may be accurately stated that **he has yet to make those distinctions**. That is, he has yet to respond consistently to these differences in letters.

(It does not necessarily mean that he is dyslexic, neurologically impaired, hypothyroid, or strabismic.)

Complete mastery of letters consists of the following:

(*1*) Naming all capital and small letters when shown examples of them, alone and in words
(*2*) Drawing legible letters when given only the letter names

Normally, complete mastery occurs toward the end of second grade.

The hardest tasks of all are naming letters and drawing letters. Naming letters requires, first, that the letter forms be clearly discriminated from one another (*d, b; n, u*); second, that their names be discriminated from one another (notice how similar these names are: *bee, dee, pee, vee*); third and finally, the name of the letter and the form of the letter must be associated.

Reading teachers would add another task to this list, straightening out the nearly universal problem called **reversal**. Reasons for reversals and a corrective technique will be discussed along with writing, in Chapter 7.

Summary

Reading has been pictured as a process by which printed messages become spoken messages. The learning-to-read process includes attending to graphic and to phonological signals, discriminating from one another similar appearing and similar sounding stimuli, recognizing a picture or word when hearing its name, and recognizing a name when seeing a picture or word representing it.

Children need to recognize common words on sight and to sound out less common words. A host of auditory and visual skills are required.

Finally, reading skills probably benefit from writing skills. At least, in the case of reversible letters, their shapes are not well recognized until children learn to draw them.

*   *   *   *   *

To learn a powerful technique for improving reading skill, read Module 4, The Talking Dictionary.

MODULE 4
The Talking Dictionary[4]

Purpose

This module is designed to train reading teachers to do an oral reading exercise, the Talking Dictionary.

Objectives

(*1*) Write the procedural steps in the Talking Dictionary.
(*2*) Given student responses during the Talking Dictionary, write the appropriate teacher response.
(*3*) Given a selection of data gathered during the Talking Dictionary, use the appropriate data to construct a feedback system.
(*4*) Construct a form for collecting data during the Talking Dictionary.

Directions

(*1*) Locate the criterion test at the end of this module (p. 210). Do it now. (If you are unable to respond to the test, go to step 4.)
(*2*) Score the test.
(*3*) If you scored 100% on the test, go on to the next section of the book (p. 213).
(*4*) If your score is less than 100%, complete this module.
(*5*) Take the test again after you complete the module.
(*6*) Score the test.
(*7*) If your score is less than 100%, recycle through the module.

Introduction

The Talking Dictionary is a corrective reading technique, an oral reading exercise designed to help the student improve his **reading rate**, his **word attack skills**, and his **sight vocabulary**. During the exercise, the student reads the same selection three times. This procedure gives the student the opportunity to use words he missed in previous trials.

The Talking Dictionary is a proven technique. It works. It can be done by a

---

[4] By Richard Ballard. Reproduced by arrangement with the author. (The original version has been modified to allow inclusion without use of an audiotape.)

student with a teacher, teacher-aide, or student-teacher serving as the listener. To learn how to do the Talking Dictionary, go to the next section.

I. Assessment and Placement

Determine the student's current reading level. You can use several assessment procedures for determining a student's current reading level.

> Check the one in each of the following two groups that would be more likely to give you information from which you could select books for the student to read:
>
> 1. a. ___ The reading section of the Wide Range Achievement Test (WRAT)
>   b. ___ Parent comments about the student's reading ability
> 2. a. ___ Information from the student's eye doctor
>   b. ___ An informal reading inventory

After you have obtained information that tells you what the student's current reading level is, you must **select books for the student to read**. Select **two** things for the student to read. The selections should (*1*) be **below** the student's current reading level, and (*2*) be of interest to the student.

> 3. Given the following student, check the two items on the list that would be most likely to be appropriate for the Talking Dictionary. Student? Male, age 9, WRAT score 2.8.
>   a. ___ *Wheels* from the *Checkered Flag* series; grade level, 2.4
>   b. ___ *Your Community and Mine*; grade level, 3.0
>   c. ___ *Reader's Digest Skill Builder*; grade level, 2.1
>   d. ___ *Exploring Science*; grade level, 3.1

Rule: The first things the teacher must do are (*1*) assess the student's current reading level and (*2*) select two items for the student to read.

II. The Listener's Role

Give the student a choice of which of the two selections he wishes to read. You could say, "John, you are going to read to me. Which of these two things would you like to use when you read to me?"

Explain the rules of the Talking Dictionary to the student after he has selected a book. The rules are

(1) The student has 1 minute to look over the material and ask for any words he does not know. (The warm-up period.)

(2) The student will read aloud for 3 minutes.

(3) When the student comes to a word he does not know, he is to say, "What's that word?"

(4) The listener will tell the student the requested word.

---

4. Given the following situations, which would be the correct response for the listener to make?

    a. ___ Sentence reads: *The dog is black*.
        Student says, "The dog is b . . . b . . . What's that word?"
        Listener says, "Black."

    b. ___ Sentence reads: *The dog is black*.
        Student says, "The dog is b . . . b . . .
        Listener says, "Sound it out."

Check the correct listener response in each of the following situations:

5. Student mispronounces word but does not ask for the word.
    a. ___ Listener supplies the word.
    b. ___ Listener makes no response.

6. Student omits word.
    a. ___ Listener makes no response.
    b. ___ Listener points out word skipped.

7. Student asks for a word.
    a. ___ Listener supplies requested word.
    b. ___ Listener says, "Sound it out."

8. Student reads without expression.
    a. ___ Listener makes no comment.
    b. ___ Listener tells student to read like he was telling someone the story.

Rule: The **only** appropriate response for the listener to make while the student is reading is the answer to the question, "What's the word?" The listener provides no prompts, asks **no** questions, makes **no** kind of verbal or nonverbal response other than the answer to the question, "What's that word?" while the student is reading.

While the student is reading, the listener must **collect data** to use as feedback for the student. The data that need to be collected are the **number of words read correctly in 3 minutes.** The listener must keep a record of the number of words read correctly in 3 minutes.

---

9. Which of the following would be an easy, efficient way of tallying the number of words read correctly in 3 minutes?

    a. ___ Words read correctly:
        The dog is black.

    b. ___ Words read correctly:
        ////

NOTE: //// = 4
      ⅃⅃ℋ = 5

---

10. Given the following data, complete the following statements:

	1st trial	2nd trial	3rd trial
Words correct	⅃ℋ ⅃ℋ ⅃ℋ ⅃ℋ II	⅃ℋ ⅃ℋ ⅃ℋ ⅃ℋ IIII	⅃ℋ ⅃ℋ ⅃ℋ ⅃ℋ ⅃ℋ III

    a. The student read _____ words correctly on the first trial and _____ words correctly on the second trial.

    b. The student increased the number of words read correctly from _____ words on the first trial to _____ on the third trial.

The student should use the number of words read correctly as feedback on his performance.

The **student** should graph the **highest** number of words read correctly during the activity. This should be the number of words read correctly during any of the three trials. A graph of words read correctly would look like this:

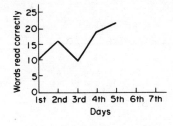

11. The most useful feedback for the student to receive would be
    a. ___ How long he read.
    b. ___ Number of words read correctly.
12. The information to record on the graph is
    a. ___ Highest number of words read correctly on any of the trials.
    b. ___ Grade level of the material read.

13. Given the following data, construct a feedback system for the student:

Day 1:	Correct
1st trial	9
2nd trial	9
3rd trial	10
Day 2:	
1st trial	10
2nd trial	13
3rd trial	18
Day 3:	
1st trial	10
2nd trial	21
3rd trial	15

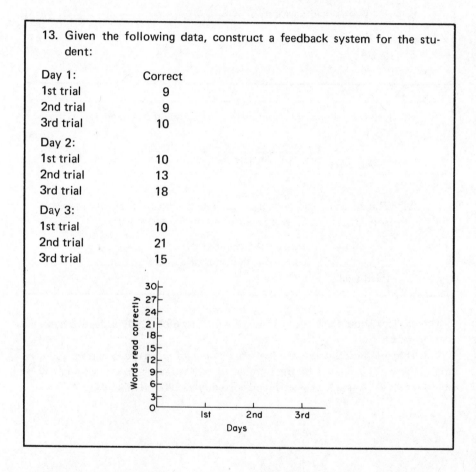

The student should set a goal of how many words he wants to read correctly each day. This goal should be recorded on the graph.

14. Given the following graph, what was the student's first goal? _____ Second goal? _____

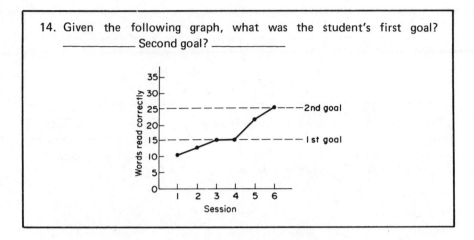

Rule: The listener has two tasks while the student is reading. These are (*1*) to supply words requested, and (*2*) to tally words read correctly.

III. The Talking Dictionary Procedure

The sequence of the steps in the Talking Dictionary begins with the warm-up period. During the warm-up period, the student has 1 minute to look over the material to be read. The student may ask for words he does not know.

After the student has looked over the material for 1 minute, he is to begin reading. The student is to read for 3 minutes.

15. While the student is reading, the listener is to do two things. These are:
   a.
   b.

At the end of the 3 minutes, the listener should do two things:

(*1*) Tell the student how many words he read correctly.

(*2*) Ask the student to set a goal for the next 3-minute period.

After the student sets a goal, the student and listener repeat the Talking Dictionary, reading the **same selection** that was read for the first 3 minutes.

16. At the end of the second 3-minute trial, the listener makes the same two responses he made at the end of the first trial. Those responses are:

a.

b.

The student reads the same selection he read during the first two trials for the third time. Once again, the listener supplies words requested and does the tallying. At the end of the third trial, the student graphs the highest number of words read correctly on any of the three trials.

Sequence:

(*1*) Warm-up time: 1 minute
(*2*) Talking Dictionary time: 3 minutes
(*3*) Talking Dictionary time: 3 minutes
(*4*) Talking Dictionary time: 3 minutes
(*5*) Feedback system

17. The first step is _____ The Talking Dictionary is done _____ times, each trial lasting _____ minutes. The final step in the activity is the _____.

Now, complete the criterion test. (The answer key is on p. 212.)

Criterion Test

1. Before beginning the Talking Dictionary the teacher must do two things:
   a.
   b.
2. The Talking Dictionary includes the following sequence. (List the steps.)
   a.   time: _____
   b.   time: _____
   c.   time: _____
   d.   time: _____
   e.
3. During the Talking Dictionary the listener's tasks are
   a.
   b.
4. The most positive information to use when giving feedback to the student would be _____

5. Given the following situations, what would be the correct listener response:
   a. The sentence reads: *The horse ran fast.*
      The student says, "The h . . . h . . . h . . ."
      The teacher response:
   b. The sentence reads: *The horse ran fast.*
      The student says, "The house ran fast."
      The teacher response:
   c. The sentence reads: *The horse ran fast.*
      The student says, "The h . . . h . . . What's that word?"
      The teacher response:
6. Design a form for collecting data during the Talking Dictionary.

Answer Key for Module 4

1. a
2. b
3. a, c
4. a
5. b
6. a
7. a
8. a
9. b
10. a. 22; 24
    b. 22; 28
11. b
12. a

13.

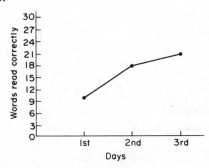

14. 15; 25
15. a. Supply requested words.
    b. Tally words read correctly.
16. a. Tell student how many words he read correctly.
    b. Ask student to set a goal for the next 3-minute period.
17. warm-up; 3; 3; graphing (or feedback)

Answer Key for Criterion Test

1. a. Assess student's reading ability.
   b. Select two things for the student to read.
2. a. Warm-up   Time: 1 minute
   b. Talking Dictionary   Time: 3 minutes
   c. Talking Dictionary   Time: 3 minutes
   d. Talking Dictionary   Time: 3 minutes
   e. Feedback
3. a. Supply requested words.
   b. Tally words read correctly.
4. The highest number of words read correctly during the three trials.
5. a. No response
   b. No response
   c. *Horse*
6. Your form should look something like the following one and **must** contain all
   of its parts.

	1st trial	2nd trial	3rd trial
Words read correctly			

WRITING

An observer of American education will note a trend in writings on curriculum, a tendency first to denigrate certain skills, then to modify the curriculum by reducing emphasis on them.[1] Such has been the case with writing—first, printing; next, cursive writing; then, spelling and punctuation; and finally, creative writing. Sommer (1965) has traced the gradual reduction in time allotted to handwriting instruction. In 1950, virtually 100% of American elementary schools reported spending 15–20 minutes a day in formal writing instruction; in 1960, fewer than 60% reported **any** instruction and those that did had a minimum requirement of 10 minutes per day.

Recently, the chairman of the English department in a distinguished university recommended that the freshman composition course be dropped from the curriculum to make room for the study of literature.

In these cases, apparently good and sound reasons are given for reducing emphasis on writing. On closer analysis, the reasons given seem suspect. It is likely that the reason for the erosion in writing instruction is lack of success in teaching those skills rather than a decreasing importance of the skills themselves.

[1] For example: "Research indicates that the whole-class approach, which dominated handwriting instruction for so many years, may actually be a waste of time for many pupils. This time could be much more profitably spent in some other area of the increasingly crowded curriculum [Burns & Broman, 1975, p. 375]."

Advances in learning technology may reverse the trend. Methods for teaching writing, from single letters to discourse, have been developed in the past 10 years. Contributions by Sommer in cursive writing (1965), by J. M. Smith, in spelling (1972), by Wilhelm (1974) in sentence writing, by Lamberg (1975) and Wolter (1975) in creative writing, all based on information feedback techniques and all successful, open a vista of possibilities for writing instruction. These methods will be detailed in this chapter.

I. The Problems with Writing

As with teaching reading, method of instruction is not by itself the principal cause of writing deficits. Rather, the key problem appears to be in measurement: Without agreed-upon standards of what constitutes acceptable writing (handwriting, creative writing, or whatever), no objective measure can be developed and no information on progress can be made available to learners. What precisely must be learned? And how can one construct an adequate measure of it? We could say, and mean the same thing, **there are no standards of good writing**.

But, the reader may say, of course we have standards. The standard in printing and handwriting is **legibility**; the standard in sentence writing is **communication of ideas**; the standard in creative writing is **good form and cohesiveness**. After all, if standards are defined further than this, we will straitjacket our children. There will be no room for "individual variation." "Handwriting is a personal thing."

But handwriting is **not** a personal thing—it is a public thing. Writing is designed to be read by others. Variations in the form of the message must be suppressed by the receiver so that he can apprehend the content, the meaning. Yes, variations in the content reflect a personal view of the world: That part of the message is what we wish to communicate. But variations in the form constitute "noise" or "static" in the system and interfere with the message.

What we need, then, to improve writing instruction are clear-cut standards and objective measures of them, thus allowing learners to shape themselves into good writing.

II. The Domain of Writing

One may view writing as including skills at the levels of letter, word, sentence, paragraph, and discourse:

- Printing letters or manuscript writing
- Orthography or cursive writing
- Spelling or writing words
- Mechanics or writing sentences

Table 7.1
Components of Training in Writing

Level	Class	Domain	Test
1	Contour	Same as reading plus cursive writing components	
2	Letter	Alphabet (capital and lowercase) Manuscript writing Cursive writing	*STARS* (Letters): Manuscript Tests 1–14, Cursive Tests 1–11
3	Word	Spelling: Coleman list Technical words from content areas Words from student writing	Words: Spelling Tests 1–5 (teacher tests)
4	Sentence	Taking dictation Punctuation Capitalization	Sentence: Dictation Punctuation Capitalization
5	Paragraph	Form convention; Phonological pattern (rhyme alliteration, rhythm) Content: topic, links, information Equivalents: summarization links induction, deduction Impact: point of view	Paragraph: Form convention, Phonological Patterns Topic, Links, Information Summarization, Links, Induction, Deduction Point of view

- Paragraphs or writing paragraphs
- Creative writing (poetry, essay, narrative and so on) (see Table 7.1)

A. Writing as Manuscript Writing

Learning to print letters is quite a formidable problem for young children. Failure to do well is usually attributed to carelessness or to immaturity. "The small muscles in the hands and arms are not well developed or controlled," and so forth. There is virtually no evidence to support the contention of a relationship between motor development and failure to learn printing. On the other hand, there **is** evidence to indicate that the principal component of writing skills is visual form perception.

Studies by Rice (1931), by Melcher (1934), and by Townsend (1951) concur in demonstrating that the visual discrimination component is the major contributor to what appear to be motor learning tasks. Melcher studied the maze learning of young children, and both Rice and Townsend studied form reproduction or copying. Rice trained some children in motor (manual) skills and others in visual skills. Four out of five instances of significant gains in copying forms were those of children given only visual training.

Townsend studied relationships between copying skill on the one hand and **form perception** and **motor skill** on the other. Whereas motor skill correlated with copying to the extent of about +.15, the form perception measure correlated +.60. These values may be translated into proportions of total score variation accounted for by each measure:

Motor skill	3%
Visual skill	36%
Unaccounted for	61%

It seems to be sensible, then, to look to training in form discrimination, that is, in letter matching, as a partial answer to the printing problem.

But there is another problem to be handled: finding one's way around a page full of white space. When Norman printed his name, it looked like this:

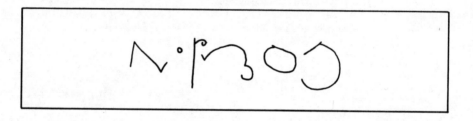

He put his pencil point on the paper. He moved his eyes from that point to some other point, the aiming point or target. His pencil point should follow his eye movement.

But there was no other point on the paper. The closest thing to a point was the edge of the paper. (Note that very young children who "draw-a-man" commonly draw the legs all the way to the bottom of the page.) When he drew the *o* in *Norman*, he had no trouble. The target was his point of origin, which he could see. Thus, he drew a creditable *o*. The *r* is acceptable except for the length of the leg.

If Norman had been able to hallucinate a point and aim for it, his printing would probably have improved. Since the accomplished artist has no difficulty in hallucinating points, we could give Norman art training.

(*1*) **Teach a matrix of points:**

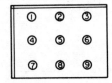

To teach the matrix, it is necessary to discriminate each point from every other one. To do that, look at the next task:

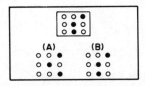

One of the patterns of points (A or B) is similar to the pattern in the top box. The child identifies the pattern (B). In the process, he has discriminated point 8 from point 9. After a series of exercises of this kind, in which every one of the points is discriminated from every other point, we ask the child to draw the matrix. He will do so very creditably. In other words, **he can now hallucinate a matrix of nine points in a square.**

(*2*) **Teach the placement of letters of the alphabet on the matrix:**

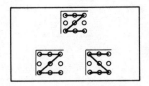

Letters are different in shape because of their relationship to certain points.

(*3*) **Discriminate letters on the matrix:**

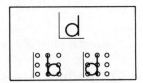

(*4*) Copy letters on the matrix:

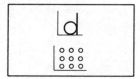

(*5*) Copy letters:

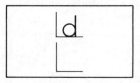

(*6*) Discriminate good letters from poor ones:

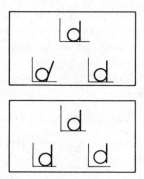

However, instruction is not yet complete. The child still needs a language of letters.

(*7*) **Teach self-evaluation**: When working with kindergarten children, we found that quality of printing tended to be erratic. Given a series of child-drawn letters, the child was perfectly capable of pointing to his good drawings and of rejecting his bad drawings. However, when asked, "What's wrong with this one?" he could not answer. Apparently, he lacked the words to describe his letters.

We then provided instruction in letter contours and gave them names: *straight line, curved line, vertical line, horizontal line, diagonal line, short vertical, long diagonal* and *on the baseline, to the topline, toward the margin line*, and so on. Next followed instruction in what was right about a good letter and what was wrong with a bad letter. Not only were children then able to tell us what was wrong, but they did not need to. They evaluated their own printing without prompting and corrected it before turning it in.

Most manuals on printing and cursive writing will recommend teaching a "direction of drawing," as follows:

The child will comply and will draw an adequate letter. Then he is told, "Draw some more the same way." The usual result will appear as follows:

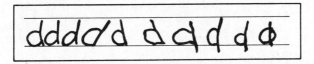

A rapid deterioration will occur. The child is incapable of doing the same movement repeatedly, without variation. One would do well to say nothing about direction of drawing. Simply require that the finished letter meet a standard of correctness.

ELIMINATING REVERSALS

There is a great diversity of opinion about the meaning of letter reversals. Most books on reading discuss the subject, national conferences have focused on it, and theories have been produced by educators, psychologists, neurologists, psychiatrists, optometrists, and ophthalmologists. The reversal is the central characteristic of conditions known as strephosymbolia ("twisted symbols"), dyslexia, alexia, primary psychogenic acathexsis, learning disability, reading disability, and others. These terms may be loosely translated: "He hasn't learned to read yet." This is the position taken by the Secretary of Health, Education, and Welfare's National Advisory Committee on Dyslexia and Related Disorders in 1969 and 1970. In brief, this interdisciplinary group of scholars and researchers eschewed any definition of reading disorder that attempts to specify its cause. They agreed, instead, to emphasize the need for methods to teach reading.

Teachers are well advised to treat reversals as a stage in learning, a point at which the form of the letter is known but its direction is yet to be learned. The simplest technique for facilitating directional learning is to provide paper like this:

Advise the child to start his writing near the double corner. Beyond that aid, he will need to have (*1*) a model alphabet available for comparison, and (*2*) a **language of letter drawing** consisting of these terms:

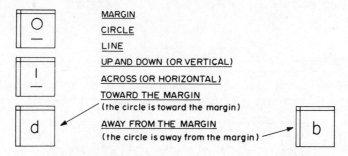

MARGIN
CIRCLE
LINE
UP AND DOWN (OR VERTICAL)
ACROSS (OR HORIZONTAL)
TOWARD THE MARGIN
(the circle is toward the margin)
AWAY FROM THE MARGIN
(the circle is away from the margin)

When a child is having trouble with a letter like *d*, the teacher may say, "*d*—circle toward the margin."

B. *Writing as Cursive Writing*

Problems in cursive writing are similar to those in manuscript writing. Many more points must be learned. Sommer developed a training program and a handwriting scale (1965). Some of her frames are reproduced here:[2]

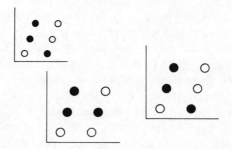

[2] Reproduced, with permission, from *Cursive Writing*, by B. Sommer (Ann Arbor, Mich.: Ann Arbor Publishers, 1965).

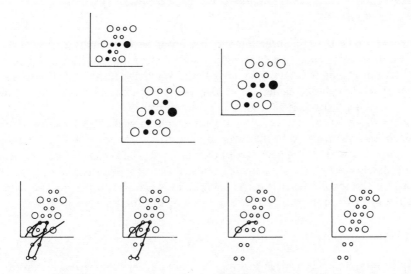

In her validation study, second grade children required 4 weeks at 15 minutes per day to achieve fourth grade proficiency. Control children showed small gains. Results of this magnitude are unusual in instructional methodology. Yet the technique, available for some 10 years, is virtually unknown. Two reasons for failure to adopt the procedure suggest themselves. First, the training material looks unusual. It is not immediately apparent that such training might make a difference to handwriting. Second, the dominant explanation of poor writing is immature muscle development, rather than visual discriminative skill, despite strong evidence for the latter explanation. Perhaps the adoption of criterion-referenced measures of cursive writing will place a premium on effective training techniques. If so, the method is available to those who wish to increase the efficiency of writing instruction.

C. Writing as Spelling

Organisms expend as much energy as is required to achieve goals.[3] Children will spell as well as they must to satisfy the standard established and enforced by the teacher. It might be enough to say only this in order to handle the spelling problem. Enforcement of standards by teachers should result in improved spelling. But there are some particular problems that cause trouble for young children and for a minority of older children and adults.

[3] This statement is based upon J. J. Gibson's discrimination rule: "... only the information required to identify a thing economically tends to be picked up from a complex of stimulus information [1966, p. 286]."

A PREREQUISITE SKILL

In our attempts to engineer spelling mastery in second-semester first graders, we were for some time singularly unsuccessful. After numerous futile attempts, we became aware of a missing ingredient. We had taught children to read **without teaching letter names**. Why? Because it was unnecessary to know letter names in order to read: letter sounds, yes—letter names, no.

But without letter names, children were unable to spell. The reason is simple enough, in retrospect. Note that, when you spell a difficult word, you dictate to yourself. As I write, I can hear myself dictate words and syllables. For a difficult word, like *hemorrhage*, I dictate and visualize, also distorting the word by sounding the second (silent) *h*. As soon as we were able to teach letter names (itself a difficult problem), problems in teaching spelling were resolved easily.

LEARNING TO SPELL

By learning to spell, I mean learning certain strategies for viewing a word that is to be spelled. The process is described at length in Volume 4. I shall summarize the paradigm here.

Step 1 Discriminate the word from other words that sound or look like the word.

Model	*onomatopoeia*
Task	
Circle the right word:	*omnipotent omniscient onomatopoeia*

Step 2 Identify all parts (letters and phonograms).

Model	*onomatopoeia*
Task	
Circle the letters in order:	*a o t n g c o n m g a f t o g d p o c e j t i a*

Task

Circle the syllables: om   on   onom   a   o   mat   matto   poeia

Step 3 Produce the parts of the word.

Model   *onomatopoeia*

Task

Complete:

onomatopoe_   onomato_ia
onomat_poeia   ono_opoeia
on_matopoeia   _matopoeia

Step 4 Discriminate the word from misspellings.

Model   *onomatopoeia*

Task

Find the word three times:

onomatopoeia   onomatapoeia   onomatopoeia
onnomatopoeia   onomatopoeia   omnoatopoeia
onamatapoeia   onomatopoea

Step 5 Produce the order of the parts.

Model   *onomatopoeia*

Task
Write the word

m   p   o   t   a   n   o   i   o   e   a   o

This procedure, called the **Michigan Spelling Algorithm**, has been used to produce instructional materials in both elementary and high schools.

A "starter" package was used by 24 second grade children to study 21 animal names. A recognition test of spelling gave a preinstruction score of 64.8% and a postinstruction score of 88.6%. Twelve of the children were able to respond to a dictated test: preinstruction score, 47.1%; postinstruction score, 90.5%.

In this study, one condition of instruction was not met. To ensure 95% mastery, learners must be required to achieve a perfect score on each unit before continuing to the next unit. The teacher did not fulfill that condition.

Steslicki (1967) reported the achievement of 100 tenth grade students on 48 words most commonly misspelled by high school and college students. On a dictated test, a preinstruction score of 50.0% was achieved; following instruction, the average score was 95.1%.

The spelling algorithm follows certain analytic steps that good spellers use. More important, it **controls attention** while the child is learning. Once more, this paradigm is not enough, by itself, to teach a word.

A MASTERY STANDARD

One of the most common questions asked by teachers about any method of teaching spelling is this: "Yes, but will he remember it?" And the answer is *no*!

Let us, for the moment, forget memory. Assume that, if the child spells a word correctly under a given set of conditions, he will continue to spell it correctly—if those conditions can be met. But they never can be met: The light will be different, the page will be different, the pencil will be different, and the child will be different.

In effect, a word must be spelled correctly under many different conditions—sentence contexts, dictation, copy editing, and so on—before it will reliably be spelled correctly. Therefore, we are always learning to spell words. And we should not be upset if a child spells a word wrong on occasion. Rather, such errors provide opportunities for teaching.

What we must do, however, is require mastery—the word must be spelled correctly before the paper is accepted.

D. Writing as Mechanics

The conventions constituting rules for punctuation and capitalization overwhelm one by their complexity, unless they are used constantly. By and large, children do not write often enough to master these intricacies, and for good reason: Teachers do not have that much time to read and feed back information.

If mastery of mechanics is a goal, and I see no reason why it should not be, teachers need some efficient techniques for providing instruction.

One procedure is to develop copy-editing tasks, as described in Volume 4. Such tasks will not only teach the conventions, but they will also increase the power of the child to express his thoughts by providing sentence structures not found in ordinary conversation.

Another procedure found to be very powerful is the controlled feedback found in the module, The Writing Dictionary.

Also, the sentence level tests of *STARS* can be used. These tests include the total domain of competencies in the test subsets of dictation, capitalization, and punctuation.

E. Writing as Composition

Two authors (Lamberg, 1975; Wolter, 1975) who have surveyed attempts to improve writing instruction have been led to the same conclusion—that techniques used to improve writing have one of two results: They either have no measurable effect or they have a measurable negative effect. The venerable technique of **grading papers** seems to be the worst offender. **Discussion followed by rewriting** is about as effective as simply having students write without feedback: i.e., no effect.

In other aspects of writing, learning increased rapidly when students were fed back information on (*1*) closeness to standards and (*2*) progress toward a goal of mastery. Those results led Lamberg and, later, Wolter, to apply positive feedback procedures to instruction in narrative writing for sixth and seventh grade students. Lamberg provided self-instructional material on how to write narratives, i.e., the standards by which narrative writing is judged. He demonstrated improvements in both quantity and quality of writing over several weeks.

Wolter carried the work further. He made it possible for children to apply standards to their own writing immediately after completing a narrative—and demonstrated increases in quality and quantity on the very next production. Wolter's "mini-program" for narratives follows.[4] Learners chart two scores, Quantity (section A) and Quality (section B).

STUDENT WRITING TASK

Instructions:

Write a true story about an interesting incident or event that happened to you. Write on one side of the paper. Use as many pieces of paper as you want. You have 35 minutes to finish your story.

When you finish your real life short story, turn to the *Real Life (Autobiographical) Checklist* and evaluate your story.

[4] Adapted, with permission, from Wolter (1975).

[blank box]

Real Life (Autobiographical) Short Story Checklist

_____
Name

   Now that you've written your story, you will see how to check it. By answering the questions that follow, you can see how **complete** and **detailed** a story is.

   First, read and score the sample story at the end of this checklist. The directions below will tell you what to do.

A. How many words in the story?
   Put the number in the box.

[ ] Box A

B. See how well the story answers these questions. Put the points for each question in the box.

   1. *What was it about?*
      a. Did it tell about one experience? [ ]
         Then give 2 points.
      b. Did it happen in 1 day or less? [ ]
         Then give 2 points.
      c. Did it happen to "I" or "I" and [ ]
         someone else ("we")?
         Then give 2 points.
   Add the boxes.

   [ ] → [ ] Box 1

2. *What happened?*

Give 1 point for each thing that happened. (Stop counting if you get 10.)

☐ Box 2

Check your scoring with the answers:

Sample story answers

Total words 62 Box A

B. 1. *What was it about?*
   a. 2
   b. 1
   c. 2
   5   5 Box 1

   2. *What happened?* 4   Box 2 (If you count 5, that could be right also.)

---

3. *Why did it happen?*

Reasons or causes that tell why are often signaled by words like *since, because, so*.

☐ Box 3

Give 1 point each time you see these words. (Stop if you get 5 points.)

4. *Who did it happen to?*

Each piece of information about the main person like *name, age, appearance, relationship with others*.

☐ Box 4

Give 1 point for each. (Stop if you get 5 points.)

5. *Who else was involved?*

Each piece of information that tells some person's relationship to the main person, or tells of an action done by that other person.

☐ Box 5

Give 1 point for each. (Stop if you get 2 points.)

6. *When did it happen?*

a. Time words like *morning, night, day, evening, 10 o'clock, 5 minutes*.

☐

b. Also time signal words like *when, after, later, before, soon.*

Give 1 point for each.

Add the boxes. (Stop at 5 points.)

Box 6

Check your scoring with the answers:

B. 3. *Why did it happen?*   1   Box 3

4. *Who did it happen to?*   2   Box 4 (1 point could be right also)

5. *Who else was involved?*   2   Box 5 (1 point could be right also)

6. *When did it happen?*

a.   2
    0
_____
  2   2   Box 6

7. *Where did it happen?*

Give 1 point for each detail about the place where the story happened. (Up to 5 points.)

Box 7

NOW ADD POINTS IN BOXES 1 TO 7. TOTAL: Box B

Check your scoring with the answer:

B. 7. *Where did it happen?*   1   Box 7

TOTAL POINTS,
BOXES 1–7   17   Box B

Sample Story

This happened last summer while my frield and I were in camp. We were hiking and we found a friend. Her name was Kim. Kim told us a lot of stories which we knew were not true at all. We decided to walk her back to her camp. Kim didn't know where her camp was, so we had to walk around till evening.

Wolter's mini-program is deceptively simple. The characteristics of a narrative used for assessing quality are the result of a painstaking search for agreement in the literature on creative writing by both Lamberg and Wolter. Those characteristics are as follows: definition of character(s), relationship among characters, description of event(s), motive, time, and setting.

After this task analysis, Wolter developed his program, tried it out with members of a target group, revised it on the basis of student errors, tried it again, and so on, until it worked.

The task analysis can be simplified by using *STARS* paragraph- and book-level tests to identify necessary skill components. It seems very likely that such efforts will have a substantial effect on student writing skill.

* * * * *

We have reviewed, in this and preceding chapters, the domains of skills in reading, writing, listening, and speaking. Some little-known techniques for teaching may be gleaned by reviewing these chapters. Perhaps, more important, the interrelatedness of the skills, as well as the lawfulness of the processes by which the skills are mastered, will become apparent.

* * * * *

We turn now to methods of teaching, reading, and writing: tutorial (Chapter 8), basal reader (Chapter 9), an individualized, language experience, or combined method (Chapter 10), and programmed or computer presentations (Chapter 11). Each method will be described and assessed against the requirements of an adaptive classroom so that missing characteristics may be added. (Before proceeding, complete Modules 5 and 6.)

MODULE 5
Teaching the Picture and Text Survey[5]

Purpose

This module is designed to train a teacher to teach the survey or question-directed reading technique. The technique has a number of applications but its primary purpose is to develop comprehension skills.

[5] By Walter Lamberg and Richard Ballard. Reprinted by arrangement with the authors.

Objectives

At the completion of this module the teacher will

(*1*) Write the instructions for each step of the survey technique.
(*2*) Use the survey technique on material designed for a target student.
(*3*) Describe the instructional plan that provides for
   • setting objectives
   • teaching a strategy for predicting questions
   • modeling responses
   • reinforcing responses
   • modifying instruction

Directions

(*1*) Locate the test for this module (below). Look through the test. If you can respond to all questions, take the test and score it against the answer key on p. 231. If you score less than 100%, go to step 2.
(*2*) Complete the module.
(*3*) Take the test after completing the module.

Materials

(*1*) A text for a target student. If you are a teaching or tutoring, select a text you might use with your student(s), such as a textbook, reader, or magazine. If you are not teaching at present, select your text from some reading you are doing now, for example, textbooks you are using in some courses or magazines.
(*2*) A picture. Choose the picture on the same basis as you chose the text. (You could use a picture in a textbook.)

Criterion Test

Task 1—Conducting a Pretest

Write out the instructions you would give a student in pretesting him on the steps in the Picture Survey.

Step 1

Step 2

Step 3

Step 4

Go on to the next part of the test.

Given: You gave a pretest for the Picture Survey to a student. The picture was of a small boy who was riding a pony. The only response the student made was to predict one question: "What is he riding?"

Task 2—Setting Objectives

Write an objective for the student for his first lesson in the Picture Survey.

Task 3—Teaching a Strategy for Predicting Questions

Describe a strategy you could teach to the student to help him predict more questions.

Task 4—Modeling

Describe and give examples of how you would model the behavior of predicting questions.

Task 5—Reinforcement

Describe a feedback form for reinforcing the student's question-predicting responses.

Task 6—Modifying Instruction

If the student failed to meet the objective you set (see task 2), what is one way you could modify your instruction? Describe the modification.

Answer Key for Criterion Test

Task 1

Step 1 The first step is to survey this picture so that you can answer the question, What is it about? You'll have 1 minute.

Step 2 Write a summary that answers the question, What is it about? You'll have 2 minutes.

Step 3 Write questions that might be asnwered in the picture. You'll have 2 minutes.

Step 4 Write answers to the questions you just wrote. You'll have 5 minutes.

Task 2

The student will predict at least two questions.

Task 3

Provide the six question words as a stimulus for generating questions.

Task 4

a. By reinforcing approximations.
b. By providing visual and auditory cues (say the question word—write it on the board).
c. By asking questions that use the words.
d. By providing the question word in writing with a blank for the student to complete the question.

Task 5

The form should have spaces for the student to check off each step in the survey as he completes the step. It should also have a space for setting objectives.

Task 6

a. By providing a model of a specific question.
b. By having the student set a goal in terms of questions.

Introduction

The Text Survey and Picture Survey are techniques for developing comprehension skills. The two techniques are essentially the same with one difference: The Text Survey uses a printed passage, whereas the Picture Survey uses a picture.

The techniques can be used with students of any age and any ability (including nonreaders). The techniques can be adapted to any type of reading material and to numerous reading skills, from reading sentences to study-reading textbooks.

The essence of the technique is that it provides for question-directed reading.

I. What You Should Do
   A. Doing the Picture Survey
   B. Applying the Technique
   C. Doing the Text Survey
   D. Applying the Technique
II. What Did You Do? Why Did You Do It? (Review, Explanation, and Rationale of the Technique)
III. From Picture Survey to Text Survey (When to Teach Which Technique)
IV. Teaching the Survey
   A. Assessment (Pretesting)
   B. Setting Objectives
   C. Providing Instruction (Treatment)

I. What You Should Do

A. Doing the Picture Survey

Descriptive Statement. You will be surveying a picture. You will be asked to predict five questions that might be answered in the picture.

INSTRUCTIONS

1. Survey (look at) the following picture to find the answer to the question: What is the picture about?

2. Write a summary that answers the question: What is the picture about? (Don't look back at the picture.)

3. Using your summary and any other information you picked up from the picture, predict at least five specific questions that might be answered in the picture. (Don't look back at the picture.)

   a.

   b.

   c.

   d.

   e.

Answers

2. Here are three possible summary statements:

   What Was It About?

   a. The picture is about two guys shooting at each other.

   b. It was about a duel.

   c. Two men were having a duel in the park. One man shot the other man.

3. Here are some possible questions that might have been predicted:

   a. Who is in the picture?

   b. What are the men doing?

   c. Why are they shooting at each other?

   d. When did it happen?

   e. Where did it happen?

   f. How many men are in the picture?

4. Predict answers. Without looking back at the picture, predict—guess—the answers to the questions **you** wrote. Write the answers below:

   a.

   b.

   c.

   d.

   e.

Compare your answers to your summary. Notice that your answers provide more specific information than your summary. Now look at the five questions you wrote. Compare them to the question, What was the picture about? Circle the correct response in each of the statements below.

5. The question, What is it about? is—more general/more specific—than your five questions. (Circle one.)

6. Your five questions are—more general/more specific—than the question, What is it about? (Circle one.)

B. Applying the Technique

Task: Select a picture to use for a picture survey. (Hint: A picture that has one central idea and some action is a good choice.) Do all the steps in a picture survey:

1. Survey by looking at the picture. (Check when completed.)

2. Summary.

3. Predict questions.
    a.
    b.
    c.
    d.
    e.

4. Predict answers.
    a.
    b.
    c.
    d.
    e.

A picture survey is the first step in teaching students to read textbooks, magazines, newspapers, etc. and to process information from what they read. Students, once they have mastered the skills in the picture survey, must learn to transfer the skills to their textbooks. The next section of this module deals with the survey with written material. Go to the next section, now. (NOTE: You will need the textbook or magazine you selected.)

C. Doing the Text Survey

Descriptive Statement. You will be surveying a passage to predict specific questions that might be answered in the passage.

INSTRUCTIONS

1. Survey the passage below. Look through it as fast as you can to find out what it is about. Don't worry about the details; just get a general idea.

THE AMERICAN REVOLUTION

Would there be war? The question on the minds of every American colonists was to be answered that fateful morning of April 19, 1775. At 3:00 that morning, near Boston, British soldiers, who had occupied Boston since 1774, were engaged in battle by the minutemen. Those American colonists, long chafing under the arrogance of the British occupation forces, had gathered at Lexington. Rumors followed of a possible British military action. Some spoke of a concerted drive in Boston to root out the revolutionaries, of house-by-house searches. Others warned that more British soldiers would be landing at Boston and that the occupation would be extended to all surrounding communities. Those with more reliable information were convinced that the British action would be smaller, but no less significant. It was believed that the British planned to seek out and destroy arms and ammunition stored by the revolutionaries in Concord.

On an ironically pleasant, peaceful morning, the British force moved out of Boston, 700 well-trained, well-disciplined regulars. The colonists were ready; they were warned by William Dawes and Paul Revere. The colonists were ready, but at first greatly outnumbered. With the first firing, it appeared this initial engagement might be the last. Then, as more and more colonists joined in the battle, the fortunes of the British quickly and dramatically changed. What appeared an easy victory turned into a clear-cut defeat for the British, as they were driven back to Boston. The original force of colonists eventually doubled in size, then tripled in size. The British were saved only by the arrival of reinforcements.

The shots heard round the world echoed into May, with the Battle of Bunker Hill, then into June, with the battle at Ticonderoga.

2. Summarize. Write a summary (at least one sentence) that answers the question below:

   What is it about?

3. Predict questions. Using your summary, any other information you picked up from the text, and your past experience with the subject of the text, predict at least five specific questions that might be answered in the text. Don't look back at the text. (If you know for sure that a question is answered in the text, great! Write it down anyway. If you have a question but don't know the answer, write the question anyway.)

   a.

   b.

> c.
> d.
> e.

Answers

2. Here are three possible summary statements:

What is it about?

   a. The passage is about the American Revolution.
   b. The passage is about the start of the American Revolution.
   c. The American Revolutionary War began with the fighting in New England.

3. Here are possible questions that might be predicted:

   a. When did the first battle start? (the date)
   b. Where did the first fighting occur? (city)
   c. What happened to the British?
   d. Why did the colonists engage the British in battle?
   e. Who warned the colonists?
   f. How did the colonists defeat the British?
   g. How many British soldiers were there?

> 4. Predict answers. Without looking at the text, predict—guess—at the answers to your questions. Write your answers here.
>
>   a.
>   b.
>   c.
>   d.
>   e.

NOTE: Compare your answers to your summary statement. Notice that your five answers are more specific than your summary statement. Compare your five questions to the question, What is it about? Which is/are more specific? Circle one:

- What is it about? (more general/more specific).
- Your five questions? (more general/more specific).

> 5. Confirm answers. Now go back to the text and read it quickly just to confirm (or check) your answers. Make any additions, revisions, corrections that are needed in your answers from the information you pick up by rereading the article quickly.

D. Applying the Technique

Task: Do a complete survey using a chapter of the textbook or an article in the magazine you selected for your target student.

1. Survey.

2. Summary.

3. Predict questions (without looking at text).
   a.
   b.
   c.
   d.
   e.
4. Predict answers.
   a.
   b.
   c.
   d.
   e.
5. Confirm answers. (If your answer was correct, place a check beside the letter. Write any revisions, additions, or corrections.)
   a.
   b.
   c.
   d.
   e.

II. What Did You Do?
Why Should You Do It?

What Did You Do?

There are many variations of the survey technique, but the heart of the technique is in these two steps: surveying and predicting questions. Some people say that surveying is a kind of reading; some people say it is simply looking. Some have called the survey step a *preview, prereading*, a *sizing up*, or an *advance organizer*. Those terms suggest what is important about surveying—that is, what the reader **does**. What the reader does is to give himself a general idea of what is in a passage (or chapter or book): what the subject is and how it is organized, an answer to the question, What is it about?

Why Should You Do That?

700 Britishers   April, 1775   Concord   defeated

Those pieces of information make sense to you because you have a general idea of the subject—the beginning of the American Revolutionary War. The human mind needs a "box"—a category, a frame, an organizer, in which to put specific details. Without the general idea, the details are not processed by the mind, are not comprehended.

Then What Did You Do?

You summarized. Your summary statement was the product of your surveying, a record in writing of what you got out of the text while surveying.

Why Should You Summarize?

Surveying is a covert behavior. It happens inside your head, hidden from others and maybe from yourself as well. By writing or uttering a summary statement, you make an overt behavior that serves as a representation of your covert behavior. It's the difference between feeling that you got something out of the passage (or that you didn't) and having a bit of concrete evidence of just what you did or didn't get. An overt response can be measured, evaluated, and brought under control by the responder.

Then What Did You Do?

Once you had that general idea, you went to the specific information. The general idea—your summary statement—was a response to a general question, What was it about? So, the specific information would come as responses to specific questions—*who, what, why, when, how, where, how many*. In a sense, you broke that general question, What was it about?, into a set of more specific questions.

If you knew a good deal of American history, your questions might have been highly specific, as you called upon your previous experience: Why did the British go to Concord? How many British soldiers were there? What prevented a total defeat by the British? (Note how much information is in the questions themselves.)

If you did not know too much history, you might have relied on the five interrogatives: What happened? Why did it happen? Who was involved? When did it happen? Where did it happen? How did it end? (NOTE: There's less information in these questions but they are still more specific than What was it about?)

Why Should You Do It?

Once you had the general idea, you were ready to process or comprehend the specific information. Having the general idea helps. Another thing that helps is having specific purposes in mind. The relatively specific questions you generated gave you relatively specific purposes for reading the passage. You wanted, perhaps, to know the date of the first battle—that's a purpose, so you asked, "When did it happen?" You wanted to know if Paul Revere really did what the legend says he did—that's a purpose, so you asked, "Was Paul Revere involved?" or "Did Paul really warn the colonists?"

One More Why

The business of predicting questions and answers seems to be a reasonable description of what really goes on in the mind of a mature reader. According to a number of theorists the mature reader does not read word for word but rather picks up just enough letters, words, parts of sentences, to make and confirm predictions as to the meaning. To do that, the reader must have some experiences with the subject or related subjects or with similar kinds of reading (textbooks, novels, etc.).

Task: Now that you know how the survey works with a text, explain how the survey worked with the picture:

Task: Based on the foregoing discussion, rewrite the following reading assignment:

Read pp. 1–15 in your book for next week. Really read carefully, get into the material. I will test you on the material by asking you a number of questions.

III. From Picture Survey to Text Survey

You now know how to do a picture and text survey. The questions you need to consider now are these:

(*1*) How do you know if you should start with a picture survey or a text survey?

(*2*) How do you know when to switch from a picture survey to a text survey?

The answers to these questions require the teacher to exercise judgment and common sense, as illustrated in the following question:

---

1. If you are working with a group of nonreaders, would you begin with a picture or a textbook? (Circle the correct response.)

   a. Picture
   b. Textbook

So one criterion for deciding if you should begin with a textbook or a picture is the reading ability of the student:

(*1*) The student has some reading skills but cannot function as an independent reader. (Rule of thumb: below 4.5 on the WRAT, begin with a picture.)

(*2*) Finally, if the student is unable to respond on a text-survey pretest, instruction should begin with a picture. If the student is able to make any response on a text-survey pretest, instruction should begin with a text.

Student A has a reading grade level score of 3.2. On a survey pretest, using the student's science book, the student made no response. Instruction in survey should begin with a:

a. Picture
b. Text

Student B scores at a kindergarten level on a reading test. Instruction in survey should begin with a:

a. Picture
b. Text

Use the criteria for both picture and textbook instruction to solve the following problems. (Write *picture* or *textbook* in the blank.)

1. Student C is in fourth grade; has a reading level of 2.3; was unable to write anything on a picture-survey pretest.

_____

2. Student D is in the ninth grade; has a reading level of 6.7; wrote a two-sentence summary, three questions, and one answer on a textbook-survey pretest.

_____

In the foregoing problems, student C was given a picture-survey pretest and student D was given a textbook-survey pretest. The decision on whether to use a picture pretest or a textbook pretest should be made on the basis of the teacher's judgment about the entering skills of the student. When in doubt about which pretest to begin with, begin with a picture pretest.

How do you know when to switch from a picture survey to a test survey?

Consider for a moment what you want students to learn from doing a picture survey. You want students to demonstrate that they can

(*1*) Write a summary.
(*2*) Predict questions.
(*3*) Answer questions.

Task: After one week of picture-survey instruction, you note that John writes good summaries, predicts four questions that are either *who, what, when, why, or how*, and can answer all the questions. Mary, after a week's instruction, writes fair summaries, predicts four questions (usually yes or no questions), and is not sure of the answers.

a. Would you move John to a text survey? (Yes or No)

b. Explain your reasons why or why not.

c. Would you move Mary to a text survey? (Yes or No)

d. Explain your reasons why or why not.

Goal Behavior of the Picture Survey

The criteria on which you decide to move to a text survey must be based on the student's performance. Does the student write a good summary? Does the student predict questions using the five interrogatives? Can the student predict answers to those questions? Does the student do a complete picture survey without teacher direction? If you can answer yes to each of these questions, then move the student to a text survey.

Task: Write four questions that will help you to decide if you should move a student from a picture survey to a text survey.

1.

2.

3.

4.

IV. Teaching the Survey

Teaching the survey involves the following responsibilities:

(*1*) Assessing the student's survey skills through a pretest
(*2*) Setting objectives
(*3*) Providing instruction in the technique

Some of the responsibilities should be taken over by the student as quickly as possible. He should learn not only to perform the basic steps of the survey but also to

(*1*) Provide his own feedback, which in turn will provide him with reinforcement.
(*2*) Set his own objectives.
(*3*) Modify his own instructional activities.

Assessment

Back a few pages, you were asked to do a survey. That introduction to the technique is also a pretest. The first lesson is used to establish what the student can and cannot do before receiving instruction.

A good pretest, then, should include the following:

(1) A very brief statement of what you want the student to do; the briefer, the better
(2) A simple statement of the instructions for each step
(3) A specified amount of time provided for doing each step

A good pretest **will not** include the following:

(1) Attempt to explain the idea of each step
(2) Examples of correct responses (modeling)
(3) Statements of objectives
(4) Exhortations to do a good job

Task: Below are two pretest situations. Which represents the right approach to pretesting? Circle the letter.

a. Teacher: Now, the first step is to survey this passage so that you can answer the question, What is it about? You'll have 30 seconds. Go ahead.

Student: (Looks at passage, for 30 seconds.)

Teacher: Now write an answer to the question, What was it about? You have 1 minute.

Student: (Doesn't respond.)

Teacher: (Does nothing for 1 minute.) Now, try to think of some questions that might be answered in the passage. Write the questions down.

Student: (Writes one question, then writes an answer, then stops.)

b. Teacher: Now, the first step is to survey this passage so that you can answer the question, What is it about? You have 30 seconds. Go ahead.

Student: (Looks at passage for 30 seconds.)

Teacher: Now write an answer to the question, What is it about?

Student: (Doesn't respond for 30 seconds.)

Teacher: Are you writing your summary? Did you hear what I said?

Student: (No response.)

Teacher: A summary, like one summary could be—this passage is about the start of the American Revolution. Get the idea?

> *Student*: (Writes, "about the American Revolution.")
> *Teacher*: Now try to think of some question that might be answered in the passage. Write down your question.
> *Student*: (Writes one question, then writes an answer, then stops.)
> *Teacher*: Good, no the second one isn't a question. Another question could be a when-question. Like when did it happen?
> *Student*: (Writes, "When was it?")

Setting Objectives

After administering the pretest, your next responsibility is to set objectives. (Eventually, the student should learn to set his own objectives.)

The objectives should be suited to the particular student's needs. There are some general guidelines that are applicable to all students:

(*1*) Objectives should always be determined from the information you obtain through the pretest.

(*2*) Objectives should provide for an improvement that can be measured quantitatively (an increase in number of pages covered in the survey, an increase in number of questions predicted, etc.)

(*3*) Generally, it is a good idea to start by focusing on one step in the survey technique at a time, (an increase in questions predicted, first; then an increase in answers predicted, etc.)

(*4*) Generally, it is a good idea to start by **focusing on the question-predicting step**, because it is the most important step in the technique.

Given: A student scored the following on his pretest:

Survey	Summary	Questions	Answers	Answers Confirmed
2 pages	6 words	predicted 3	predicted 3	2

Which one of the following objectives best reflects the guidelines stated above?

a. Student will improve his ability in surveying.

b. Student will increase number of pages in survey to 10.

c. Student will increase number of questions predicted from 3 to 5.

A student scored the following on his pretest:

Survey	*Summary*	*Questions*	*Answers*	*Answers Confirmed*
5 pages	5 words	0	0	0

Task: Write an objective for the student's first lesson.

Providing Instruction

QUESTIONS

One form of instruction is to provide students with a strategy for performing a certain behavior. A basic strategy for predicting questions is to use the six interrogatives as a guide or stimulus for generating questions. Generally a complete survey will have questions that begin with

> *who*
> *what*
> *where*
> *when*
> *why*
> *how*

Our student predicted the following question:

Who was fighting?

Task: What other interrogatives should the student use in predicting questions?

1.
2.
3.
4.
5.

MODELING

In presenting the strategy for generating questions via the six interrogatives, you could also fulfill another, crucial teaching role, modeling. In modeling, you perform the correct or desired response. A model is an example of the response you want the student to make.

Task: Provide models of the questions the student could have predicted with the passage that follows.

1. *What*
2. *Where*
3. *When*
4. *Why*
5. *How*

Would there be a war? The question on the minds of every American colonist was to be answered that fateful morning of April 19, 1775. At 3:00 that morning, near Boston, British soldiers, who had occupied Boston since 1774, were engaged in battle by the minutemen. Those American colonists, long chafing under the arrogance of the British occupation forces, had gathered at Lexington. Rumors flew of a possible British military action. Some spoke of a concerted drive in Boston to root out the revolutionaries, of house-by-house searches. Others warned that more British soldiers would be landing at Boston and that the occupation would be extended to all surrounding communities. Those with more reliable information were convinced that the British action would be smaller, but no less significant. It was believed that the British planned to seek out and destroy arms and ammunition stored by the revolutionaries in Concord.

REINFORCEMENT

Another major teaching responsibility is to provide for reinforcement. Any positive feedback will reinforce (strengthen) a desired response. A highly effective kind of feedback is that which is not only positive but which also gives the student **objective, specific** information about his performance.

Task: Which of the examples of feedback is **positive** and **specific** and **objective**? (Circle one.)

1. You did a really fine job on the survey.
2. You failed to get five questions.
3. You predicted five questions.

REINFORCEMENT THROUGH RECORDING FEEDBACK

Receiving positive, objective, specific information is good. Recording that information is even better. By recording the information from each lesson on a graph or chart, a student can see his progress over a period of time. Also, by learning to measure and record his own performance, the student learns to give himself his own feedback, thus to evaluate and control his own performance.

The chart on page 249 is one way of recording feedback for the survey. Note that the form provides for recording information about the performance at each of the steps (so many questions predicted, so many answers predicted, etc.). It also provides a place to note the overall performance for a particular lesson by means of a total number of points (one point for doing the survey, one point for doing the summary, then one point for each question and each answer predicted, and each answer confirmed).

Task: Look at the sample information in the form. Then, record the following information (in line 3).

The student did another 15-minute lesson in his history text. His objective was to increase the number of answers predicted from three to five. This time, he surveyed five pages, wrote a 20-word summary, predicted five questions, predicted five answers, and confirmed five answers.

REINFORCEMENT OF APPROXIMATIONS

For a student to be reinforced, he must first make a desired response. For example, if a student predicts one question, you can reinforce that response and chances are good that he will predict more questions the next time.

Some students may not make a desired response at first. But they will make some kind of response which could lead to that desired response. That "some kind of response" can be considered an **approximation** of the desired response.

In the survey technique, a desired response is five questions. A student may approximate that response in a number of ways:

- Before a student can predict five questions, he can predict less than five.
- Before a student can predict any questions, he can state (or write) a correct answer to a possible question.
- Before he can state a correct answer, he can state any answer (correct or incorrect).
- Before he can state any answer, he can say anything at all in response to a text or picture.
- Before he can say anything at all, he can look at the text or picture.

The ineffective way to handle approximations is to yell at the student, tell him he was wrong, or insist that he do it again (with no help).

The effective way is to lead the student from an approximation to the desired

SURVEY FEEDBACK AND PLANNING

Objective	$\frac{\text{Text}}{\text{Time}}$	Survey No. Pages	$\frac{\text{Summary}}{\text{No. Words}}$	Questions predicted	Answers predicted	Answers confirmed	Total points
1. Pretest	$\frac{\text{History}}{15\text{ min.}}$	3 pages	6 words	3	2	1	8
2. Increase number of questions to 5	$\frac{\text{History}}{15\text{ min.}}$	4 pages	8 words	5	3	2	12
3. Increase number of answers to 5							
4.							
5.							
6.							
7.							
8.							
9.							
10.							

response by (*1*) reinforcing the approximation by giving some positive feedback, and (*2*) giving a model of the desired response.

Task: Which of the following situations illustrates reinforcement of approximations of the correct response?

a. *Teacher*: Now, I want you to think of some questions that are answered by the picture.

   Student: (Looks at picture, says nothing.)

   Teacher: Johnny, give us a question?

   Student: (Looks away from picture.)

   Teacher: Johnny, pay attention! What is a question?

   Student: Uh, they're fighting.

   Teacher: No, that's not a question. Give me a question.

b. *Teacher*: Now, I want you to think of some questions that are answered by the picture.

   Student: (Looks at picture, says nothing.)

   Teacher: Good, you're looking carefully at the picture.

   Student: Uh, the men are fighting.

   Teacher: Very good, the men are fighting. Now, you could turn that into a question—What are the men doing? Some other questions?

   Student: Who, uh, the men are boxers.

   Teacher: Good, that could be a *who*-question—Who are the men?

   Student: Why are they fighting?

   Teacher: Excellent! Why are the men fighting?

MODIFYING INSTRUCTION

After fulfilling the responsibilities discussed up to this point, you may have one more responsibility to meet, that of modifying your instruction. If a student does not meet his objectives, you should modify your instructional design: the objectives, the instruction provided, the kind of models you provide, the reading material, the feedback system. Some examples follow.

Task: Johnny predicted one question on his pretest. However, when you explained and modeled the five-interrogative approach, Johnny **said** six questions of his own. You set his objective, as follows: Johnny will increase number of questions predicted from one to five. You then have Johnny go through the survey steps. He predicts zero questions.

Modification: It's one thing for Johnny to say a lot of questions; it's another thing for him to predict questions from a text. A reasonable modification would be to lower the objective to an increase of one question per lesson.

Task: Mary is failing history. She says she hates the class, the teacher, and her history textbook. You want to teach her to use the survey technique on her history text. She refuses. What would be a possible modification? (Hint: Mary probably finds the history book to be punishing. Where could you start?)

Modification:

Task: Wayne has increased the number of questions he asks about a picture. However, the questions call for only one-word responses: *yes, no* answers. What would be a possible modification? (Hint: How could you model questions that would help Wayne?)

Modification:

Task: Tom has increased the number of questions predicted from two to five. Most of his questions are of the *what happened*?, *who, when, where* kind. You want him to increase the variety of his questions and ask **discussion-type** questions: *why* (was it important), *why* or *how* (did it happen). But Tom continues to ask just the *what, who, when*, and *where* type. What would be a possible modification? (Hint: How could Tom be directed toward asking discussion-type questions?

Modification:

Task: Sally has been working on increasing the number of questions predicted. She has increased the questions from three to six..However, the number of answers predicted has dropped from three to one. What would be a possible modification?

Modification:

---

* * * * *

You have completed the module. Take the test on p. 230.[6]

MODULE 6
The Writing Dictionary[7]

Purpose

This module is designed to provide teachers with competency in using a technique for developing student writing skills.

Objective

Having identified a student, the learner will

(*1*) Assess the student's current skill level
(*2*) Establish an objective for the initial exercise
(*3*) Teach the initial exercise

Materials

(*1*) Pictures (for elementary students only)
(*2*) Additional paper
(*3*) A student

[6] There is no answer key for this module.
[7] By Rowena Wilhelm and Wayne A. King. Reprinted by arrangement with the authors.

Directions

(*1*) Locate the criterion test for this module (below). Do it now if you can. If you cannot complete it with 100% mastery, continue with step 2.

(*2*) Work through the module.

(*3*) Complete the criterion test.

Criterion Test[8]

Find a school-aged child (or an adult if a child is not available). Administer the pretest Writing Dictionary exercise. Proceed as follows:

1. How old is your student? _____

2. What is the student's reading level? _____

3. How did you determine the reading level?

4. What stimulus material will you use?

5. What is the time limit for the exercise? _____

6. Administer the pretest. Attach the stimulus material (pictures or topics) and the student's written response to these sheets.

7. Analyze the student's current skill level:

    a.   How many words were written? _____

    b.   What is the percentage of correctly spelled words?_____

    c.   What is the percentage of correctly used end punctuation? _____

8. At what stage will you begin the first exercise (after the pretest)?_____ Write the objective next:

Administer the initial learning exercise. Proceed as follows:

9. In order to do the task, what five factors must the student know?

    a.

    b.

[8] There is no answer key for this criterion test.

    c.

    d.

    e.

10. Write an example of how you would provide your student with each of the foregoing requirements. Use **modeling**.

    a.

    b.

    c.

    d.

    e.

11. Design an appropriate feedback graph.
12. Do the exercise, using the examples from step 10 to provide instruction.
13. Did the student progress beyond pretest performance?

Introduction

The Writing Dictionary is a developmental technique designed to help students improve the quality and quantity of their writing. These goals are accomplished by focusing first on quantity and later on quality.

The Writing Dictionary is a person, one who provides the student with requested words. This person can be a teacher, a paraprofessional, a student teacher, or even another student. In addition, students are encouraged to use printed sources of information.

This exercise is appropriate for students at any age or ability level. It can be used with nonreaders or students who can print only a few words.

This module contains three parts:

   I. Doing the Writing Dictionary
  II. Following a Developmental Sequence
 III. Teaching the Procedure

I. Doing the Writing Dictionary

The Writing Dictionary requires five teacher behaviors: (*1*) providing stimulus materials, (*2*) giving instructions, (*3*) being a dictionary, (*4*) providing feedback, and (*5*) establishing the next goal.

A. Provide the Stimulus Material

The success of the Writing Dictionary is largely dependent upon stimulating exciting and interesting thoughts that the student can write about. One way to produce interesting thoughts is to provide an interesting picture to look at. To ensure that the student is actually interested, he should be provided with more than one picture.

Which is the best way to present the writing stimulus? Check one choice in each exercise.

  1. a. ___ Give John a picture of cowboys on a roundup, which you think he will be interested in.

     b. ___ Give John three pictures, one about cowboys, one about kids playing at the beach, and one about camping. Ask him to choose one.

  2. a. ___ Ask Daryl to choose any topic that she wants to write about.

     b. ___ Give Daryl a list of topics. Ask her to choose one or write about a topic she has already decided upon.

B. Give Instructions

In order to get to work, the student will need to know

(*1*) What to do (the objective)
(*2*) How to proceed to do it (instructions)
(*3*) How much time is available for doing it

3. Which is the best way to state the task guidelines? Check.

a. ___ Today you should try to write more words than you did yesterday. Ask me any words you need. You will have exactly 5 minutes.

b. ___ Today you should try to write more words than you did yesterday. You will have exactly 5 minutes.

C. Provide the Dictionary

A teacher, another adult, a child, or printed material may act as a dictionary, depending on the skill level of the student. You yourself should work with younger or less skilled students, i.e., you are the dictionary. If a student does not know a word he wishes to write, he **must request** that word. Then, write the word on a slip of paper and give it to the student. Provide words whenever requested, but only when requested.

For each of the following exercises, check the appropriate response:

4. Carrie asks for a word you know she has written before. You should

a. ___ Write the word on a slip of paper and hand it to her.

b. ___ Say, "Carrie, you know how to write that word. Think a minute."

5. Rich asks, "How do you spell *mountain*?" You should

a. ___ Say, "It's spelled *m-o-u-n-t-a-i-n*."

b. ___ Say, "The word is spelled like this," and hand him a piece of paper with the word on it.

With older or more skilled students, the resource person can be replaced by resources that the student can use independently. Also, as the student progresses, he will need information other than spelling. For example, the student may need sample adjectives and adverbs when working on increasing the use of descriptive words.

6. What additional resources could you use as the Writing Dictionary? Check all that apply.

a. ___ A dictionary

b. ___ A list of adjectives and adverbs

c. ___ A thesaurus

d. ___ Other (specify)

D. Provide Feedback

When the student has finished writing, he must have feedback on how well he has performed. If the student is at a stage where he can count up points independently, then all you need do is to provide the correct graph and be available if a question occurs.

At other times, you may be required to participate partially. For example, you may be required to circle correct punctuation marks. Then the student takes over, counts them, and puts them on the graph.

---

7. Which is the correct way to provide feedback?

    a.   ___ When Lisa has finished, wait until she counts up her words and plots the number on her graph. Then you can go over, look, and say, "You did very well today!"

    b.   ___ When Lisa has finished, take her paper, add up her words, record them on your record, and tell her, "You did very well today."

E. Establish the Next Objective

Before the task can be considered complete, the student must know what the goal will be the next time he does the activity. This is another task for which the student should take responsibility. Students quickly learn to establish reasonable goals. They can look at a graph that demonstrates that they wrote 37 words today and decide, "I will write 40 words tomorrow."

Within one stage of work, the student should set his own goals. When changing to a new stage in learning, the student may need help. This is when you should be available to aid in setting reasonable goals.

---

8. Jim has tried to increase the length of his stories all week. What should your feedback response be? Check.

    a.   ___ "Very nice, Jim! How many words do you think you can write next time? Good!"

    b.   ___ "Very nice, Jim! Next time you should try to write 85 words. I think you can do it."

II. The Developmental Sequence

One sequence of goals is as follows: (*1*) quantity, (*2*) punctuation, (*3*) descriptive words, (*4*) spelling, and (*5*) organization.

Stage 1: Quantity—Number of Words

Increasing the flow of words is the most important stage in the writing sequence. Typically, students have been concerned about qualitative features too early in the learning process. The emphasis upon spelling, punctuation, and the like rewards brevity: the fewer words used, the less the chance of errors. By removing all qualitative factors, the student can be freed to write, can be allowed to transfer thoughts to written words.

OBJECTIVE

Given a time limit (held constant), the student will increase the number of words written over successive practice sessions.

FEEDBACK MEASURE

One point per word written during the allowed time.

Assume that you are the resource person for a group of students working on quantity only. In each exercise, check the instructions that are appropriate.

9. a. ____ "Today you will have 5–10 minutes to work on your writing. Don't worry about spelling or punctuation; simply write as much as you can."

   b. ____ "Today you will have 5 minutes to work on your writing. Don't worry about spelling or punctuation; simply write as much as you can."

10. a. ____ "Now it's time to do our writing exercise. See if you can write more words today than you did yesterday. You have 10 minutes as always."

    b. ____ "Now it's time to do our writing exercise. See if you can write more words than you did yesterday. Watch your spelling! You have 10 minutes, as always."

TRANSITION

Use the following criteria to advance the student to the next stage. Note that more than one may be appropriate.

(1) Number of words written: The student reaches the goal originally suggested by the teacher (perhaps twice the original number of words). More important, the teacher watches for an easy flow of words, occupying the total time.

(*2*) Redundancy: The student is not unnecessarily using the same words many times in one writing period.

(*3*) Independence: The student is asking for only a few words during a writing period (no more than 1 in 10).

(*4*) Boredom: The student is writing so freely that the task is no longer challenging.

---

11. Given the following situations, would you move the student to stage 2? Circle *yes* or *no* for each example.

    a. David works the entire 5 minutes and has increased the number of words written from 12 to 37. Today 16 of the 37 words were requested from the teacher. (Yes, No)

    b. Gavin wrote 134 words Monday, 142 Tuesday, and 149 Wednesday. Each day he used the same words over and over. (Yes, No)

    c. Shelly started writing 24 words in 10 minutes and now writes 143 but stops after about 7 minutes. (Yes, No)

    d. Heather has increased from baseline (11) to 45 words in 5 minutes. She works steadily and requests only a few words. (Yes, No)

Stage 2: End Punctuation

The addition of simple punctuation as point-earners allows the student to progress with the least amount of strain. The rules for end punctuation can be learned easily. From this stage on, the student should at least maintain quantity while receiving points for the **correct** use of:

(*1*) Capitals
(*2*) Periods
(*3*) Question marks

OBJECTIVE

Given the same conditions as stage 1, the students will increase the number of points earned by increasing the number of instances of correct end punctuation.

FEEDBACK MEASURE

One point for each word written and one point for every correct period, question mark, or capitalized letter. (Include capitals other than the first word of the sentence.)

TRANSITION

When the student is placing capital letters, periods, and question marks with 95% accuracy and has maintained quantity, he should progress to the next stage.

---

12. Given the following situations, would you advance the student to stage 3? Circle *yes* or *no*.

    a. Babs entered stage 2 writing 135 words in 10 minutes. Today she wrote 142 words with 48 of 50 capitals, periods, and question marks placed correctly. (Yes, No)

    b. Mark entered stage 2 writing 76 words in 5 minutes. Today he wrote 48 words with 15 of 16 capitals, periods, etc. correctly placed. (Yes, No)

    c. Gail entered stage 2 writing 84 words in 5 minutes. She is now writing 118 words with 24 of 38 capitals, periods, and question marks placed correctly. (Yes, No)

Stage 3: Descriptive Words

At the completion of the first two stages, the student should be writing freely with correct end punctuation. Stage 3 provides students with a tool to increase both the quantity and quality of their writing. The student now receives a bonus point for each adjective and adverb written. Students make use of those words to increase length and to add color to the story.

OBJECTIVE

Given the same task conditions, the student will increase the number of descriptive terms written while maintaining quantity and correct punctuation.

FEEDBACK MEASURE

One point: each word written
One point: each correct capital, period, question mark
One point: each adjective or adverb written

TRANSITION

Advance the student to the next stage when the number of descriptives has increased by 100% and total quantity and punctuation have been maintained.

13. Given the following situations, would you advance the student to the next stage? Circle *yes* or *no*.

   a. Jason entered this stage obtaining a total of 153 points in a 10-minute writing exercise. The passage included 6 descriptives. Today he obtained 155 points with 15 descriptives. (Yes, No)
   b. Karen entered this stage with a total of 180 points for a 10-minute writing exercise that included 11 descriptives. Today she obtained 196 points, including 14 descriptives. (Yes, No)

Note: At this stage in the instructional process, it becomes difficult and unnecessary to evaluate writing performance by separating the criteria at each stage. The student will be quite consistent at employing the skills developed and an occasional error is not significant. Therefore, one should concentrate on **total points earned**. The student may no longer increase the number of words written. In fact, he may have to decrease the number of raw words in order to devote attention to other aspects. Nevertheless, the total number of points will increase because of the increasing number of ways to gain points.

Stage 4: Spelling

If spelling is a problem, now is the time to devote attention to it. If the student is spelling many words incorrectly, attention can be directed to it by giving points for **every word spelled correctly**. However, if the student spells most words correctly, points can be given for "editing," i.e., having completed the exercise, the student circles all misspelled words and corrects them. Points are then given for identifying (one point) and correcting (one point) errors.

OBJECTIVE

The student will increase the number of points earned by increasing the number of words spelled correctly.

FEEDBACK MEASURE

One point: each word written
One point: each correct capital, period, question mark
One point: each adjective or adverb
One point: each correctly spelled or edited word

The recording of points may be done in various ways from this point on. One way is to add the points to the current graph. Another is to begin a new graph for bonus points.

Advance the student to the next stage when he spells most words correctly.

Stage 5: Organization

At this stage the student begins attending to the presentation of ideas in an organized manner. This includes breaking the story into three parts:

(1) Opening paragraph
(2) Body
(3) Closing paragraph

The student will increase the number of points earned by correctly including (1) an opening paragraph, (2) the body of the story, and (3) a closing paragraph.

As before, with the addition of five bonus points for including each of the three parts of the story.

There will not be another stage presented in this module. However, this type of writing exercise need not be discontinued. A number of directions are opened to the instructor and student: Report writing, poetry, narratives, and other forms of rhetoric can be taught using variations on these procedures.

The stages of the Writing Dictionary have been presented in a convenient sequence one might employ when starting with the early elementary child and continuing for a long period of time. Certainly a student may not progress through a number of stages during the time you are responsible for his learning.

You may find that a student already has sufficient skill at a particular task. You could then disregard that stage until a time when it may be needed, and go on to another. For example, with older or more skilled students, you might start with the number of words produced and then go directly to stage 4, spelling.

Punctuation was the second stage and involved only periods, capital letters, and question marks. As students become more skilled or if you begin with students who are more skilled, you may add commas, colons, semicolons, quotation marks, etc., to the list.

Finally, something has been neglected that you feel is important. Find a place in the sequence and add it!

III. Teaching the Procedure

One cannot assume that a student will be able to perform the task simply by being told to do it. You will find that it is often necessary to provide instruction on **how** to do the task, especially with younger students. Teaching how to do the Writing Dictionary involves the following steps:

(*1*) Assessing the student's current writing skills
(*2*) Establishing objectives
(*3*) Introducing the task to the learner
(*4*) Modeling **how to**

Some of this information you already know from previous modules, therefore it will not be repeated here in full. However, we will cover these steps as they relate specifically to this activity.

A. Assessment

In order to assess the learner's writing skills, you first need to assess a general skill level in order to choose appropriate stimulus material. If you are familiar with the student, you may already have the necessary information. However, if the student is new to you, his reading level is a useful gauge.

---

14. Where can you obtain information about the student's reading level? Check all that apply.

   a. ___ Look in the student's permanent file.
   b. ___ I already know from recent work.
   c. ___ Give the reading subtest of the WRAT (Wide Range Achievement Test).
   d. ___ Other (specify).

When you know the student's grade level, you can choose (*1*) the stimulus material and (*2*) the time length for the pretest.

Good readers, especially if they are older students, may be able to write a story if they are given a topic. For example, "My favorite pastime is . . ." or "What the Bill of Rights means to women." Poor readers usually need more than a topic to provide things to write about. Pictures provide a rich stimulus. The student does not need to spend time fabricating a story; he need only recount what is happening in the picture.

As far as time is concerned, younger students and students with lower reading levels are given a short time for writing. Older students and better readers can write for longer periods. The following table will serve as a guide for choosing the appropriate stimulus material and time length for assessment.

Reading grade[a]	Stimulus material	Minutes
1–4	picture	3–5
5–8	picture–topic	5–15
9–12	topic	15–30

[a]Regardless of age.

---

15. For each of the following, choose the appropriate stimulus material. Enter *P* for picture, *T* for topic. Then choose the appropriate time limit. Circle the number.

   a. ___ John is in the eighth grade. His reading level as measured by the WRAT is Grade 2.7.
      Minutes: 5   10   15   20

   b. ___ Bill is a tenth grade student with above-average reading and writing skills.
      Minutes: 5   10   15   20

   c. ___ Karen is a seventh grader who reads well and completes all writing assignments.
      Minutes: 5   10   15   20

   d. ___ Pam is an average fourth grader.
      Minutes: 5   10   15   20

   e. ___ Ron is a tenth grade student who has yet to complete a written assignment, and reads at a level of Grade 5.6.
      Minutes: 5   10   15   20

After you choose the appropriate material and time limit, administer the pretest. Now you have information for establishing an instructional objective.

B. Establishing an Objective

Every student who has been selected to use the Writing Dictionary will begin by working on quantity as an initial objective. It is the task at which all students can progress most rapidly, regardless of current skill, and thereby provides the learner with plenty of positive feedback.

---

16. Clark is in the fourth grade. Given a picture stimulus, he wrote 8 words in 5 minutes on the pretest. Which objective would you select?

    a. ___ Given 5 minutes and a picture, Clark will increase the number of words written from 8 to 20.
    b. ___ Given 5 minutes and a picture, Clark will increase the number of words from 8 to 20 and will decrease his spelling errors by 10%.

---

17. Alicia is in the ninth grade and is an average reader. On the pretest, she wrote 237 words in 15 minutes. Punctuation, etc., was about 60% correct.

    a. ___ Given a topic and 15 minutes, Alicia will increase punctuation from 60 to 90% correct, while maintaining at least 237 words written.
    b. ___ Given a topic and 15 minutes, Alicia will increase the number of words written from 237 to 350.

C. Provide Instruction

Having conducted the pretest and established the initial objective, you can begin the Writing Dictionary with the student. You will remember that the pretest does not provide the student with instruction about how to do the task. Now is the time. The student needs to know

(1) The objective—what is to be done.
(2) How it is to be done, i.e., how to:
    (a) Use the stimulus to write from
    (b) Use the Dictionary
    (c) Plot progress (self-feedback)
    (d) Set a goal for next time

A very efficient means of instruction is **modeling**. To model, you perform the desired response, i.e., you provide an example of how it should be done. The easiest way to accomplish this is to make the first task period following pretesting a modeling session. More time must be allowed because of the demonstration. However, the students will be able to perform these tasks on their own in the future.

For each of the following pairs of instructions, check the one that is an example of modeling:

18. a. ____ I have given you each three pictures. I want you to choose one to write a story about, then write down what you think is happening in the picture. Tell as much as you can about it.

    b. ____ You each have three pictures on your desk. Look at them and pick **one** that you like. [pause] OK, does everyone have one? I have a picture here on the board. Can anyone tell me what is happening in the picture? Good! I will write that down. Now look at your picture.

19. a. ____ When you are finished writing count all the words you wrote, then put the number on your graph. Start at the bottom and count up to your number and put a line there. Then fill in the column with . . .

    b. ____ Everyone stop writing please. Count how many words you wrote. I counted the words in the story we wrote on the board. There are 12. How many do you have? Good. You have a graph on your desk just like this one [point to board]. I would put my 12 words on it like this. Now you do yours . . .

Turn to the criterion test (p. 253) and follow instructions.[9]

---

[9] There is no answer key for this module.

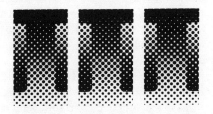

Making Teaching Methods Adaptive

Tutorial
Basal Reader
Language Experience
Programmed and Computer

Part I presented the concept of an adaptive classroom system. Essential characteristics were (1) provision for mastery of subroutines, (2) goal measures, (3) a safe environment, (4) self-instructional materials, (5) self-evaluation, and (6) a mastery requirement.

Any method of teaching seems to be successful with some children, probably those who are maximally ready to learn. But the position taken here is that all the common methods can be **made to work** for all children—simply by making the classroom adaptive.

Our task, then, is to determine what would be required to make each method adaptive—or to determine for each method which characteristics are intrinsic to the method and which must be supplied. The following chart has been started for you. Presence of a condition is indicated by X; absence by 0. As you read the following chapters, fill in the chart. (My version follows Chapter 11—but I am hopelessly biased. The only sure way to evaluate your analysis is by operating a successful classroom.)

CHARACTERISTICS OF AN ADAPTIVE CLASSROOM
INTRINSIC TO VARIOUS TEACHING METHODS

| Characteristics | Method | | | | |
| | | | | Programmed | |
	Fernald	Basal	Individualized language experience	Book	Computer
Subroutines	X	0			
Goal measures					
Controlled environment					
Self-instructional materials					
Self-evaluation by feedback Task success Progress					
Mastery required					

A TUTORIAL METHOD

RESOURCES

> Paper
> Black crayon (or grease pencil, china marker)
> Shoe box
> "Teacher" (any person who is literate)

Teaching any nonliterate person to read is both simpler and more complex than is commonly realized—simpler, because there is a method that claims to be **universally successful**, if used properly; more complex, because it is so easy to go wrong, and thus to fail, using this method.

First, I shall present a brief historical note; next, I shall specify assumptions, describe the method, and show the forces that interfere with success.

Dr. Grace Fernald was to this country what Maria Montessori was to Italy. Her book, *Remedial Techniques in Basic School Subjects* is a classic of pedagogy. In fact, after I had first read it in 1950, I assumed that "the reading problem" was solved and we could go on to other educational problems.

No less an authority than Lewis M. Terman—that remarkable student of the gifted—wrote, in a foreword to Fernald's book, "It is my considered judgment that Dr. Fernald's conquest of word-blindness [alexia, dyslexia] is an achievement comparable with that of Miss [Anne] Sullivan [the teacher of Helen Keller].... The fact is that the method she has devised is successful; and not sometimes, but always."

I used the Fernald method for about 5 years in clinical work with considerable success, and was continually surprised to find that some of my student–clinicians were less successful. For some time, I assumed that I was not teaching them properly. Only gradually did I come to realize that the teacher's conviction that it will work is critical and that, for certain kinds of children, no shortcut will work. In other words, faith in the method is necessary in the face of counterforces in the child.

I. Assumptions

Fernald made certain assumptions:

(*1*) **Any child can learn to read up to the limit of his intellectual capacity**. Reasons for failure, such as visual defects, neurological impairment, emotional problems, and the like, are interesting excuses—interesting enough to justify looking at the evidence. The "evidence" did not impress Fernald, probably because she had taught these same kinds of people to read.

(*2*) **Learning to write precedes learning to read**. That is to say, the easiest way to learn to read is to write a message, then to read the message one has produced. Thus, primary emphasis is placed on writing stories.

(*3*) **Learning to write is a multimodality process**. Visual, auditory, and kinesthetic signals must occur concurrently, in a natural way, for literate behavior to take place.

(*4*) **The only appropriate material to be used in reading and writing instruction is the creative output of the child**. Using child-generated materials in a systematic way, the child will spontaneously develop all the reading skills of a mature reader. (Thus the teacher is not required to know phonics rules, to search out spelling lists, to check progress with reading tests—although the last is not forbidden.)

(*5*) **At all times, the child must have free access to information, must be allowed to pace himself, and must be free from teacher pressure to succeed**. The teacher's role is carefully prescribed. The teacher may not deviate from that role.

II. Procedure

Step 1 **Assurance**. The learner is told that he is going to learn to read. The method used works with everyone. If the learner has failed in the past, that is because some other method was used that was not right for **him**.

Step 2 **Generation**. "Tell me a word you would like to know—to be able to read and write. **Any** word." The learner will produce a word (perhaps **antidisestablishmentarianism**).

Step 3 **Modeling**. Using shoe-box-sized paper (approximately 4 by 10 inches) or larger if necessary, the teacher writes the word with black crayon (or china marker). Write large.[1]

Step 4 **Tracing**. The learner is told the following:

    (*a*) "Trace the word with your [index] finger [or two fingers] ."

    (*b*) "Once you start tracing, keep on going."

    (*c*) "While tracing, say the word **once, slowly**. Start the word when you start tracing; finish it when you finish tracing."

    (*d*) "Trace it as many times as you need to, but **say** the word **slowly** each time. Now, go ahead."

    (*e*) Optional: "Close your eyes and try to see the word. If you can see it, try tracing it in the air. Remember to say it as you trace it. If you can't see it, or part of it, trace it on the paper again."

    (*f*) "If you think you can write it, try to write it on this scrap paper. Say the word—not the letters—as you write it." (Turn over the original. The child must write the word without help.)

Things to watch for during step 4:

- Tracing **must** be done with the finger(s), not a pencil. Never mind dirty fingers.
- The word must be enunciated clearly: All the sounds, with no undue distortion. (*Must* is *mmmuusssttt*, not *mmm–uhhh–sss–tih*. There must be no junctures in one-syllable words. In polysyllabic words, each syllable is enunciated. The syllables need not conform exactly in time with the tracing to begin with. That will come.)
- When the child writes the word, the complete word must be written. If he has trouble, let him go back to trace again, then start the word over—on another paper. (No corrections, erasures, etc.)
- Copying (looking back and forth) is never allowed.

* * * * *

The child has discovered that he can learn to read and write a word. Now he is ready for the next step.

Step 5, **Story**. "Let's write a story. You think of something you'd like to write. Here's some paper. Any word you don't know, just tell me; I'll

---

[1] Fernald said cursive **or** printing. In fact, all her many illustrations are in cursive form, even those of first graders. She was concerned with the flow of the movements, broken up by printing.

write it on one of these sheets of paper, and you can trace it, then put it in your story."

Step 6 **Generation**. He formulates the story and writes the first word if he knows it. (If he cannot write the first word, he learns it by tracing, then tries it on scrap paper, then puts it on his story sheet.) The procedure puts a strain on his memory, so he tends to keep rehearsing the story. The rehearsal is a necessary condition for success. A one-line story may be enough, at first.

Step 7 **Reading**. The teacher now **types the story** (perhaps on an index card). The child "reads" the story.

Step 8 **Filing**. The learner files all new words alphabetically in a shoe box for future reference. (End of lesson.)

The procedure is continued each day using stories generated by the learner. When an old word is to be used but the learner has forgotten it, he may look it up in his file and relearn it.

III. Stages of Learning

Stage 1 According to Fernald, the initial stage lasts from 1 to 8 months, with an average of 2 months. Long words tend to be remembered, short words to be forgotten. Words are simply relearned each time (no matter how many times) without fuss or panic.

Stage 2 Tracing tends to drop out bit by bit. The student learns some new words simply by looking at the model, then writing independently (not copying), saying each part of the word as he writes it. During stage 2, he will begin reading books of interest to him. As he reads, he may ask you to identify any words he does not know. You simply **tell him the word** (do not ask him to sound it out!) and make a note of the word. After his reading, he learns these words by tracing and writing them.

Stage 3 Most new words are learned by writing them once. Reading is still primitive. Many small words are yet to be learned.

Stage 4 He begins to identify new words on the basis of similarity of parts to known words. He begins to sound out words. He scans a paragraph to identify unknown words before reading. If he wants to sound out words, ask him to do so before reading the paragraph. **Keep the focus on the message, not on the skill.**

Stage 4 is complete when the learner is able to function in the same kind of material as others his age. In the process of reaching that point, he masters most of the standard spelling lists and simple punctuation and capitalization. (For further work, see the module, The Writing Dictionary, which conforms to the Fernald procedure.)

IV. Pitfalls

As mentioned earlier, this powerful and complete tutorial method seems not to work for some teachers.

Condition 1 The child is making progress. On a given day, he refuses to work, complaining that he is bored, his hands get dirty, it is a stupid way to learn, and so on. The teacher responds by changing the method (**wrong**). *Interpretation*: The child is rule testing. Correct response: "Let me know when you're ready to work."

Condition 2 The child is making progress. On a given day, the teacher decides to "speed things up" by introducing phonics; or he decides to find out how much the learner "really knows." and introduces spelling tests, reading tests, and so on; or he undermines the child's confidence in other subtle ways. *Interpretation*: The teacher is bored or angry and attacks the child in these ways.

Condition 3 The child is not making progress. He continues to trace words over and over and seems unable to learn the words well enough to write them. *Interpretation*: (*1*) Some part of the method is being carried out improperly or (*2*) the child is highly emotional in the presence of the teacher. (See Chapter 11, on programmed instruction.)

V. Discussion

After more than 10 years of engineering the reading and writing processes, I remain convinced of the validity and effectiveness of Fernald's procedures. The "hand-kinesthetic" method provides all the conditions for learning of which I am aware:

(*1*) Adequate associative strength (meaning): The learner generates the words and stories from his own experience.

(*2*) Adequate subroutines: The learner receives both auditory and visual training during the tracing step; he learns to impose letters on space during the writing step; and he has maximum opportunity for immediate feedback.

(*3*) Self-selection and self-pacing: He chooses his own words and stories and practices until he achieves mastery (one perfect rendering in writing and in reading).

(*4*) Rule enforcement: The teacher insists on the correct procedure.
(*5*) An adaptive system: The product consists of stories or essays, each of which the learner can read, and separation when the learner can operate independently. The primary resource, the teacher, varies his input as demanded by the learner (just as the fetus takes what it needs from its host).

One deficit in the procedure as described by Fernald is clear-cut evidence of progress. In fact, she kept extensive charts of learner productivity and undoubtedly fulfilled that condition, perhaps without realizing that it is an integral part of the method. Learner boredom, we have discovered, is eliminated when charts **are kept by the learner himself**. Teacher boredom is reduced or eliminated when teachers have information on learner progress.

Therefore, use the techniques described in Module 1, Designing and Using Feedback Forms and Module 6, The Writing Dictionary. Module 6 requires that the teacher select the learning units on which to give feedback. Appropriate units and order of units are as follows: (*1*) words, (*2*) new words, (*3*) length of stories (either the number of words or the number of sentences), (*4*) words spelled correctly, and (*5*) simple punctuation.

THE BASAL READER
METHOD

MATERIALS[1]

Graded Series
    Prereading (2)
    Preprimer (3)
    Primer
    First reader
    Second reader (2)
    Etc.
Teacher manuals
Supplementary
    Initial reading inventory
    Workbook
    Duplicating masters
    Skill chart
    Word cards
    End-of-level tests

[1] Example is taken from Houghton Mifflin readers.

Basal reader systems consist of a graded series of reading books and supporting materials. The "basal system" has been evolving for more than 150 years, according to Spache and Spache (1973, pp. 146–147), and now provides the primary method of instruction in more than 90% of the first grade classrooms in the United States.

I. Problems with Basals

Let us be agreed at the outset that although groups of children may receive instruction, individual children learn to read (or fail to learn). Basal readers are designed for group instruction. With 25 to 50 children in a room, the teacher needs printed material that will control the attention of most of the children. Since most children are illiterate when they enter first grade, authors appear to be safe in assuming that first materials, usually stories, ought to consist of the **most commonly used words**, that is, words that appear most often in print. Therefore, reading books are gradated, by selecting words from frequency tables of word usage and by introducing new words in the order of most common to least common.

This clever strategem is not without its problems. An unseemly number of children have difficulty remembering these early words. Authors of basals have responded to this difficulty in several ways:

(*1*) They have slowed down the rate at which new words are introduced.
(*2*) They have added easier stories before the first reader; first a primer, then a preprimer, than another preprimer (and usually **another** preprimer).
(*3*) They have increased the number of repetitions of a word, with new words being repeated from 20 to 40 times in slightly differing contexts.
(*4*) They have added word cards (**flash cards**), workbooks, toys, and games to reinforce[2] instruction and to bolster the flagging attention that inevitably accompanies repetition.

These efforts have undoubtedly had some effect, but they cannot, by themselves, resolve the word-learning problems for the lower 30% of the group. If we are to make the basal system work for them, we must take advantage of learning principles unused by present materials and techniques.

---

[2] Educators use the term *reinforce* to mean "give practice in." Psychologists use the term to refer to the use of a stimulus following a response to increase the probability of occurrence of the response.

II. Making Basals Work

A review of the strategies used by authors to improve word learning will demonstrate an unstated assumption: **Retention depends upon frequency of use.** No psychologist will argue with that assumption. But—retention does not depend on frequency alone.

There are three other principles that can be put to work:

- Retention of a word is a function of the number of its associations (its meanings).
- Retention of a word is a function of its discriminability (how clearly it is heard and seen).
- Retention of a word is a function of its reproducibility (whether or not it can be written).

You may remember that Fernald's procedure required all three of these conditions, with repetition taking care of itself, i.e., children tend to include words they know in their stories.

Associations. Selecting words to be learned from a word-frequency list, as clever as that may seem, puts children at a disadvantage. Here are the first (i.e., most frequent) 20 words from one such list (Johnson, 1971):

the	*in*	*for*	*on*
of	*that*	*it*	*be*
and	*is*	*with*	*at*
to	*was*	*as*	*by*
a	*he*	*his*	*I*

Examination of the words reveals at least two characteristics:

(*1*) The words are short. Short words are, in general, hard to remember. They have fewer identifying characteristics than do long words.

(*2*) They are mainly **function** words, connectives (prepositions, conjunctions, verb auxiliaries) and pronouns.

By their nature they have only grammatical meaning. Nouns and many verbs refer to things, actions, and events, many of which can be visualized (and thus have **referential** meaning), but connectives and auxiliaries are relationship terms with little or no substantive meaning.

Compare the "meaning" of these words to the "meaning" of words in Dan's first Fernald story: "My aunt works in a restaurant. She cooks hamburgers and many other objects."

To maximize the meaning of a story in a preprimer or primer, **the child must learn whole sentences.** In a sense, the sentence "stores" words like *in* and *the*.

The child can recognize such a word in a new context by recalling the original sentence and by matching the word in the new context to the same word in the known context. **Technique I**: Require children to learn early stories by rote (by auditory training, by dramatization, by "reading" to their friends).

Discriminability. The expression **discriminability of a word** refers to its uniqueness, its unlikelihood of being confused with words similar in form or in sound. (See Chapter 2 for an extensive discussion of auditory training.) The first few sight words the child encounters will be recognized easily. **Thereafter, each new word must be discriminated from every other word** in the child's repertoire of sight words. That is, the new word must be placed side by side with known words so that points of difference[3] can be discovered.[4]

Within the frequency list just referred to, the following words have the ranks shown (a rank of 1 is most frequent):

was (9)	*would* (39)
with (13)	*their* (40)
which (31)	*when* (45)
were (34)	*who* (46)
there (38)	*what* (54)

Note the similarity in appearance (the confusability) of these words.

One eighth grade illiterate I saw recently was attempting to read words aloud from a test. Each time he tried an unknown word, no matter what its initial letters, his first sound was *wh-h-h*. Judging from the number of [w] and [wh] words in the basic list, his attempt is understandable though futile. The oral response, /name of word/, must be controlled both by **common features** [wh-] and by **distinctive features** [-at] rather than [-ere]. **Technique II**: Provide opportunities for children to discriminate new words from old ones in several sentence contexts. (As pointed out earlier a word looks different and sounds different in different contexts.)

Reproducibility. Formal spelling instruction with word lists is usually begun toward the end of first grade. But, ideally, each child should learn to write each word that he can read. Certain practical problems interfere with realization of this ideal.

 • First, with current instructional practices, printing tends to lag behind reading by at least one semester. To introduce word writing concurrently with word reading, methods of instruction in printing must be improved.

---

[3] "Distinctive cues." See Gates (1955).
[4] A simple technique: When a new word is met, have each child page **forward** in his reader and find the word four to six times.

- Second, imperfect knowledge of word spelling tends to inhibit creative writing—not only for college students but also for first graders. (How many of us have not, at one time or another, chosen an easier word to write down rather than look up the spelling of our preferred word?) Thus, a technique must be developed that will allow both creative writing and noncreative spelling.
- Third, children are seriously hampered in spelling unless they are able to name all the letters of the alphabet. And there is ample evidence to show that a substantial proportion of children have not mastered letter names by the end of first grade—much less at the **beginning** of first grade. So, techniques must be developed for teaching letter names within the first semester of first grade. **Technique III:**

(*1*) Printing letters (see Chapter 3).

(*2*) Creative writing: Demonstrate to children how they may write using their own guesses at spelling, including blanks: *I m go___kamp___w___mi dad*. This constitutes a first draft. Next, words are written out by teacher or aide on cards. The child learns the word by tracing (see Fernald procedure, in Chapter 8) and writes a better draft for his log.

(*3*) Letter names are most easily learned and retrieved by using the following procedure:

(*a*) Teach the following key words:[5]

cat	gun	pie	key
tree	bell	box	wave
man	dog	fish	
jet	queen	zebra	

(*b*) Each word is learned in two ways. First, as a sight word:

$$[cat] \equiv /cat/$$

Second, letter by letter:

$$[cat] \equiv /see \cdot ay \cdot tee/$$

Only these words are taught letter by letter. That is, spelling of other words is handled by the spelling paradigm in Chapter 7. When a child wishes to remember a letter name, he will retrieve the word, and then select the letter name:

$$/tree/, /tee \cdot r \cdot ee \cdot ee/.$$

To summarize: Several steps can be taken to increase the efficiency of word learning if the basal system is to work:

(*1*) Children must learn whole sentences in which new words are embedded.

---

[5] To teach both *letter names* and *printing*, see *DIDAC* (D. E. P. Smith & J. M. Smith, 1975).

(*2*) New words must be discriminated visually and aurally from similar words already known.

(*3*) New words must be written. To do so, the child must be able to print and name letters. (To name letters, teach words in which letter names are embedded.)

These techniques will get children off to a good start. But success, by itself, will not sustain effort. To maintain motivation, the child will need evidence of progress toward goals. Enter the adaptive classroom.

III. Basals in an Adaptive Classroom

Let us assume that children are learning to read and write letters and words successfully. They have also discovered that stories have meaning, i.e., that they are fun to read. Now it remains only to fulfill the conditions of an adaptive classroom in order to ensure the success of our children:

(*1*) The classroom is a self-modifying system. Both teacher and children modify their behavior to reach measured goals. Need: goal measures.

(*2*) The classroom is a stable environment. Need: teacher training in classroom management.

(*3*) The learner is trained to be independent. Need: opportunity for self-selection of tasks; feedback using goal measures.

(*4*) All subroutines are established. (Visual discrimination of form and space; auditory discrimination of utterances, words, and sounds in words; verbal fluency; then, analogous training on the materials within a given lesson.)

What stands out from this analysis is that children need **goal measures, self-selection**, and **feedback on progress**.

One characteristic of the basal system is contradictory to these conditions. Teachers typically group children for instruction and conduct groups in such a way that children **within** the group—

- use the same materials;
- move at the same rate;
- receive the same instruction (whether they need it or not);
- are dependent upon the teacher for diagnosis and prescription.

Children **outside** the group are usually required to complete workbook materials, many of which consist of make-work designed to keep children quiet.

Since the conduct of group instruction is carefully specified in all teacher manuals accompanying basals, we shall not recommend changes. Rather, to produce an adaptive classroom, institute the following procedures:

(*1*) Use a system of **pacing tests** to provide feedback on progress.

(*2*) Provide independent work periods to allow for self-selection and practice.

(*3*) Develop self-evaluation and peer-evaluation procedures to decrease dependency on the teacher.

(*4*) Abjure round-robin reading.

Pacing tests. Perhaps the most persistent problem of instruction in all areas is that of knowing what to teach. Teachers look to textbook writers and test makers. Textbook writers look to other authors and to test makers. And test makers look to authors and teachers. And each group assumes that the other group is looking at children. As a result, we have 50 years of what Gesell, in another context, called **cauliflower overgrowth** of curriculums.

In fact, the children shall lead us if we ask them the right questions. The engineering strategies described in Volume 1 of this series revealed a series of sufficient skills underlying the total reading and writing acts. Graduated tests representing every skill have been constructed under the title *Standard Achievement Reporting System* (*STARS*), found in Volume 2.

Tests selected from this series or others like it in scope and depth may be used to pace or monitor children. *Pacing* here means "continuous estimates of progress." **The tests do not constitute a curriculum.** Rather, like a medical checkup, they are designed to reveal normal progress and to point out deficiencies. If a serious deficiency develops, the instructional diet may be modified to handle it.

What I have described is a feedback system with goal measures. The teacher's record for each child, the Language Arts Competency Profile, appears on pp. 22–26. A progress chart to be kept by the child is described in Volume 2.

Children take tests at any level—letter, word, sentence, paragraph, or book, 1 or 2 days each week. The child is free to select his test but there is one constraint: He may not take a second test in any sequence until he has passed the first test in the sequence. Tests are graded from easy to difficult.

Figure 9.1 demonstrates the impact on achievement when children have an opportunity to use pacing tests. Two first grade classes ($N = 50$) took the Matching Letters tests from *STARS* in April of 1972. They completed all six tests within a 2-week period, and 98% passed Test 1, about 95% passed Test 2, and so on, with 36% passing Test 6. Adding up all the percentages passing, we may divide by 6 (tests) to find a **percent mastery** of 74%.

The 1973 first grade classes were given **their own packages of tests** in the fall and were allowed to take tests as they were ready for them. By April, they had achieved 90% of mastery. In the meantime, the original 1972 first grade classes moved to second grade where they also received their own tests. By April, they had achieved 96.5% of mastery.

MATCHING LETTERS

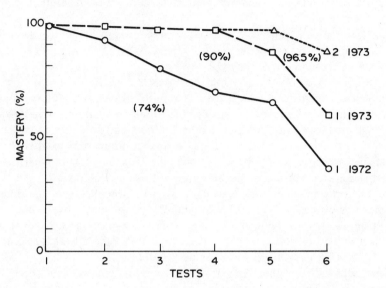

Figure 9.1 Proportion of first and second grade children who achieved 100% scores on Matching Letters tests with (1973) and without (1972) use of criterion-referenced tests.

This evidence suggests that self-pacing and self-testing pay off in higher achievement, as inferred from test scores.

Independent work periods. If children are to become responsible for their own achievement, they must have an opportunity to choose goals, to select materials, and to evaluate and chart their progress.

The independent work period, 20–30 minutes, twice a day, provides time for those activities. It is an **independent** work period, thus does not require the teacher to be available except for well-defined tasks, such as record keeping.

On the other hand, independent work does not preclude children from using other children to facilitate some of their activities, for example, to supply words in a Talking Dictionary activity, to administer tests, or to take part in a dramatization. Arrangements should be made before the period begins.

Self- and peer-evaluation. Before any work is accepted for record keeping, it must reach some agreed-upon level of excellence labeled **mastery**. Since teacher time is quite limited relative to the time of peers, it is sensible for children to use answer keys, where appropriate, and peers as test monitors before asking the teacher for the final evaluative step.

Practice in test taking and practice in assessing one's own readiness for a performance are desirable skills. The problem of test-panic among college students is largely a problem of lack of knowledge: "I don't know what I know and I don't know what I don't know." Treatment for college students and treatment for first graders is the same: First, determine what the standard of adequacy will be; second, study and test yourself to determine whether you can meet the standard; third, restudy to remedy deficiencies; fourth, take the test.

Abjure round-robin reading. This piece of advice does not derive from the earlier description of an adaptive classroom. Rather, it derives from decades of observing teachers, aides, and clinicians "hearing the child read." Teachers say, "But that's how I do my diagnosis. And besides, the child models for other children." The practice is ill advised on both counts. First, we do not ask a musician to **practice** on the stage before an audience; when he reaches the stage, he should be ready to perform. The surest way to kill a child's interest in reading is to have him expose his inexpertness before his peers. And if he is a good reader, the surest way to kill his interest is to require him to endure the inexpertness of others, which also summarizes the counterargument to oral reading "in the circle" as modeling. What is modeled is seldom an exemplar of good reading.

Round-robin reading probably persists because it serves certain teacher needs: (*1*) a need to classify children as bright, average, and dull; (*2*) a need to attack children by means of "constructive criticism"; and (*3*) a need to fill time with apparently reading-related activity.

Let us, by all means, use oral reading in front of the class to entertain, to inform, to dramatize, to persuade—but **not** to practice word recognition.

MAKING PHONICS SYSTEMS WORK[6]

We have carried out extensive trials with phonics methods to determine why children founder with them. Some of the conclusions we reached are as follows:

(*1*) Children must have moderate skill in segmenting words within sentences, in discriminating sounds within spoken words and in recognizing letters within printed words.

---

[6] This section is taken, with minor changes, from *Tutorphonics*, by J. M. Smith and D. E. P. Smith (Ironridge, Wis.: Enrichment Reading Corporation of America, 1975), pp. 2–3, by permission.

(2) A "sight" vocabulary of 50–100 words appears to be necessary, for several reasons:

   (a) To allow the child to read sentence contexts—in order to use context clues.

   (b) To provide "homes" for phonograms, i.e., key words that contain the phonogram and may be recalled in order to identify a sound.

   (c) To avoid the need for sounding short words, especially function words, which tend not to be phonemically regular anyway.

   But even when these conditions are met, many children will still have difficulties.

(3) One final problem: Many children who have been taught phonics and apparently "know their sounds" are unable to use them in sounding out words.

Why should that be? What would keep a child from using sounding skills successfully after thorough training? After much trial and error, we discovered three conditions that, if present, allow children to succeed:

· First, minimize phonic distortions.
· Second, maximize the meaning of the phonic "chunk."
· Third, teach sound–symbol correspondences **within the sounding-out process.**

Phonic Distortion. As noted earlier, the term *phonics* refers to a set of conventions, a set of tools for unlocking words. The teacher and the children are aware that the sound /puh/ is not the same as the /p/ in /pet/. To say "[p] says /puh/" is to say that we have agreed to tolerate some sound distortion in the interest of unlocking words. But the amount of distortion a word can tolerate and still be recognizable is limited.

Least distortion occurs with three-letter groups, syllables or words; more distortion occurs with two-letter groups; most occurs with single letters. Therefore, to reduce distortion, train children to use the largest possible unit for decoding.

Maximize the Meaning. When a phonogram is isolated in a word, its sound must be retrieved from memory storage. Single letters, consonant blends, and digraphs have sounds that are hard to remember. They have very few associations.

But three-letter words, like *cat, pop, bun,* and *can* are easily retrieved and can be used as cues for identifying many long words in which they appear. Furthermore, their parts (*ca* in *cat*) can become usable units.

The Learning Context. When sound–symbol correspondences are learned in isolation, their use is likely to be limited. Such learnings should occur within tasks relevant to the sounding process.

To train children properly, then, materials should be designed so that learners begin by learning three-letter units (short words) that appear in other words. Then two-letter chunks (taken from the three-letter words) are presented. Finally single letters (from the known words) are presented. (Sample exercises appear in Volume 4.)

AN INDIVIDUALIZED
LANGUAGE EXPERIENCE
METHOD

RESOURCES

Chalkboard or newsprint stock
Chalk or grease pencil
Trade books and easy-to-read informational books
Reference books
Assorted skill-drills

The individualized language experience method—a "best of both worlds" plan—is well defined by Spache and Spache (1973) who call it a **combined program**.[1] They recommend it in preference to basal or other "structured" methods, including, presumably, programmed or computer methods.

Language experience methods, developed largely by Claryce Allen and Roach Van Allen (1961, 1966), by Harry Hahn (1967), and by others, are strongly supported by both linguists and reading specialists. These methods derive from the Fernald procedure and are, in effect, a "group Fernald"—if that is not a contradiction in terms.

---

[1] For details, helpful references, and a summary of research, see Spache and Spache (1973), pp. 293–447).

The various versions begin with children's oral productions, show and tell reports, group story telling, news reports, and the like. Therefore they have many of the advantages of Fernald's tutorial (children's own oral language patterns, varied vocabulary, rich associations) and few of the problems of the basal (repetition, narrow vocabulary, stilted, book language).

There are roughly three stages of development:

Stage 1 The group dictates a story to the teacher who prints it (as given) on the board or on paper (usually large sheets of newsprint, which allows large lettering). Children practice reading it, copy it in order to read it to parents, disassemble the words and assemble them, and, finally, put a book-size version of it on the reading table. The teacher may use the story to give instruction in printing, phonics, comprehension, and so on, although some writers see little need for such teaching.

Stage 2 Small, homogeneous groups do the same thing as the large group. Now, individual children have an opportunity to have their own stories transcribed.

Stage 3 Children write their own stories, reports, poetry, etc., illustrate them, and produce books for other children to read.

An essential component of this method and of the individualized program into which it can be transformed is the teacher–child conference. Here, ideally, the child's work is evaluated once or twice a week, as needed, and individual prescriptions are given—toward more basic skill work, or toward upward expansion of skills.

I. Problems

This combined program has unlimited possibilities for exploiting the creative impulse of both children and teacher—if certain problems intrinsic to the method can be resolved. Three conditions are lacking and must be remedied:

(*1*) A controlled environment
(*2*) Subroutines
(*3*) A feedback method

The environment. The teacher's functions as scribe for several groups, as diagnostician for every child, and as keeper of the extensive records required by the method leave little time for classroom management.

Subroutines. One powerful advantage of the Fernald tutorial method is lost in group administration. Note that the teacher writes all stories until children reach stage 3. It is predictable that the lower 30% will reach stage 3 without substantial effort on visual and auditory subroutines. With the Fernald tutorial method, children trace and say words under conditions that develop form, space, and sound discriminations. In the group version, this training will not occur under normal conditions.

Feedback. What many people see as the heart of the method, its lack of structure and opportunity for creativity, also constitutes the seeds of its own destruction.

The problem is **not** that the children may fail to develop certain word-attack skills, certain comprehension skills, spelling competency, and the like. In fact, there is ample evidence that all these skills develop spontaneously when children become deeply engrossed in reading and writing. (See Cramer, 1970, for example.) **That is not the problem**.

Rather the problem is one of motivation. For many children, success in a task is not enough (D. E. P. Smith, Brethower, & Cabot, 1969). They must also see **evidence of progress**. And showing the child his growth by putting early and later productions side by side fails to convince such children. Those who slow down in work behavior constitute a serious threat to the instructional system.

II. Making the Combined Program Work

An adaptive classroom can be engineered by resolving the three problems—environment, subroutines, and feedback. First, the teacher must procure (or develop) effective self-instruction on basic skills: letter matching, printing, letter naming, and auditory discrimination of words and parts of words. (See Chapter 11.) With these resources, the lower 30% problem will be reduced, though it will not be eliminated. (The lower 30% includes those with dialect differences and others who cannot function in a noisy environment. Thus, subroutines are not enough.)

Next, a system of pacing tests (like *STARS*) may be instituted to supplement the teacher's diagnostic skill. Subjective estimates of progress can be reduced, as can record keeping, thus increasing teacher efficiency. At the same time, the learner feedback afforded by the tests allows the child an opportunity to be responsible for his own skill development.

Finally, the teacher need not be scribe for all groups. A Talking Dictionary function can be handled by the more advanced children in the class, thereby increasing their productivity while freeing the teacher for management functions. Management functions, of course, refer to environmental control, which, along with providing resources, is a major teacher responsibility.

PROGRAMMED LEARNING
AND COMPUTER PROGRAMS

The phrases **technology of learning** and **programmed reading** mean computers to some people. To others, they mean mind control. They are neither the one nor the other. They refer, rather, to how materials are produced.

Strictly speaking, there is no **method** of reading instruction that can be called a programmed method; neither is there one that can be called a computer method. If these terms were correct, consistency would require us to call a basal procedure a book method and an experience story a blackboard method. Programmed materials and computer displays do not constitute methods of teaching reading.

However, paper-and-pencil programs and computer programs designed to support instruction do have a method in common. That method is the way in which they are developed. It is called **behavioral engineering**. It begins with explicit statements of assumptions about learners, the learning process, and/or the goals of learning. The following are examples of such statements:

- Given alternative courses of action, children tend to choose those that lead most directly to their goals.
- Attentional control is a primary condition of learning.
- A terminal behavior or set of behaviors called reading can be defined, and such behaviors can be attained by some specified proportion of learners (such as 80% or 90% or 95%).

After stating his assumptions, the behavioral engineer defines his target population: "entering first graders" or "illiterate, English-speaking adults." Next, he defines goal behaviors, usually in terms of a criterion test. Only then does he begin construction of a program to be used with the target population.

To construct the program, he must make decisions about stimuli, responses, and their relationships. He specifies a domain of stimuli to which children must respond when reading; he specifies the kinds of responses desired; he then develops instructional **formats** or tasks designed to produce those responses in the presence of those stimuli. The occurrence of an appropriate response in the presence of a stimulus is called a **skill**. When a sufficient number of skills are attained, the target person will demonstrate attainment of the goal by passing the criterion test.

In the process of building the materials, the developer expects to enter many cul-de-sacs, to suffer many failures. He expects to encounter some sacred cows in current practices and some inefficiencies. But when he is completely blocked, he will turn to his expert resource, the teacher, for ideas on how to proceed.

Perhaps most important, he assumes that his goal is attainable, that the moon can be reached, and that his job is not done until he reaches that goal.

The end result of these efforts is a total system that produces literate behavior in a reliable way. It is not far different from previous methods in appearance. Compared with prior methods there may be as many options for children (or more), as many opportunities for creativity (or more). Materials may not look very different. In fact, the main difference between prior methods and an engineered method is reliability of results. To produce those results reliably, the engineer finds that he must add some things to current methods and, perhaps, subtract some things.

Curriculum developers who have used engineering procedures have followed one or another of two primary routes: They have developed either (*1*) programmed materials (books, teacher scripts, audio tapes, transparencies) or (*2*) computer programs with audio and visual components. Let us first review programmed materials, which have the longer history, then look at computer programs, the hope of the future.

I. A Programmed Learning Strategy

Prior chapters have described several methods of teaching reading—tutorial, basal reader, and individualized language experience. The present chapter, as noted, does not concern a method of **teaching**. Rather, it will focus first on the method of development of programmed materials and of computer programs. That information will help to account for the resulting instructional materials. Then, in place of a method of teaching, a method of **learning** will be described.

That is, the role of the child as **pupil**, receiver of instruction, decreases and his role as **student** expands. The teaching role of the teacher decreases and his role as manager of instruction expands.

Program developers have typically taken on only one or two aspects of the language process for programming. For example, Susan Markle spent several years developing a vocabulary program called *Words* (1968), perhaps the most thorough and extensively evaluated of all published programs. S. Taylor, H. Frankenpohl, and A. McDonald also developed an extensive vocabulary program (1962), quite different from Markle's in its initial assumptions and therefore in its final form. J. M. and D. E. P. Smith produced a three-volume programmed phonics curriculum called *Tutorphonics* (1975b), which provides all necessary word analysis skills by means of audiotape cassettes and response pages. Sommer developed a program to teach cursive writing (in press).

A few attempts have been made to program the entire learning-to-read process (Sullivan, 1968; Research for Better Schools, Inc., 1971).

So far as I know, only one project has targeted on language arts *in toto,* that is, on reading, writing, listening, and speaking, including provision for perceptual subroutines at entry and on control of the total learning environment. That project produced the *Michigan Language Program* with *DIDAC* and teacher training materials (D. E. P. Smith & J. M. Smith, 1975). On the basis of its engineering data, it has been included in a group of six superior reading systems studied by Ellson.[1]

A. Method of Development[2]

The term **empirical development** refers to the systematic tryout of learning tasks under actual classroom conditions, with revisions based on tryout results. This method increases the likelihood of developing materials that work properly. These steps are usually followed:

(1) Specify the goal behavior.
(2) Define the target population.
(3) Adopt a criterion of effectiveness.
(4) Construct materials.
(5) Validate the system.

---

[1] Douglas Ellson, Department of Psychology, Indiana University, personal communication.
[2] Adapted, by permission, from "The Michigan Language Program: A Case Study in Development," by D. E. P. Smith and J. M. Smith, *AV Communication Review,* 1970, *18* (4), 446–454.

STEP 1. SPECIFY THE GOAL BEHAVIOR

Objective: The child will read paragraphs with no more than 10% unknown words (must be sounded out) and will demonstrate comprehension by answering questions on them; he will write paragraphs with a spelling accuracy of no less than 90%.

STEP 2. DEFINE THE TARGET POPULATION

(1) People who cannot read English
(2) Most first grade children. (We expected to be unable to reach 5% of the children. Special procedures now make it possible to reach some of that 5%.)
(3) Those who attend reading clinics
(4) Adult illiterates
(5) Those for whom English is a second language

STEP 3. ADOPT A CRITERION OF EFFECTIVENESS
(OR A MINIMAL LEVEL OF ACHIEVEMENT)

The developers may require that 50% of the target population (such as first grade children) must do 50% of the tasks correctly. If unsuccessful, the tasks must be revised or expanded and tried again, each time with a new or inexperienced group, until the criterion is reached.

A more common criterion is 70%/70%. Most basal reader workbooks approach that criterion, even without extensive development, because of the skill and experience of their authors.

The developers of the *Michigan Language Program* adopted a standard of 95%/95%. Ninety-five percent of an untrained first grade class, heterogeneously grouped, must do 95% of the tasks correctly within any lesson or else that lesson must go back to the drawing board. Furthermore, the final or "criterion" task, the goal of instruction, must be done correctly by 100% of the group. If, in fact, 1 or 2 or 3 children in a group of 30 do not achieve the mastery criterion, they are not allowed to continue in new materials until they do achieve mastery. Failure is not allowed.

STEP 4. CONSTRUCT MATERIALS

Task and sequence formats are described in Volumes 1 and 4 of this series. Summarized briefly, all learnings were viewed as recognitions and reproductions. Any particular stimulus (a letter, a sound, a word, a sentence) or response (naming or drawing a letter, naming or writing a word, transforming a question and matching it to a sentence in a paragraph, etc.), any unit sooner or later went through three steps: copying, recognizing, and reproducing. Usually, the learning took place within a larger task. For example, one sounds out a word in order to complete a sentence, all the other words of which are known. Stated another way, virtually all learnings beyond the subroutines were made functional by teaching **processes** rather than **products**.

Program development took 6 years of intensive work. Problems that arose led to new discoveries. We found that some children constantly demand help even though they do not need it. Encouragement and support had no appreciable effect on their dependency. They discovered that they could do the work "all by themselves" only when their teacher refused to help them. In desperation, they tried, were successful (because tasks were carefully constructed), and gained quickly in independence.

We found that the classroom is a system in which absence of any critical condition of learning results in lost children. For example, we found that effective materials are not enough. Two other conditions were critical: a stable environment and feedback. To enable the lowest 30% to achieve, the classroom **must** be stable and predictable, most easily achieved by consistent enforcement of **no more than** two rules. Consistent enforcement is defined as **restatement of the rule** (enforcement) on at least four infractions—or rule tests—out of five. The second condition, feedback or knowledge of results, has long been known as a condition for learning. But **visible** feedback on **progress toward a goal** turned out to be even more critical for unmotivated students (D. E. P. Smith *et al.*, 1969). To say it another way, success in the immediate task was not a sufficient incentive for disturbed, acting-out, passive–aggressive, and mentally retarded children. The necessary and sufficient condition was goal setting and record keeping—**with the children keeping their own records** (Chapman, 1973).

Many of the problems were stubborn. The motivation problem previously described consumed 2 years of experiments. The learning-to-spell problem took 3 years during which four complete programmed spelling books were developed and discarded. The final solution turned out to be a combination of steps, one of which we had consistently overlooked. We had been laboring over programs on such evanescent topics as "visual memory" and "auditory memory"; it turned out that the actual missing component was the **names of letters**. Suspecting that to be the case, we began to try teaching letter names. Several programs were written and discarded. Out of their ashes arose *DIDAC* (directed developmental activity), which solved the letter-naming problem—which, in turn, solved the spelling problem.

The last problem to arise was that of measurement. Educational technologists generally agree that the measurement of achievement should be done by a "criterion test" or "criterion-referenced test," an assessment of the specific goals of instruction. Necessarily, such a measure looks like the instructional material itself. If we were to teach 10 spelling words, the criterion would consist of those 10 spelling words, rather than a sampling of them as in a standardized test of "spelling ability."

The criterion tests developed for the *Michigan Language Program* exactly reflect the curriculum and, at the same time, correlate highly with standardized tests. A wide spread of scores is found before instruction; a narrow spread clustering about 95% correct is found after the program is completed.

STEP 5. VALIDATE THE SYSTEM

The term *validity* refers to the extent to which some item or set of items does what it purports to do. Programmed materials require three kinds of validity: task validity, program validity, and external validity.

Task validity. Each of the several thousand tasks comprising the program reached or exceeded the 95% criterion of correctness.

Program validity. It is conceivable that a child might respond correctly to program tasks singly and yet fail to demonstrate learning on the total program. That might occur if the program tasks were trivial or failed to teach anything new. To determine the extent to which the various programs actually teach reading and writing, a series of criterion tests was prepared (*Standard Mastery Tasks in Language*).

These mastery tasks measure competency in visual discrimination of letters, auditory discrimination of words, recognition of letter names, manuscript writing, word recognition (sight words), word writing (spelling from dictation), and word-attack skills ("phonics" plus context clues).

Mastery tasks look much like standardized achievement tests but are, in fact, quite different. Standardized tests include a sampling of tasks in some skill area and rank students relative to one another. Mastery tasks measure all tasks in a skill area and, in addition to ranking students, measure the absolute amount learned (e.g., spells correctly 143 words of the 150 words taught, or 95%). Further, standardized tests are designed to maximize the spread of scores and, therefore, items learned by virtually all children are discarded and items not usually taught are included on the test. Mastery tests, on the other hand, reflect the actual curriculum.

Program validity has been assessed in a number of studies by using *Standard Mastery Tasks in Language*:

(*1*) Auditory Discrimination of Words (Task I-B: related to Listening I): Consolidated School Study

Population: Thirty first grade children, heterogeneously grouped, from a consolidated school district in the Midwest.

Training: Four hours, consisting of sessions lasting 10 to 12 minutes, five sessions per week for 4 weeks.

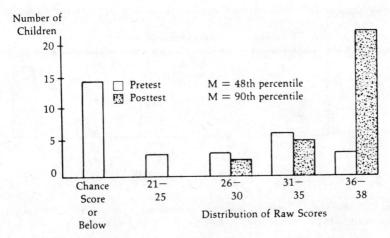

Figure 11.1. Results of tests on auditory discrimination of words, consolidated school study. (Reproduced, with permission, from D. E. P. Smith & J. M. Smith, 1970.)

Results: (Figure 11.1.) Before training, half the children received chance scores or below while 3 scored at or near perfect scores. The group was typical of first grade groups on the pretest (48th percentile). After training, 2 scored average for first graders, 5 were above average, and 23 of the group scored at or near perfect scores. At that point, the average score was at the 90th percentile.

(2) Auditory Discrimination of Words: Rural Town Study

Population: Twenty-five kindergarten children, the lower half of the total kindergarten population in a small midwestern rural town.

Training: Four hours, consisting of sessions lasting from 6 to 12 minutes, five sessions per week for 6 weeks.

Results: (Figure 11.2.) Before training, the children were unable to respond to the auditory discrimination test. Following training, 12 of the 25 achieved at or near perfect scores, 7 scored above average for first graders, and 6 scored average. The lowest score was at the 55th percentile for Grade 1.

(3) Visual Discrimination of Letters (Task 1-B: related to Reading 1 and Reading 2): Rural Town Study

Population: The same 25 kindergarten children reported previously participated in this training concurrent with their auditory training.

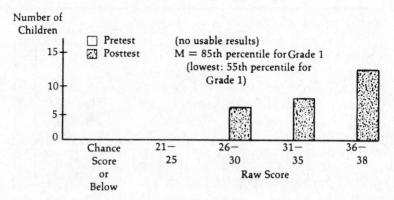

Figure 11.2. Results of tests on auditory discrimination of words, rural town study. (Reproduced, with permission, from D. E. P. Smith & J. M. Smith, 1970.)

Training: The children used Reading 1 and Reading 2 self-selectively under conditions described in the Program Administration Manual. All children completed the two books within 6 weeks.

Results: (Figure 11.3.) Before training, the children were unable to respond to the test of letter discrimination. Following training, 12 achieved at or near perfect scores, 7 scored above average for first grade, 4 scored average, and 2 scored below average. (Note that the norm for first grade is used here although these are below-average kindergarten children.)

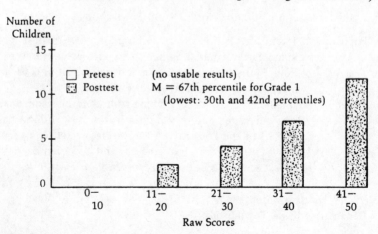

Figure 11.3. Results of tests on visual discrimination of letters, rural town study. (Reproduced, with permission, from D. E. P. Smith & J. M. Smith, 1970.)

External validity. Let us assume that task validity and program validity are satisfactory. The question would still remain: "Are the skills developed by these materials what most people interpret as reading and writing? Is the learner able to carry out school tasks requiring reading and writing?"

One way to answer these kinds of questions would be to observe the learner's success in school tasks. Another way is to assess his skills by using a measure that itself predicts school success. The validity of standardized tests depends on their predictive value. Although they do not mirror the curriculum very well, they do tend to predict school success moderately well. The external validity of the *Michigan Language Program* has been assessed in two studies by using the Gates Primary Reading Test, one study with a clinic population and the other with a classroom group.

(*1*) Word Recognition and Word Analysis: Clinical Study (Smith, Brethower, & Cabot, 1969)

    Population: Five children taken in order from a waiting list ranged in age from 8.5 to 11.4 years. Reading skill deficiencies ranged from 1.1 years to 2.7 years. The children were described by their teachers as hyperactive (2), anxious (1), passive-aggressive (1), aggressive, acting-out (1). Two were in third grade, one in fourth, one in fifth.

    Training: Classes were held for 45 minutes, 4 days per week, for 14 weeks. The children completed the total program through Word Attack and Comprehension.

    Results: (Figure 11.4.) The children all approximated a Grade 4.0 reading level after training, with an average gain of 1.4 grades. There was virtually no misbehavior. Average amount of time spent working exceeded 90% for all the children.

(*2*) Word Recognition and Word Analysis: Class Group Study

    Population: Eighteen third grade children, heterogeneously grouped, from a suburb of a midwestern industrial community. Average IQ (California Test of Mental Maturity) was 99.5 (range: 83–112). Average reading level (Gates Advanced Primary) was Grade 3.5 (range: 2.8–4.5).

    Training: The children received 8 hours of instruction over 8 weeks using Word Attack and Comprehension only. (Four of the group did not meet the entering requirements for that book, i.e., adequate visual and auditory discrimination and 150 sight words. Nevertheless, they participated.)

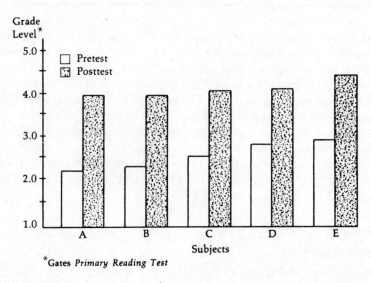

Figure 11.4. Results of tests on reading. (Reproduced, with permission, from D. E. P. Smith & J. M. Smith, 1970.)

Results: Pretest: Grade 3.5
         Posttest: Grade 4.1
         Change: + .6 grades
         Range: + 1.7 grades to −.3 grades
         Major gains were achieved by children who had scored at Grade 3.3 or below on the pretest.

COMMENT

As teachers and supervisors are well aware, statistics tell only a small part of the story. Each of the studies reported was carried out under nearly ideal conditions: The teacher operated the group precisely as directed in the teacher's manual. Other teachers using their own procedures might well find results differing somewhat from these. But more important, and left untold by the statistics, was the tone of these classes: Children working industriously and independently, with virtually no misbehavior, were characteristic of each class. This result deserves a separate heading: Teacher Validation.

B. Method of Instruction

MATERIALS

	Learners	Teacher
Readiness:	Group activity Individual: follow on (response book)	*DIDAC*: 300 transparencies and teacher script
Listening:	Group activity: 2 response books	14 tape cassettes (or teacher script)
Speaking:	Group activity	Teacher script for fluency; conversational exercises
Reading:	Individual: 10 prereaders; 5 response books; 4 mastery readers	
	Group activity	Tape or script for aural–visual training
Independent reading:	Individual: Response book; trade books (e.g. *High Intensity Program*, Random House)	Tape cassette
Writing:	Individual: 5 workbooks	
Program Administration Manual; Classroom Management; Performance Tasks (daily); *Standard Mastery Tasks in Language*: 1 and 2		

There are several characteristics of the materials and their sequencing that teachers recognize as desirable, but which are usually unavailable with conventional materials.

Task formats. Virtually all responses are taught first as recognition tasks. Thus, letter shapes are discriminated from one another before children are asked to produce them. Names of words are discriminated and their shapes are discriminated before the child attempts to associate name and shape to produce sight words.

Whole-to-part learning. Whole stories are learned aurally and sentences are identified within stories; words are identified within those same sentences; and letters are identified within words, as are the sounds used in phonics conventions. Thus newly learned letters and words are virtually always retrievable by reference to larger, meaningful wholes.

Discriminations rather than repetitions. Repetition of words and letters and letter–sound equivalents do occur, but to a much lesser extent than in conventional materials. The reason for that is the emphasis on discriminative tasks. Repetition occurs only to allow new units to be discriminated from similar looking or sounding old units. Thus repetition as an end in itself does not occur.

Independence. It is unusual for a child to be **unable** to do any task. If such a problem does occur, however, chances are very good that it also occurred during the 6-year development stage. Therefore, a corrective procedure for it is likely to be provided in the teacher's manual. As a result, teachers do not need to help children and, in fact, are strongly encouraged to avoid helping. Within a few weeks, children are truly instructing themselves.

Mastery. Mastery tasks appear throughout the materials and in a separate mastery task booklet. Each mastery task within any series of booklets must be completed before new work is provided **in that series**. Children are always free to work in alternative series.

Self-pacing. The self-pacing characteristic of programmed material is well known. What is less well known is the gradual increase in rate of work by slower children, estimated by one observer as a threefold increase (Bloom, 1974). For example, at the beginning of training, fast children outstrip slow ones at a ratio of 5:1 (five tasks completed by fast learners to one task by slow learners). Within a period of weeks, that ratio drops to $2\frac{1}{2}$:1 and finally to $1\frac{1}{2}$:1. The fast learners have not necessarily slowed down. What happens is that, when deficits of slow learners are remedied, productivity tends to speed up.

Self-selection. Perhaps the most common criticism of programmed materials heard from professionals is as follows: Such a slow, step-by-step, drill-like procedure has to be dull and boring. Many of the materials developed in the first decade of programmed instruction (1957–1967) deserved such criticism. The criticism need never have been justified, however: If learners are indeed bored by the material, then it is not ready for use. A student's desire to complete the work or to return to it at the earliest opportunity is typical of a well-designed program.

Certainly if the principle of self-selection is allowed to operate, children will select *only* what interests them. And self-selection is one of the conditions specified for the *Michigan Language Program*. Thus, if the criticism were justified, we should find proportion of time spent working to approximate 0–10%. However, the children referred to in Figure 11.4 had not been functioning in school, and, using these materials, self-selection, and feedback, and with strict timing procedures used by observers, all of the children worked beyond 90% of total class time.

Reinforcement. One identifying characteristic of programmed material is the availability of the answer following each task or "frame." At one time, it was thought that looking at the answer and finding that it matched the learner's response was a reinforcing or rewarding event. It was thought that the correct answer was analogous to food or water reinforcers in animal studies. That position is no longer widely held. Many studies demonstrated that the answer key was seldom used in good programs and often used when tasks were ambiguous.

The *Michigan Language Program* was commonly criticized in its early days for its failure to include any answers. "Where is the reinforcer?" critics asked. We took the position that, if a task is well designed, the answer will be self-evident. Furthermore, if an answer is not self-evident, the task is not well designed. "But where is the reinforcer?" The reinforcer in such tasks is thought to be the reduction of uncertainty at the moment of discovery. Whether or not that interpretation is correct, some reinforcer must be present since the tasks control the children's attention better than do conventional materials (see the rate-of-work data given previously), and at least as well as games, modeling clay, and the throwing of paper airplanes.

The foregoing analysis has focused on system characteristics rather than on teacher role or other aspects of method. To a large extent, the teacher's role is that of manager of the enterprise and troubleshooter.

Note the similarities and differences between programmed materials and computer materials as we turn to an examination of two computer projects.

II. Computer Program Strategies

The two major engineering efforts to teach reading via computer have been carried on at Stanford University (Atkinson, 1968, 1974) and at the University of Illinois (Obertino, 1974; Riskin & Webber, 1974). The Stanford project began about 1964 and the Illinois, PLATO-based project began in 1971. Let us first examine each project, then compare them for similarities and differences, and finally, speculate about the future of reading instruction via computer.

A. *The Stanford Project*

According to Atkinson (1974), the initial attempts to teach reading by computer were aimed at a total curriculum, with no input by the teacher.

Experience demonstrated that this was likely to be an inefficient use of both teacher and computer. The most obvious capability of the computer is that of individualizing certain self-study activities. The computer is presently unable to lead a group discussion or to operate a group verbal fluency training session.

The original terminal consisted of a cathode-ray tube, a light pen, teletypewriter, audio headset, and a slide projector. Equipment now consists of a teletypewriter and headset. The typewriter uses only capital letters.

The program as presently constituted is used by children for 15 to 30 minutes a day. Instruction is provided in letter naming, phonics (called **decoding**), and sentence comprehension (called **communication**), with decoding occupying most of the instructional time.

METHOD OF INSTRUCTION

Presumably, development of instruction was similar to that of the programming procedure. Instructional formats appear to follow the copy, recognize, reproduce (or test) sequence described in the programming section. Copying is done by typing out a word shown on the printout; recognition requires choosing a word as heard (through the headset) from choices presented on the printout. Reproduction consists of typing words from dictation.

Several sequences (called **strands**) are available:

(*1*) Orientation to the device
(*2*) Letter identification
(*3*) Sight words
(*4*) Spelling patterns
(*5*) Phonics
(*6*) Spelling
(*7*) Word comprehension (presumably word analysis)
(*8*) Sentence comprehension

Entry to higher strands is contingent upon reaching critical levels on lower strands. Tasks on several strands may be met in the same sitting.

It may be inferred, then, that the sequence of learnings adopted by the developers proceeds synthetically, from letters to sight words to word analysis to sentences. Word analysis is assumed to comprise acquisition and use of letter group–sound correspondence (letter group = spelling patterns).

Reinforcement consists of verbal praise, applause, cheering emanating from the headset. Errors are pointed out without requiring corrections.

The most difficult problems facing the developers, according to Atkinson (1974, p. 172), concern sequencing of activities:

(*1*) Within a strand, which items and formats should be used and when should review be scheduled?

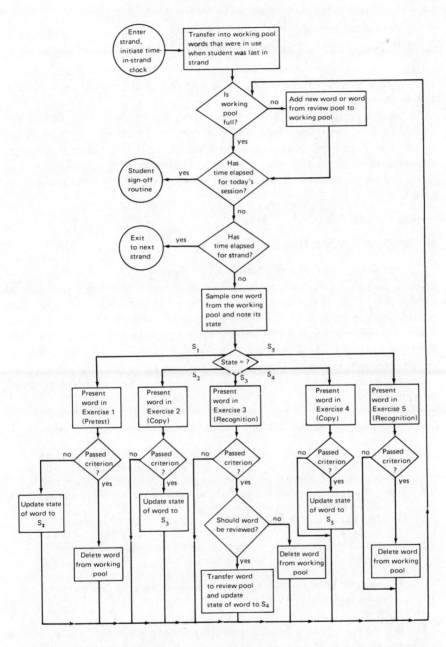

Figure 11.5. Sample flowchart for sight-word recognition. (From "Teaching Children to Read Using the Computer" by R. C. Atkinson, *American Psychologist,* 1974, *29,* 169–178. Copyright 1974 by the American Psychological Association. Reprinted by permission.)

(*2*) How much time should be allocated to each strand?

(*3*) How much time should be allocated to a given student?

Each learner's response history is stored and various formulas are used for making decisions about sequencing. A sample flowchart for sight-word recognition is shown in Figure 11.5.

Atkinson reports a 5-month superiority of his first grade subjects over equivalent control students and predicts that, if similar instruction were available at upper levels, the superiority would be a full grade by the end of third grade. Although that may be the case, increases in skill complexity from first to third grade not accounted for in the present learning model leave the question in doubt.

B. The PLATO Project (PERC)

The long-range goal of the PLATO Early Reading Curriculum Project is to create a complete K–6 curriculum. In the short range, the plan is to make the capabilities of the device available to teachers. Certain lesson and curriculum management techniques combined with a relatively simple computer language (TUTOR) makes it possible for teachers to design their own curricula. "In fact, the only curricula which are ever effective in a classroom are those that the teacher **perceives** as being effective [Riskin & Obertino, in preparation]."

Certain other assumptions that have guided the work of the team are of interest:

(*1*) . . . reading can be defined in terms of observable, measurable behaviors. . . .

(*2*) Different children learn in different ways and at different rates. An effective reading program will allow the child to proceed at his own pace and will offer him learning experiences which capitalize on his natural style. [This assumption is taken very seriously: Variety, multiple options and creative responses typify the materials.]

(*3*) Children do not profit from public exposure of their "mistakes" and "weaknesses."

(*4*) [Tests should be used to adapt materials to children rather than to measure children's failure to adapt to a standard.]

(*5*) No computer based curriculum will gain . . . acceptance unless it is sufficiently flexible to allow teachers to shape it to their own classroom practices [Obertino, 1974].

The equipment consists of a display panel, slide projector, headphones, a touch panel, and a typewriter. Children use the device self-selectively, doing lessons that run about 4 minutes; they spend from 10 to 20 minutes a day at the console.

The program presently offers instruction in letter naming, auditory discrimination of words, sight words, phonics, concept development, and story writing.

METHOD OF INSTRUCTION

All lessons are self-contained, with pretest, instruction, posttest, and remedial follow-up. Although several formats are used, they do not reflect (to me) any clear assumptions about how children learn. Since all lessons reach some criterion of adequacy, presumably enough material is offered in displays to allow children to learn. As in the previous examples of learning technology, opportunities are available for matching (discrimination), recognition, and reproduction, although tasks may not require precisely those responses.

As in the Stanford program, several strands are now available:[3]

(*1*) Orientation (for teaching the child how to interact with the device and to load audio discs and microfiche)
(*2*) Visual skills
(*3*) Letter naming
(*4*) Phonics
(*5*) Auditory skills
(*6*) Sight words
(*7*) Vocabulary
(*8*) Concept development
(*9*) Stories
(*10*) Games

Unlike the Stanford program, this group has moved **away** from sequencing across strands, allowing children to self-select their paths almost completely. For that reason, the structure of objectives presented here is already out of date. But the kinds of skills included are of interest (see Figure 11.6).

Certain discoveries reported by the group bear reporting:

(*1*) Children's responses to the device itself suggest a two-by-two classification (Obertino, 1974):
 (*a*) **Active nonconventional.** In effect, these children explore the consistencies of the device by poking, pounding, flicking buttons on and off, punching the keys at a furious rate, and paying no attention to the instructional signals until they "know" the machine.
 (*b*) **Active conventional.** The good child, who goes to work and uses the device as he would a teacher.

---

[3] Bob Yeager, personal communication.

THE PLATO ELEMENTARY READING CURRICULUM
STRUCTURE OF OBJECTIVES

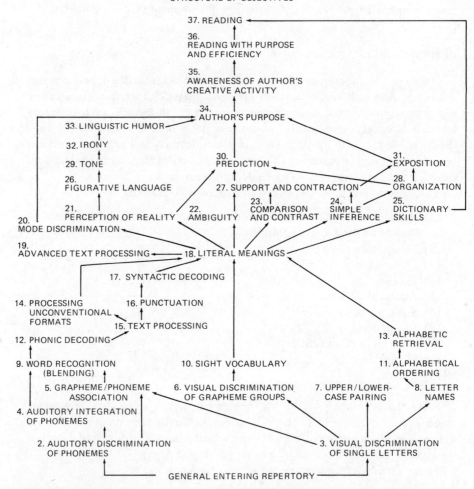

Figure 11.6. Kinds of skills included in the PLATO Project. (From "The PLATO Reading Project: An Overview" by Priscilla Obertino, *Educational Technology*, 1974, 8–13. Reprinted by permission.)

    (*c*) **Passive conventional**. Dependent, cautious but productive, he responds when he hears directions such as "Go ahead—try."

    (*d*) **Passive, nonconventional**. Nonresponsive, apparently overwhelmed by the complexity of the display, this child must be taken by the hand.

(*2*) Any feedback tends to be reinforcing. According to Yeager (in preparation), the student "makes his response in order to make the computer terminal **do something**." **Any** feedback tends to be positively reinforcing, even negative feedback such as "No, you're wrong." Thus, **no feedback** appears to be more likely to elicit a different response than will negative feedback. (Similarly, teachers have discovered that ignoring many mis-behaviors tends to eliminate them more quickly than does actively punishing them.) Thus, ". . . the general principle [is] that the best re-mediation for a student's error is no remediation at all" (in most cases).

(*3*) Interactive instruction is possible. It is usual to attempt to build flexibility into a computer–child interaction by allocating the decision-making func-tion to the computer. Thus, programmers attempt to anticipate all re-sponses likely to be made by learners and to build in appropriate machine responses. This is the "father-knows-best" posture of our culture.

The PLATO–PERC group has, instead, taken a cautious step in the other direction. Where possible, they have given the decision function to the student—for example, by allowing self-selection of strands.

Formal evaluative data on PERC efforts are not yet available. However, it seems self-evident that these workers are constructing the future. The only clear weakness in the project is the instructional formats, which can be modified easily, if necessary. The number of positives provides reason for an optimistic outlook.

C. Stanford–PERC Strategies Compared

Two substantial efforts at early reading instruction via computer have been described. The similarities are not unexpected, because of the nature of man, the capabilities of the computer, and the state of knowledge of language and learning:

- Both began by planning a total curriculum and, as a result of experience, lowered their sights to first grade reading.
- Both intended to operate without the teacher and wisely moved into a role subservient to the teacher.
- Both adopted a synthetic method of teaching (letter–word–sentence) and have yet to modify that position.
- Both have sequenced learning in hierarchies.
- Both provide numerous kinds of extrinsic reinforcement, from cheering to games.
- Both concluded that presentation of the correct response after an error is the most efficient corrective procedure.

Differences are even more interesting, as the table shows.

	Stanford	PERC
Sequence	Entry to a higher level is contingent upon achievement of critical subskills.	Self-selective across strands.
Variety	Five formats, Few activities.	Many formats. Many activities.
Scope	Initial: letters. Final: sentences.	Initial: letters and sounds. Final: stories.
Process	Explicit (association: copy, recognize, reproduce).	Nonexplicit (combined: discriminative, associative).
Phonics	Syllable method.	Letter method (now in revision).
Options	Program-controlled.	Student-controlled.

One of the values of this kind of analysis of developing programs is that it provides places to look when improvements are required. And both projects look sufficiently vigorous that continued development is likely. By consistent use of engineering strategies, each is likely to produce a powerful, effective program.

One might ask, "Why have you not applied the six characteristics of an adaptive classroom to computer programs?" Computer programs are in development, thus have yet to report their failures, if any. But there is no reason to think that they should be exempt. The way in which the "active, nonconventional" child responds to the hardware is vaguely reminiscent of the rule-testing behavior in ordinary classrooms. So far, both computer programs play a supporting role in a total classroom, and their contribution to an adaptive system is largely determined by the teacher who uses them.

III. Futures

The safest prediction for the future of reading instruction is that basal readers will continue to dominate early reading instruction. It is the safest prediction because today's condition is the best predictor of tomorrow's condition. Change will occur when events require change. When we can no longer afford the waste of 30% of our children, change will occur.

When that time comes, I suspect that we will find a marriage of programming methodology with computer capabilities for handling well-defined basic skills. I do not foresee any greater achievement resulting from that marriage than is now possible with programmed materials alone. But the increase in efficiency will result in a substantial reduction in the cost of instruction. That outcome will lead, in turn, to universal availability of effective instruction.

**CHARACTERISTICS OF AN ADAPTIVE CLASSROOM
INTRINSIC TO VARIOUS TEACHING METHODS**

Characteristics	Method				
			Individualized language experience	Programmed	
	Fernald	Basal		Book	Computer
Subroutines	X	0	0	X	X
Goal measures	X	X	0	X	X
Controlled environment	X	0	0	X	X
Self-instructional materials	X	0	X	X	X
Self-evaluation by feedback					
Task success	X	0	X	X	X
Progress	0	0	0	X	0
Mastery required	X	0	0	X	X

REFERENCES

Allen, R. Van. *Report of the reading study project*. Monograph No. 1. San Diego, Calif.: Department of Education, 1961.

Allen, R. Van, & Allen, C. *Language experiences in reading: Teacher resource book.* Chicago: Encyclopedia Brittanica Press, 1966.

Atkinson, R. C. Computerized instruction and the learning process. *American Psychologist*, 1968, *23*, 225–239.

Atkinson, R. C. Teaching children to read using a computer. *American Psychologist*, 1974, *29*, 169–178.

Baratz, J. C. A bi-dialectal task for determining language proficiency in economically disadvantaged Negro children. *Child Development*, 1969, *40* (3), 889–901.

Baratz, J. C. Beginning readers for speakers of divergent dialects. In J. A. Figurel (Ed.), *Reading goals for the disadvantaged*. Neward, Del.: International Reading Association, 1970. (a)

Baratz, J. C. Teaching reading in an urban Negro school system. In F. Williams (Ed.), *Language and poverty*. Chicago: Markham, 1970. (b)

Baratz, J., & Povich, E. *Grammatical constructions in the language of the Negro preschool child*. Washington, D.C.: American Speech and Hearing Association, 1968.

Baratz, J. C., & Shuy, R. W. (Eds.). *Teaching black children to read*. Washington, D.C.: Center for Applied Linguistics, 1969.

Bereiter, C., & Englemann, S. *Teaching disadvantaged children in the preschool*. Englewood Cliffs, N.J.: Prentice-Hall, 1966.

313

Bernstein, B. Social structure, language, and learning. *Educational Research,* 1961, *3.*

Blank, M., & Solomon, F. A tutorial language program to develop abstract thinking in socially disadvantaged preschool children. *Child Development,* 1968, *40,* 47–61.

Bloom, B. S. Time and learning. *American Psychologist,* 1974, *29,* 682–688.

Brethower, D. The classroom as a self-modifying system (Ph.D. dissertation, University of Michigan, 1970). *Dissertation Abstracts International,* 1971, *31,* 2168A.

Burns, P. C., & Broman, B. L. *The language arts in childhood education* (3rd ed.). Chicago: Rand McNally College Publishing Company, 1975.

Cazden, C. B. Subcultural differences in child language: An interdisciplinary review. *Merrill-Palmer Quarterly of Behavior and Development,* 1966, *12,* 185–219.

Chapman, R. E. Evaluation as feedback in innovative school programs. Ph.D. dissertation, University of Michigan, 1973 (Univ. Microfilm No. *34,* 1472A, 1974).

Cohen, S. A. The taxonomy of instructional treatments in reading: Its uses and its implications as a classroom analysis scheme. *Journal of the Reading Specialist,* 1971, *11,* 5–23.

Cramer, L. C. An investigation of first grade spelling achievement. *Elementary English,* 1970, *47* (2), 230–237.

Dale, P. S. *Language development.* Hinsdale, Ill.: Dryden, 1972.

Deutsch, M., & associates. *The disadvantaged child.* New York: Basic Books, 1967.

Dolch, W. *A manual for remedial reading* (2nd ed.). Champaign, Ill.: Garrard, 1945.

Fernald, G. *Remedial techniques in basic school subjects.* New York: McGraw-Hill, 1943.

Figurel, J. A. (Ed.). *Reading goals for the disadvantaged.* Newark, Del.: International Reading Association, 1970.

Gates, A. I. Implications of the psychology of perception for word study. *Education,* 1955, *75,* 589–595.

Gibson, J. J. *The senses considered as perceptual systems.* Boston: Houghton Mifflin, 1966.

Goldiamond, I. Stuttering and fluency as manipulative operant response classes. In L. Krasner & L. P. Ullmann (Eds.), *Research in behavior modification.* New York: Holt, 1965, 106–156.

Goodman, K. S. Reading: A psycholinguistic guessing game. In H. Singer & R. B. Ruddell (Eds.), *Theoretical models and processes of reading.* Newark, Del.: Reading Association, 1970.

Goodman, K. S. Dialect barriers to reading comprehension. In J. Baratz & R. Shuy (Eds.), *Teaching black children to read.* Washington, D.C.: Center for Applied Linguistics, 1969.

Hahn, H. T. Three approaches to beginning reading instruction. *Reading Teacher,* 1967, *20,* 711–715.

Hess, R. D., & Shipman, V. Early experience and the socialization of cognitive modes in children. *Child Development,* 1965, *36,* 869–886.

Horn, T. D. (Ed.). *Reading for the disadvantaged.* New York: Harcourt, Brace & World, 1970.

Houston, S. H. A reexamination of some assumptions about the language of the disadvantaged child. *Child Development,* 1970, *41,* 947–961.

Jensen, A. R. How much can we boost I.Q. and scholastic achievement? *Harvard Educational Review,* 1969, *39,* 1–123.

Johnson, D. D. The Dolch list reexamined. *Reading Teacher,* 1971, *24,* 455–456.

Knudsvig, G. Cross-dialect learning (Ph.D. dissertation, University of Michigan). *Dissertation Abstracts International,* 1975, *35,* 2539A.

Labov, W. The logic of nonstandard English. In F. Williams (Ed.), *Language and poverty.* Chicago: Markham, 1970. (a)

Labov, W. *Study of non-standard English*. Champaign, Ill.: National Council of Teachers of English and Center for Applied Linguistics, 1970. (b)

Labov, W. *Language in the inner city*. Philadelphia: University of Pennsylvania Press, 1972.

Labov, W., & Cohen, P. Systematic relations of standard and non-standard rules in the grammars of Negro speakers. *Project Literacy Reports*, 1967, *8*.

Lamberg, W. Design and validation of instruction in question-directed narrative writing, developed through discrimination programming (Ph.D. dissertation, University of Michigan). *Dissertation Abstracts International*, 1975, *35*, 2839A.

Lenneberg, E. H. *Biological foundations of language*. New York: Wiley, 1967.

Lewis, B. N., & Dask, G. The theory and practice of adaptive teaching systems. In R. Glaser (Ed.), *Teaching machines and programmed learning II*. Washington, D.C.: DAVI-NEA, 1966. Pp. 213–266.

Markle, S. M. *Words: A programmed course in vocabulary development*. Chicago: Science Research Associates, 1968.

McNeill, D. Developmental psycholinguistics. In F. Smith & G. A. Miller (Eds.), *The genesis of language: A psycholinguistic approach*. Cambridge, Mass.: MIT Press, 1966.

Melcher, R. T. Children's motor learning with and without vision. *Child Development*, 1934, *5*, 315–350.

Obertino, P. The PLATO reading project: An overview. *Educational Technology*, 1974, 8–13.

Research for Better Schools, Inc. *Teaching in IPI reading: Volume 3, Stage IV*. Philadelphia: Research for Better Schools, Inc., 1971.

Rice, C. Eye and hand movements in the training of perception. *Child Development*, 1931, *2*, 30–48.

Riskin, J., & Obertino, P. *Scope of the PLATO elementary reading project*, in preparation.

Riskin, J., & Webber, E. A computer based curriculum management system. *Educational Technology*, 1974, 38–41.

Rutherford, W. Teaching reading to children with dialect differences. In J. A. Figurel (Ed.), *Reading goals for the disadvantaged*. Newark, Del.: International Reading Association, 1970.

Shuy, R. W. Language variation and literacy. In J. A. Figurel (Ed.), *Reading goals for the disadvantaged*. Newark, Del.: International Reading Association, 1970. (a)

Shuy, R. W. Teacher training and urban language problems. In R. W. Fasold & R. W. Shuy (Eds.), *Teaching standard English in the inner city*. Washington, D.C.: Center for Applied Linguistics, 1970. (b)

Smith, D. E. P. *Learning to read and write: A task analysis*. In *A technology of reading and writing (Vol. 1)*. New York: Academic Press, 1976.

Smith, D. E. P., Brethower, D., & Cabot, R. Increasing task behavior in a language arts program by providing reinforcement. *Journal of Experimental Child Psychology*, 1969, *8* (1), 45–62.

Smith, D. E. P., & Smith, J. M. The Michigan language program: A case study in development. *AV Communication Review*, 1970, *18* (4), 446–454.

Smith, D. E. P., & Smith, J. M. *Michigan language program*. New York: Random House, 1975.

Smith, D. E. P., & Smith, J. M. *Child management* (rev. ed.). Champaign, Ill.: Research Press, 1976.

Smith, D. E. P., & Walter, T. Experimental classroom: Minutes of meetings. Unpublished manuscript, 1972.

Smith, J. M. *Curriculum developer's handbook for spelling*. Ferndale, Mich.: Tri-Level, 1972.

Smith, J. M. *Preparing instructional tasks*. In *A technology of reading and writing* (Vol. 4). New York: Academic Press, in press.

Smith, J. M., & Smith, D. E. P. *Classroom management*. New York: Random House, 1975.

Smith, J. M., & Smith, D. E. P. *Tutorphonics* (3 vols.). Ironridge, Wis.: Enrichment Reading Corporation of America, 1975. (b)

Smith, J. M., Smith, D. E. P., & Brink, J. R. *Criterion-referenced tests for reading and writing*. In *A technology of reading and writing* (Vol. 2). New York: Academic Press, 1977.

Sommer, B. *A learning program in cursive writing*. Unpublished Ph.D. dissertation, University of Michigan, 1965.

Sommer, B. *Cursive writing*. New York: Random House, in press.

Spache, G. D., & Spache, E. B. *Reading in the elementary school* (3rd ed.). Boston: Allyn and Bacon, 1973.

Steslicki, W. *Programmed spelling for high school and college*. Ann Arbor, Mich.: Ann Arbor Publishers, 1967.

Stewart, N. A. Negro dialect in the teaching of reading. In J. C. Baratz & R. W. Shuy (Eds.), *Teaching black children to read*. Washington, D.C.: Center for Applied Linguistics, 1969.

Sullivan, J. *Programmed reading*. New York: McGraw-Hill, 1968.

Taylor, S., Frankenpohl, H., & McDonald, A. *Word clues*. Huntington, N.J.: Educational Developmental Laboratories, 1962.

Townsend, E. A. A study of copying ability in children. *Genetic Psychology Monographs*, 1951, *43*, 3–51.

Wardhaugh, R. Theories of language acquisition in relation to beginning reading instruction. In F. B. Davis (Ed.), *The literature of research in reading with emphasis upon models*. New Brunswick, N.J.: Iris, 1971.

Wilhelm, R., & King, W. *An exercise to improve quantity and quality of writing*. Ann Arbor, Mich.: University of Michigan School of Education, Office of Instructional Services, 1974.

Williams, F. (Ed.) *Language and poverty*. Chicago: Markham, 1970.

Wolfram, W. A. *A sociolinguistic description of Detroit Negro speech*. Washington, D.C.: Center for Applied Linguistics, 1969.

Wolfram, W. A. The nature of nonstandard dialect divergence. In J. F. Savage (Ed.), *Linguistics for teachers*. Chicago: Science Research Associates, 1973.

Wolter, D. *Effect of feedback on performance of a creative writing task*. Unpublished Ph.D. dissertation, University of Michigan, 1975.

Yeager, Bob. *A decision model to handle student errors*, in preparation.

Zintz, M. V. *The reading process*. Dubuque, Iowa: Wm. C. Brown, 1970.

INDEX

A 7
B 8
C 9
D 0
E 1
F 2
G 3
H 4
I 5
J

Date Due